The British Machine Tool Industry, 1850–1914

The British Machine Tool Industry, 1850-1914

RODERICK FLOUD

Professor of Modern History
Birkbeck College, London

CAMBRIDGE UNIVERSITY PRESS

Cambridge
London   New York   Melbourne

Published by the Syndics of the Cambridge University Press
The Pitt Building, Trumpington Street, Cambridge CB2 1RP
Bentley House, 200 Euston Road, London NW1 2DB
32 East 57th Street, New York, NY 10022, USA
296 Beaconsfield Parade, Middle Park, Melbourne 3206, Australia

ISBN 0 521 21203 0

First published 1976

Printed and bound in Great Britain by
Billing and Sons Ltd, Guilford and London

Library of Congress Cataloguing in Publication Data
Floud, Roderick.
The British machine tool industry, 1850–1914.
'This book began as a D.Phil. thesis
for the University of Oxford.'
Includes bibliographical references and index.
1. Machine-tools – Trade and manufacture
– Great Britain – History. I. Title.
HD9703.G72F55   338.4'7'6589020941   75-46133
ISBN 0 521 21203 0

To Cynthia

Contents

Tables, figures and appendices

Tables, figures and appendices

Preface

I have received intellectual and financial support in the writing of this book from many people and institutions. In particular, I should like to thank Nuffield College, Oxford, University College London and the Central Research Fund of London University, Cambridge University and Emmanuel College, Cambridge, and Birkbeck College, London, for help in the form of facilities for research, research assistance, and sabbatical leave. I am also grateful to Methuen and Co. Ltd and the editors of the *Economic History Review* for their permission to reprint sections of this work which have previously been published.

Many members of firms in the machine tool industry helped me and gave me advice and hospitality during the course of my research. In particular, I should like to thank Mr R. C. Bragger and Mr J. T. Clements of James Archdale and Co. Ltd, Mr D. Mitchell and Mr G. C. Butler of the Butler Machine Tool Co. Ltd, Mr J. H. Hartopp, Mr J. D. Ellson and Mr J. Hugo of Alfred Herbert Ltd, Sir Stanley Harley of Coventry Gauge and Tool Co. Ltd, and Mr R. Gibson of A. A. Jones and Shipman Ltd. Others who gave me much help were Mr H. O. Barrett of the Machine Tool Trades Association, Mr P. A. Sidders of *Machinery*, and Mr F. G. Barkway of Kelly's Directories. I should also like to thank Mr Ian Hollick for permission to use the papers of Sir Alfred Herbert.

Much of this work would have been impossible without the help of Greenwood and Batley Ltd, and in particular of Mr L. Haberman and Dr Charles Greenwood. The archives of the firm have now been deposited with Leeds Central Library (Archives Department) and I should like to thank Mr Collinson of that department for his help.

I owe a great deal to many people who have criticised my work, and I should like to thank in particular R. M. Hartwell, P. Mathias, S. Nicholas, N. Rosenberg and S. B. Saul. My greatest debts, however, are threefold. This book began as a D.Phil thesis for the University of Oxford, and my supervisor as a research student was H. J. Habakkuk. To him I owe the suggestion of a topic, constant stimulus and encouragement, and the privilege of contact with an exemplar of the crafts of economic historian and research supervisor. Stanley Engerman not only examined my thesis, but has discussed successive drafts of this book many times since, and its present shape, though not its deficiencies, owes much to his suggestions

xiii

and advice. Lastly, my wife has lived with the history of machine tools throughout our married life; she has despaired and exulted with me, supported and criticised. It is for this and much else that this book is dedicated to her.

R.C.F.

October 1975

Introduction

Modern industrial society could not exist without machine tools. The transformation of metals from their origin as ore to their finished state is completed by metal-working machine tools, and the invention and innovation of efficient and effective machine tools, largely during the nineteenth century, made possible the production of the multifarious machines on which nineteenth- and twentieth-century economy and society has been based. The machine tool industry in any country, and particularly in such an advanced industrial country as Britain, has therefore always been at the forefront of technical progress; in spite of this, it has normally been small, the employer of a few highly skilled men rather than of a vast labour force, and the monetary value of its products has always seemed low compared to the output of the many other engineering and metal processing industries who use its products. Perhaps for this reason, there have been few studies of the machine tool industry; yet study of it is important not only because of its intrinsic significance but also for the light which study of it can throw on the wider context of manufacturing industry, and on the process of invention and innovation which is a constant feature of industrial change.

This study is intended to do three things: to throw light on the history of a neglected but important industry, to discuss the relevance of the experience of the machine tool industry to a controversial period of British economic history, and, most generally, to discuss how it is possible to describe and explain invention, innovation, technical and technological change and its causes and consequences. These three topics are primarily studied through the use of quantitative data, analysed and organised by simple economic analysis and statistical method. This methodological bias, as it will seem to be to many historians, was not deliberate at the beginning of the research which led to this book; it arose instead from the discovery that quantitative data existed which might reveal more about the history of the industry than would the books, articles and other literary materials with which the research began. This was partly because the literary sources for the history of the industry were so incomplete, and so uneven in quality, and partly because the quantitative data which became available seemed so much more suitable for answering what were essentially aggregative and quantitative questions — how many machine tools did the

1

industry make, how many firms were there, how much of their production did they export, what rates of growth of productivity did they achieve? Not all these questions can be answered, but the use of extensive quantitative data allows for a closer approach to the answers than would otherwise have been possible.

To throw light, by whatever means, on the history of an important industry, is in itself a worthwhile task for an economic historian. To do so for the machine tool industry in Britain between 1850 and 1914 is worthwhile also because the economic history of Britain in that period is both complex and controversial. It is now generally accepted that Britain suffered, in that period, a decline in the rates of growth of its total output and of labour and 'total' productivity, even if the exact magnitude of the decline is still disputed. Numerous theories have been advanced to account for this decline, including a decline in the quality of entrepreneurship, a decline in inventiveness, a failure to invest in domestic industry, a resistance to change on the part of organised labour, a structural weakness of British industry, and many others. What has sometimes been lacking, in the discussion of these theories, is evidence drawn from more than a handful of industries, which might enable problems of aggregate decline to be explained or discussed at a disaggregated or micro level. The machine tool industry is particularly appropriate for a micro level study of this kind, because of its central role as a supplier of capital goods to so many of the industries which were experiencing technical and economic change at this period.

Answering many interesting questions about the role of the machine tool industry in promoting or aiding technical change is difficult, however, partly because of the current state of economic theories of technological change. It is clearly sensible for an economic historian to borrow from such theories, and to organise his work to take full advantage of their insights, but it has rightly been said that economic theory, and in particular the neo-classical theory which has often recently been applied to problems of economic history, provides no satisfactory explanation of technological change defined narrowly as 'a change of a neo-classical production function – an alteration of relationships between inputs and outputs across the whole array of known techniques' (David, 1975, p. 2). Even problems of choice of technique within an existing array of production methods have often proved intractable because of the range and complexity of the factors involved, because of the existence of 'learning by doing', and because analysis of technical and technological changes has often been carried out at too aggregate a level. This study makes use, at several points, of the

2

existing theories of technological change, but it also seeks to show how study of the process of innovation has to be linked to the structure of the innovating industry and firm and its relationship with its customers. It is necessary, in fact, to consider the cumulative impact and the separate causes of a whole range of decisions by firms to produce at particular levels of scale and specialisation.

The first two chapters set the context within which the machine tool industry operated, within the engineering industry and within the limits of the technical characteristics of the major products which it made. In the third chapter the growth and changing structure of the industry is described, while the fourth chapter discusses the British role in international trade in machine tools. The final chapters consider the experience of one leading machine tool firm, Greenwood and Batley of Leeds, and its relevance to the history of the machine tool industry as a whole.

1. The engineering industries

The mechanical engineering industry is at once one of the most important of modern industries, and one of the most difficult to define. The first British Census of Production, taken in 1907, classified the output of the engineering industry (including electrical engineering) under forty separate headings; even these headings are often merely broad descriptions – for example 'agricultural machinery', 'textile machinery', 'railway and tramway equipment and parts' – which conceal the operations of hundreds of firms producing thousands of separately named pieces of equipment (P.P. 1912–13b). Perhaps the most important single unifying factor, linking these thousands of disparate products, however, is that the mechanical engineering industry is concerned with the processing of metals, and in particular with the transformation of metals into machinery, for further use in the operations of a myriad other industries. This transformation of raw or semi-finished metals into machinery is carried out by machine tools, defined 'as briefly as possible' by one writer as

> contrivances in which a cutting tool is used to bring a piece of metal to the shape, size and degree of finish required by the operator and which to some degree reduce the manipulative skill and physical strength he needs to achieve his object. (Steeds, 1969, p. xix)

The machine tool industry thus occupies a central place within the mechanical engineering industry. At the same time, it cannot easily be distinguished from other branches of mechanical engineering, since the processes of production are very similar, since most engineering firms are capable of making or at least modifying machine tools to suit their own purposes, and since historically many machine tool firms have also made other types of engineering products, or have turned to machine tool production from other branches of engineering. The process by which the machine tool industry has developed, and the process by which it has developed its products is therefore one of constant interaction with the many other branches of engineering which supply its customers, inspire its inventions, and train its labour force, and on whose investment plans its prosperity depends.

For all these reasons, it is important to begin a study of the machine tool industry by setting it firmly in its place among the other branches of engineering. Unfortunately our knowledge of the development of the

4

mechanical engineering industries is incomplete; for an industry which in 1907 employed about 8% of the labour force engaged in manufacturing industry, surprisingly incomplete. As Professor Saul, who has himself made a number of pioneer studies of the industry, has pointed out, we need detailed studies of the various branches of engineering before we can discuss the development of the industry as a whole, and most of these detailed studies have not been written (Saul, 1967, p. 111). Nevertheless, the work of Professor Saul and others, and the various contemporary accounts of engineering in the nineteenth century, enables us to construct at least an outline of its history.

It is generally accepted that the evolution of the engineering industries in Britain during and after the industrial revolution was one of change from unspecialised jobbing metal working to highly specialised engineering in which firms made one, or at least only a small number, of types of machines, often in only a small range of sizes. The engineers of the industrial revolution, such men as James Watt, Henry Maudslay, Robert Stephenson, Joshua Field or John Rennie, were prepared to design and make machinery of all kinds, from steam engines to Babbage's calculating engine, but during the first half of the nineteenth century more specialised production became normal. As Saul puts it:

> During the third and fourth decades of the century the industry had begun to develop away from the earlier pattern, whereby all manner of metal jobbing was undertaken, into more specialised organisations. Complete specialisation was still rare, but makers of locomotives, textile machinery and heavy machine tools came closest to it, though there was little or no concentration within a particular field of activity. (Saul, 1968a, p. 186)

The trend to specialisation continued up to the first world war and beyond, urged on by those who saw the lack of it as one of the factors responsible for the declining competitive position of the British engineering industry. Specialisation was greater in some industries than in others, and the size of engineering firms also varied greatly, from the giant railway workshops to the small businesses of the Birmingham hardware districts and the scattered makers of agricultural machinery, many of them not far removed from blacksmiths. The trend towards 'modern' specialised units of production was, however, clear in many fields, however slow the progress towards it.[1]

This description has at least the attractions of simplicity, but it needs further examination. It says very little about the actual process by which the industry was transformed. It cannot tell us whether the process was one by which old firms gradually narrowed their range of products, or whether they were superseded and forced out by new firms entering already specialised. It cannot tell us whether the size of the industry changed as its structure was changing, and how these developments interacted. It cannot tell us what kind of specialisation was achieved, whether it was specialisation in the production of one commodity, or in the production of a range of technically similar products, or in the production of a range of goods for one consumer industry, or some sub-division of one of these.

These questions must be answered however imperfectly, before the place of the machine tool industry in the whole process, and the structure of that industry, can be discussed. It is necessary to know whether the changes in machine tool production, which are to be studied in detail, were typical of the industry as a whole, or whether its progress was entirely heterodox, in relation to all these questions.

It is difficult to answer these questions. Traditionally, the history of British industries has been approached as if it were a type of aggregated business history; one might add up the histories of all the firms, and then one would have the history of the industry. This approach has been forced on economic historians by the nature of the available data, which has normally been the records of individual firms; the findings from these have been combined with scanty aggregate production and trade statistics, and the whole seasoned with the qualitative comments of contemporary observers. A great deal of illumination has been gained by such methods, but they are of limited value unless they can be complete and can cover all firms in the industry. Furthermore, the data available refer to the leading firms, to the firms whose records have survived, to the firms which attracted press attention, to the firms who made important technical progress.

These methods cannot illuminate the submerged section of the industry, technically less progressive, with smaller workshops, less efficient bookkeepers and less enterprising managers; yet these firms have been responsible for the bulk of production. As an illustration of the difficulties of the traditional method, which Saul himself is the first to admit, one can cite Professor Saul's work on the machine tool industry; he identified 129 firms 'in the four main areas of machine tool production' in 1913, but was unable to discover even the minimum of information about 69 of them (Saul, 1968b, p. 42). He was able to obtain figures of output for only 10 firms, responsible between them for only 29% of the total output of the industry as it was recorded in the 1907 Census of Production.[2] It is

possible that in some of the engineering industries which had a smaller
number of units, for instance locomotive production, wider coverage might
be achieved, but it is likely that Professor Saul's experience is not untypical; it has also to be remembered that securing the necessary information
becomes progressively more difficult as the enquiry is pushed back into the
nineteenth century.

In order to answer the questions which have been posed about the
developing structure of the engineering industries, it is necessary to adopt
different methods, since the traditional methods help us to understand
only the probably untypical experience of a few firms. In the rest of this
discussion of the structure of the engineering industries, therefore, an
attempt will be made to describe the industries through material gathered
from contemporary trade directories. The data from these sources will be
used to discuss the accepted view, stated in summary above, of the changing structure of the engineering industry during the period up to 1914.

The difficulties associated with the use of directory material in eluci-
dating the development of an industry are as numerous, and as severe, as
those associated with the methods which have just been described, and a
discussion of these difficulties must precede the use of the data. The directories used in this study were those produced by Kelly and Co., called the
(*Post Office*) *Directory of Merchants, Manufacturers and Traders*. They
were compiled by agents, employed by the publishers, each of whom
covered a particular area of the country. The agents were directed to get in
touch with every business concern in their area, to inform them that each
firm was entitled to a free entry in the directory under every heading with
which it was concerned, and to collect this information on products or
types of business for inclusion in the directory. This procedure was
repeated every time the directory was published, at first every two or three
years, but by the 1890s annually. The cost of the publication was covered
by sales and by advertisements; firms could pay for advertising space in the
directory, or for the printing of their entry in a heavier or larger type than
the normal entries, or for the insertion with their entry of some extended
description or praise of their product.[3]

The accuracy of information gathered from these directories is directly
dependent on the accuracy with which they were compiled. It can plaus-
ibly be argued that it was in the interests of all concerned to ensure that
the directory was as comprehensive as possible. The publishers had this aim
because of their wish to ensure that the directory was as useful as possible,
and thus a more attractive purchase. Each individual firm had an interest in
seeing that it was included, particularly if its competitors were, and an

interest in seeing that it was listed under as many headings as it had products. This raises the question of whether the directory might be over-comprehensive, might include firms under headings in which they were not really competent. It is again true that the publishers would have an interest in avoiding such exaggeration, which would reduce the attractions of the directory. Secondly, it can be argued that no firm would seek business in a field in which it was totally incompetent, since the costs of undertaking stray orders in such fields would be very high. It is possible, in other words, that firms may be listed under headings in which they were not normally employed, but they would be at least potential producers in that field, while the interests of the publishers would exert pressure on them not to exaggerate their skills. On these grounds, therefore, it seems reasonable to treat the directories as reasonably accurate evidence; it will be shown later that the information from them on the machine tool trade is consistent with other evidence about the size of the industry.

Given therefore that the directories are an accurate source of information it has to be asked whether they can provide answers to the questions which are to be asked. The information is incomplete in two important respects. No information is given on the size of the firms; each is given one entry, however large or small it is. Secondly, the classifications which are used by the directory compilers are in terms of industries; a firm will be listed as a maker of machine tools, not as a maker of heavy or light, cheap or expensive tools, or under particular tools. Thus the directories can give no information on whether a firm specialised within an industrial group, as we know from qualitative information many were increasingly doing.

The use of the directories does have a further drawback, which may well account for the fact that, with one exception, business directories have not normally been used in this way (Sigsworth and Blackman, 1968). Partly because of the large number of firms in the engineering industry, and partly because each firm might be listed under a number of different headings, the bulk of the material is considerable. In principle, it would have been desirable to have studied every year for which the directories were published. This would have enabled variations over time in the number of firms and in their distribution over branches of the industries to have been studied, and more information would have been available on the 'life-histories' of individual firms. In practice, because of the bulk of the material, only three years were studied, 1907 because of the availability of census output figures for that year, and 1877 and 1892 to span the period for which the directories are available. One has at best, therefore, three snapshot pictures, at fifteen-year intervals, of the engineering industry; the headings were chosen from directories to cover roughly the Census of Production definition of the engineering industries. (A list of the industries is given in appendix 1.1). In discussing the material, the following definitions will be used:

entry	the individual mention of one firm under one heading
firm	the unit of organisation, one firm having one or more entries, corresponding to the number of products made. A firm listed more than once, but at different addresses, has been treated as one firm
product	the type of engineering product produced, as defined by the compilers of the directory
sector	the set of entries concerned in the manufacture of a product
engineering industry	the set of sectors covered

Thus, the *firm* of Greenwood and Batley had an *entry* as a manufacturer of machine tools, which was therefore one of its *products*. It therefore was one firm in the machine tool *sector* of the *engineering industry*.

The evidence of the directories as to the total size of the engineering industry is given in table 1.1:

Table 1.1   *The size of the engineering industry*

In 1877	1721 firms had 2509 entries, divided among 35 sectors
In 1892	3755 firms had 5773 entries, divided among 45 sectors
In 1907	3429 firms had 5104 entries, divided among 45 sectors

Source: *Kelly's Directory of Merchants, Manufacturers and Traders.*

The expansion of the engineering industry is clear; although the number of firms contracted slightly after 1892, the growth up to that point is striking. This is entirely consistent with qualitative evidence; this was as a whole a period in which there was considerable expansion, particularly in the light engineering branches, with the rise of such new trades as cycle manufacture, sewing machines, and other Midland Industries. As these were new trades, and many of them were situated in areas of the country without an existing tradition of engineering, it is reasonable that much of the expansion of output to cater for these new demands should have come through the formation of new firms, rather than by the old engineering firms turning to new products. A further reason for the growth in total numbers can be found in the expansion of the agricultural machinery industry, which also brought engineering to many new areas of the country.

What is perhaps more surprising is that the growth in total numbers was accompanied by a substantial turnover of firms, so that both in 1892 and in 1907 the majority of firms had been founded since the preceding 'snapshot'. Only 13.2% of firms listed in 1892 had survived from 1877, and only 30.9% of the firms listed in 1907 had appeared in either or both of the lists for 1877 and 1892. This rapid turnover of firms would normally imply that the industry was highly competitive, with low barriers to entry of new firms, and this point is discussed more fully below.

It is normally accepted that this was a period in which the engineering industry showed signs of increasing specialisation. If specialisation is defined, initially, as concentration on the manufacture of one product, or alternatively as participation in only one branch of the industry, then the directory material shows that the proportion of specialised firms was indeed slightly increasing over the period under discussion, as shown in table 1.2.

Table 1.2   *The proportion of specialised firms in the engineering industry*

1877	1245 out of 1721 firms made only one product, or 72%
1892	2783 out of 3755 firms made only one product, or 74%
1907	2582 out of 3429 firms made only one product, or 75%

Source: *Kelly's Directory of Merchants, Manufacturers and Traders.*

It is, however, apparent that some sectors of the industry were much more specialised than others, as appendix 1.2 shows. If, instead of calculating the percentage of specialised firms within the industry as a whole, as was done in table 1.2, we calculate the percentage within each sector, and take the mean, the results are as in table 1.3. Again, it can be seen that on average the sectors within the engineering industry were becoming more highly specialised but that the amount of specialisation was already high by 1877, probably somewhat higher than would have been expected, which suggests that the emergence of specialised engineering manufacture was quite well advanced by the middle of the century.

The directories also produce evidence which, at first sight, appears to

Table 1.3   *An alternative calculation of the proportion of specialised firms in the engineering industry*

1877	1892	1907
47%	47%	52%

Source: *Kelly's Directory of Merchants, Manufacturers and Traders.*

contradict the picture of increased specialisation. Table 1.4 shows the average numbers of products made by all firms, and by firms making more than one product, and suggests that the trend was towards less specialisation from 1877 to 1892, although slightly towards specialisation from 1892 to 1907. In addition, it might be thought to be a corollary of the movement towards specialisation that the unspecialised firms should stand a smaller chance of survival. This does not appear to have been the case. Of the 1721 firms appearing in 1877, 496, or 28.8%, survived at least until 1892, while 976 (26.0%) of the firms appearing in 1892 survived at least until 1907. When these firms are divided into firms making one, and more than one, product, it can be seen that the unspecialised firms had only a very slightly higher chance of surviving. From 1877 to 1892 29.6% of unspecialised firms survived, as against 28.0% making more than one product, while between 1892 and 1907 the comparable figures were 28.2% and 25.2%.

Table 1.4   *Number of products made by engineering firms*

Date	No. of firms	Mean no. of products	No. of firms making more than one product	Mean no. of products
1877	1721	1.46	476	2.66
1892	3755	1.53	972	3.08
1907	3429	1.50	847	3.00

Source: *Kelly's Directory of Merchants, Manufacturers and Traders.*

A possible reason for these apparent contradictions is that the definition of specialisation which has hitherto been adopted is concealing and confusing more than it is revealing. Specialisation has been defined as the concentration by the firm on the manufacture of one of the products listed in appendix 1.1. It is clear that, by the nature of the directory material, it can reveal nothing about the decision by a firm to specialise its production within one of those branches, making, for example, only lathes instead of all machine tools. But other choices were open to the firm, under the general umbrella of a movement towards specialisation. It was, firstly, possible for a firm to specialise by concentrating on a range of products which presented technically similar problems in their design and manufacture, although they differed greatly in ultimate use and were sold to a wide variety of customers. An example of such a class of products is the range of different types of steam engines. Professor Rosenberg has suggested that the similarity of technique exhibited by many industrial processes during this period was a potent factor in the technical progress of the metal-using industries:

> Metal-using industries, therefore, were continually being confronted with similar kinds of problems which required solution and which, once solved, took their place in short order in the production of other metal-using products employing similar processes. (Rosenberg, 1963, p. 425)

In view of this 'technical convergence', it seems likely that firms would grow by the addition to the range of products which they made of other products whose manufacture involved similar problems or suggested similar solutions. Thus firms would 'specialise' not in one type of machinery, but in a range of similar types. As Professor Rosenberg points out, analysis of industry in these terms involves discarding

> the familiar Marshallian approach, involving as it does the definition of an industry as a collection of firms producing a homogeneous product, – or at least products involving some sufficiently high cross-elasticities of demand. For many analytical purposes it is necessary to group firms together on the basis of some feature of the commodity as a final product . . . (Rosenberg, 1963, p. 422)

It is not necessary, of course, for the link between the manufacture of different types of machinery to have been a technical one. A second type of specialisation would be for the firm to group its products to satisfy the requirements of a particular customer or a group of customers. Many industries require many different types of machinery to aid them in their production; the manufacture of small arms, for example, involves the use of a range of metal-forming and metal-cutting machinery, and of numerous woodworking machines. The individual machines in the range have little in common with each other, and much more in common with woodworking or metal-working machinery used in totally dissimilar processes. On the other hand, there are advantages if one machinery making firm produces all the machines, and can ensure that they fit together in the production process. Thus Greenwood and Batley of Leeds made, for example, small-arms machinery, and equipped complete factories; partly based on the 'spin-off' from this activity, they also made a wide range of wood- and metal-working tools. Other examples of such specialisation by customer occur in the textile machinery trades, and in the manufacture of such apparently disparate products as cranes, hydraulic machinery, pumping machinery and marine steam engines, all intended for the ship-building trades.

In view of these two possibilities for further types of specialisation in engineering, it is interesting to examine the directory material to see whether either type occurs. If they do, one would expect to find that patterns, explicable rationally in either of these two ways, would appear in the data; that is, there would be many cases where firms made two or more products in conjunction which were either technically similar or were directed at the same customers. Conversely, if no such systematic pattern appears, one would expect to find a large number of firms making, in conjunction, products which appeared to have very little relation to each other. At the extreme, if the connections were entirely random, one would expect to find no pattern at all, simply a random collection of choices. It can easily be shown, by a chi-square test, that the pattern differs from that which would be expected under a random choice hypothesis. (For the data for 1877 $p \leqslant 0.001$.) As table 1.5 shows, a large number of products were never made in conjunction, while, on the other hand, a number of products were made very often in conjunction.

Table 1.5   *Links between the manufacture of engineering products*

Year	No. of sectors	No. of possible links	No. of observed links	No. of single 10% links	No. of double 10% links
1877	35	595	295	116	19
1892	45	990	510	208	51
1907	45	990	419	158	41

Source: *Kelly's Directory of Merchants, Manufacturers and Traders.*

The products made most often in conjunction are those making up the 'single 10% links' and the 'double 10% links' mentioned in table 1.5. These figures are arrived at by the method shown in the following formula:

$$X = \frac{\text{No. of firms making product } A \text{ who also make product } B \times 100}{\text{No. of firms making product } A}$$

$$Y = \frac{\text{No. of firms making product } B \text{ who also made product } A \times 100}{\text{No. of firms making product } B}$$

If either X or Y is greater than 10%, the link is considered to be a single 10% link. If both X and Y are greater than 10%, the link is considered to be a double 10% link. (It should be noted that if both X and Y are greater than 10%, the link will be considered as *two* single 10% links for the purpose of table 1.5.) While it is clear that this procedure is somewhat arbitrary, in the sense that some other proportion might equally easily be held to be more significant, some such procedure is necessary to discriminate between products that are normally, or merely casually, made in conjunction. This criterion can also be used to examine in detail the inter-connections between products, allowing matrices such as that in table 1.6 to be compiled. Table 1.6 shows one group of products commonly made together in 1877, and further examples of such groups for 1877 and for 1892 and 1907 are shown in appendix 1.3. The three groups which emerge most clearly from this procedure are concerned with the manufacture of various kinds of steam-engines, with tool-making, and with the manufacture of textile machinery.

Table 1.6   *An example of links between sectors of the engineering industry in 1877*

	1	2	3	6	8	17	28
1		27	9	13	17	9	15
2	71		14	14	22	8	20
3	79	44		21	47	21	44
6	58	25	11		11	11	17
8	37	19	12	5		16	36
17	31	10	8	8	24		30
28	21	11	7	5	22	12	

Notes:

(a)   Each figure represents the percentage of the total number of firms listed in the vertical border who also made the product listed along the horizontal border. Thus 71% of firms making product 2 also made product 1, and 27% of firms making product 1 also made product 2.

(b)   The products included in the table were (numbered as in appendix 1.1):
1. Fixed steam engines, 2. Portable steam engines, 3. Pumping steam engines, 6. Marine steam engines, 8. Cranes, 17. Hydraulic machinery, 28. Pumping machinery.

In all these cases, the factor which most clearly links the products which are manufactured in conjunction is that they are technically similar, much in the way suggested by Rosenberg. This does not, however, rule out a certain amount of specialisation based on other considerations, such as the needs of potential customers, either by individual firms or by groups of firms; there are a number of strong links between products which exist other than in the three main groups, or which cut across those groups; in 1877, for example, 10% of cotton machinery makers and 20% of flax machinery makers also made machine tools, and the connections of steam machine makers with other groups is also strong. The primary purpose of this discussion is not, however, to delineate these connections in detail, but rather to emphasise that the choices made by firms were either rational, or at least customary, and that they appear to have been dictated to some considerable extent by what might be called the economics of learning-by-doing; firms applied the expertise which they had learned in one branch of manufacturing to closely related branches.

The engineering industries

The structure of the engineering industry in the late nineteenth century clearly requires further discussion which would be out of place in a work concerned largely with one branch of the industry. It has not been possible, for example, to discuss the geographical distribution of the industry nor the changes in that distribution, although such factors must have had an effect upon the industry and upon the products which it made in conjunction. What is clear, however, even from this short discussion, is that despite the fluidity and high turnover of firms which is a notable feature of the industry, its structure is in no way random; there existed, even as early as 1877, a very large number of specialised engineering firms, and in addition a number of firms who exploited their technical capabilities in the manufacture of similar products. To a considerable extent, therefore, the traditional picture of a very slow evolution from general, metal-jobbing firms to specialised firms, achieved only around 1914−18, has to be seriously modified, to take account of the very considerable progress in this direction which had been made as early as the 1870s.

Appendix 1.1   Products included in the sample from the material in *Kelly's Directory of Merchants, Manufacturers and Traders*

1. Fixed steam engines
2. Portable steam engines
3. Pumping steam engines
4. Power looms
5. Steam engines (unspecified)
6. Marine steam engines
7. Cornish steam engines
8. Cranes
9. Gun implements
10. Gun, rifle and pistol
11. Machine tools
12. Electrical machinery
13. Woollen machinery
14. Tools (unspecified)
15. Electrical dynamo
16. Mining machinery
17. Hydraulic machinery
18. Woodworking machinery
19. Printing machinery
20. Agricultural implements
21. Locomotive steam engines
22. Traction engines
23. Boot and shoe machinery
24. Lathes and tools

25. Edge tools
26. Cotton machinery
27. Joiners tools
28. Pumping machinery
29. Paper machinery
30. Rail and mine tools
31. Worsted machinery
32. Rail carriages
33. Ploughing engines
34. Rail wagons
35. Sewing machines
36. Hosiery machinery
37. Cannons
38. Ammunition
39. Hand tools
40. Agricultural engines
41. Sheep shears
42. Typewriters
43. Steam hammers
44. Flax, hemp and silk waste machinery
45. Oil mill machinery
50. Ordnance machinery
51. Shells
52. Torpedo

Note: The numbers assigned to the products are for convenience; the order has no significance.

Appendix 1.2   Percentage of specialised firms within each sector (No. of firms in sector is given in brackets)

Product	1877	1892	1907
1. Fixed steam	35.5 (286)	20.3 (389)	22.2 (275)
2. Portable steam	18.9 (114)	2.5 (161)	2.0 (101)
3. Pumping steam	11.8 (41)	5.7 (245)	5.8 (172)
4. Power loom	53.7 (54)	44.6 (56)	42.2 (45)
5. Steam engines (unspec.)	33.3 (77)	63.6 (55)	50.0 (38)
6. Marine steam	25.0 (62)	40.0 (165)	63.6 (143)
7. Cornish steam		1.8 (112)	0.0 (68)
8. Cranes	30.2 (126)	52.7 (148)	56.6 (152)
9. Gun implements	75.9 (26)	81.5 (65)	71.1 (52)
10. Gun, rifle, pistol	90.0 (130)	92.9 (435)	87.0 (308)
11. Machine tools	33.7 (167)	19.1 (236)	25.7 (222)
12. Electrical machinery		71.3 (122)	65.9 (176)
13. Woollen machinery		49.4 (168)	62.5 (160)
14. Tools (unspec.)	57.9 (128)	64.4 (45)	72.4 (58)

16

Appendix 1.2   *Continued*

Product	1877		1892		1907	
15. Electrical dynamo			63.1	(38)	16.7	(114)
16. Mining machinery			41.5	(41)	51.8	(83)
17. Hydraulic machinery	34.1	(88)	42.8	(168)	58.4	(173)
18. Woodworking machinery	53.3	(15)	41.0	(61)	64.1	(67)
19. Printing machinery	74.1	(27)	76.3	(59)	77.4	(53)
20. Agricultural impls.	81.9	(147)	91.2	(857)	95.1	(878)
21. Locomotive steam engines	0.0	(4)	20.2	(84)	42.3	(52)
22. Traction engines	16.8	(12)	1.7	(58)	0.0	(50)
23. Boot and shoe machinery	88.9	(9)	78.3	(60)	85.3	(75)
24. Lathes and tools	24.4	(125)	45.2	(186)	41.1	(190)
25. Edge tools	57.3	(173)	70.9	(271)	60.9	(220)
26. Cotton machinery	46.6	(55)	63.1	(220)	72.4	(181)
27. Joiners tools	54.6	(104)	65.8	(184)	54.4	(158)
28. Pumping machinery	53.3	(210)	36.0	(114)	44.4	(126)
29. Paper machinery	66.7	(9)	51.6	(31)	60.0	(35)
30. Rail and mine tools			32.1	(78)	35.0	(80)
31. Worsted machinery	75.9	(29)	38.3	(94)	33.3	(51)
32. Rail carriages	52.0	(25)	63.8	(47)	48.2	(27)
33. Ploughing engines			2.3	(43)	0.0	(30)
34. Rail wagons	75.0	(77)			95.9	(98)
35. Sewing machines	72.8	(60)	77.0	(152)	87.2	(47)
36. Hosiery machinery			85.3	(34)	86.7	(30)
37. Cannons	15.0	(8)	33.3	(6)	100.0	(1)
38. Ammunition	87.5	(8)	58.3	(12)	54.8	(42)
39. Hand tools			15.7	(185)	27.0	(133)
40. Agricultural engines					39.1	(23)
41. Sheep shears	52.6	(20)	60.9	(23)	52.6	(19)
42. Typewriters					100.0	(72)
43. Steam hammers	22.2	(36)	25.6	(43)	32.0	(25)
44. Flax etc. machinery	34.5	(29)	44.7	(47)	56.7	(30)
45. Oil mill machinery	8.3	(11)	52.9	(17)	33.3	(15)
50. Ordnance machinery	18.2	(6)	25.0	(8)		
51. Shells			50.0	(14)		
52. Torpedo			50.0	(2)		
N	35		45		45	
Σx	1631.9		2113.7		2333.1	
x̄	46.6		47.0		51.8	

Appendix 1.3   Inter-relationships between the production of engineering goods

This appendix presents a number of matrices showing links between the manufacture of different engineering products, on the model of table 1.6 above. As in that table, each figure in the matrices represents the percentage of the total number of firms making the product listed in the vertical border who also made the product listed in the horizontal border. (The numbers in the borders refer to the list of the products in appendix 2.1.) Thus in the first matrix, for example, 36% of firms making fixed steam engines also made Cornish engines, while 87% of the firms making Cornish engines also made fixed steam engines.

'The steam engine group' in 1892

	1	2	3	6	8	17	28
1		36	55	22	9	11	8
2	87		79	30	39	11	7
3	87	52		30	11	13	12
6	51	29	44		6	6	3
8	23	12	19	7		29	18
17	24	11	20	6	26		27
28	28	10	26	4	23	40	

'The steam engine group' in 1907

	1	2	3	6	8	17	28	7	33
1		32	54	12	8	11	13	24	9
2	87		77	15	13	8	9	39	27
3	86	45		14	12	16	18	37	15
6	22	11	17		5	5	4	6	3
8	15	9	13	5		24	12	3	1
17	17	5	16	4	21		29	6	1
28	28	7	25	5	14	40		13	3
7	97	57	94	13	7	16	24		31
33	90	90	87	17	7	3	13	70	

'The tool-making group' in 1877

	11	14	24	25	27
11		0	39	8	1
14	0		8	12	12
24	54	8		6	2
25	8	9	4		19
27	2	15	3	32	

'The tool-making group' in 1892

	11	14	24	25	27	39
11		2	28	7	5	60
14	9		20	2	4	4
24	35	4		3	2	18
25	6	0	2		17	7
27	7	1	2	25		10
39	77	1	18	10	10	

The engineering industries

'The tool-making group' in 1907

	11	14	24	25	27	30	39
11		0	41	5	4	10	37
14	0		19	3	3	5	0
24	47	6		4	2	8	15
25	5	1	4		27	8	0
27	6	1	2	37		6	8
30	29	4	20	21	11		21
39	61	0	22	8	10	13	

'The textile group' in 1877

	4	26	44	31
4		24	7	6
26	22		10	2
44	14	21		7
31	10	3	7	

'The textile group' in 1892

	4	26	44	31	13
4		46	13	38	39
26	12		7	14	25
44	15	32		19	26
31	22	33	10		64
13	13	32	7	36	

'The textile group' in 1907

	4	26	31	44	13
4		27	16	9	27
26	7		8	2	17
31	14	28		8	63
44	13	10	13		17
13	8	19	20	3	

2. The technical history of machine tools, 1850-1914

The increasing specialisation and differentiation of the engineering industry was a response to the development of many new products and techniques of manufacture in the second half of the nineteenth century. The development, for example, of the electrical industries, of cycles, typewriters, sewing machines, automobiles and boot and shoe machinery, of improved steels and alloys, and of methods of power transmission and generation, all called forth new manufacturing industries and techniques. For the machine tool industry, which was the primary supplier of machinery for these new industries, these developments implied the need for constant change in its products, and a constant readiness to respond to new opportunities and new needs. Machine tools in this period were changed, and new machine tools invented, in response to two sets of pressures; firstly, manufacturers required new tools, and modifications to old tools, to carry out new processes and to make old processes more efficient. Secondly, machine tool makers produced new tools, and modified old tools, to take advantage of developments in power generation and in metals technology. Both these sets of pressures, and the responses by machine tool makers to them, were continuous, and it is important to see the development of machine tool technology in this period as a process of constant accretion to knowledge, not as a series of discrete inventions.

This point is emphasised by the proliferation of different types of machine tools which took place after 1850. The major types of machine tool are lathes, drilling machines, boring machines, planing machines, shaping machines, slotting machines, milling machines, grinding machines, shearing and sawing machines, and some pressing machines which have a cutting action. These are not, however, discrete categories, since many machine tools combine in one machine operations which can be carried out separately by other machines. The names given to certain machines have also varied over time, and between countries.

As Steeds points out:

The machine now commonly called a 'vertical lathe' has, in the past, been called a 'circular planer', a 'turning and boring mill', and even a 'horizontal lathe', — the last because its work table was horizontal. The

20

term 'capstan lathe' has a fairly definite meaning in Britain but is not used in America, where 'screw machine' is used to describe the same thing. (Steeds, 1969, p. xix)

As will be apparent from Steeds' example, the basic name of a machine tool is normally modified by some adjective describing the alignment of one or other part, (horizontal, vertical, straight), the capacity of the machine tool to perform different jobs (plain, universal), the method by which it performs them (radial, multiple), or even the final product (screw-cutting, cutter grinding). All these modifications make it extremely difficult to describe even the most common machine tools, so that attention will be confined mainly to description of the basic types, even if these were in fact rarely if ever made without some modification.

The lathe performs the metal-cutting operation known as turning. In the basic lathe the work-piece is rotated between two supports, known as centres, while the cutting tool is held against it. The cutting tool is thus static, while the work-piece revolves, although the tool may be moved from one end to the other of the work-piece, to allow cuts to be taken at different places. Many types of lathe dispense with the two centres, the work-piece being clamped to a face plate, and the cutting tool being brought into operation against the side or edge of the work-piece, which still revolves. In the capstan turret lathe a number of different cutting tools are clamped into a tool-holder, in pre-set positions, and are then rotated or indexed to allow them to cut the work-piece one after the other. This allows a sequence of operations to be carried out without the need to remove and replace different cutting tools, and was an important aid to speeding up turning operations.

The drilling machine holds a drill or other end-cutting tool in a spindle which is rotated and fed towards the work-piece. Drilling machines thus operate on a static work-piece, while the cutting tool revolves. Boring machines operate on the same principle, but the cutting tool is differently shaped, to allow it to cut a hole of a wider radius than could be accomplished with a drill bit. In some boring machines, however, particularly those made early in the nineteenth century, the boring tool was supported on a bar placed in a hole already roughly cut or cast.

In the planing machine the cutting tool is again held static, while the work-piece, clamped on the work-table, is fed past it with a reciprocating motion. The tool may be moved transversely between each motion of the work-table, thus allowing the whole of the work-piece to be machined. Normally the work-table is horizontal, the cutting tool being suspended above it on a bar held between two standards. Various modifications of planing machines allow the cut to be taken in both directions, or provide for a quick-return motion of the work-table, thus reducing the time wasted in returning to the beginning of the stroke.

The shaping machine, like the planing machine, is used to produce flat surfaces. In the shaping machine, however, the work-piece is static, while a cutting tool attached to a ram is fed across it in a straight line with a reciprocating motion. The work-piece is fed transversely on each return stroke, the ram head being hinged to allow the cutting tool to pass over the work-piece on the return stroke. The slotting machine is essentially a version of the shaping machine, but the vertical rather than the horizontal face of the work-piece is machined.

The basic feature of the many types of milling machines is that the cutting tool is a rotary cutter with multiple teeth, unlike the single-edged or double-edged cutters used in all the machine tools previously mentioned. Milling machines can however, by the use of different shapes of rotary cutters mounted in different positions with respect to the work-piece, perform many of the operations of the other machine tools, and are one of the most versatile of machine tools.

The grinding machine employs an abrasive wheel or wheels to remove metal through the contact with the work-piece of 'thousands of points simultaneously and millions of points continually' (Woodbury, 1959, p. 8). The cutting tool is thus entirely unlike the cutting tools used in other machine tools. In other respects, however, in the methods by which the cutting tool is applied to the work-piece, many grinding machines employ virtually the same mechanisms as those used in other tools; early grinding machines in fact consisted of grinding wheels fixed to the tool-holder of a lathe. In some grinding machines the work-piece revolves while the tool is fixed, but in most the work-piece is held steady while the tool revolves; in the cylindrical grinder both the work-piece and the cutting wheels revolve.

The other machine tools are relatively familiar. Shearing machines operate with a guillotine motion to cut metal, partially through the force of their own weight. Sawing machines use multiple cutters arranged on a metal band which is reciprocated across the work-piece. Pressing machines (other than those which utilise the plastic properties of metal to form a shape) again cut with a guillotine motion.

One extremely important machine tool has not so far been mentioned, since it is distinguished from those already considered rather by its function than by its methods of cutting. This is the gear-cutting machine, which almost always uses the cutting methods of milling, shaping or slotting machines. As Woodbury says, however, 'Probably none of the machine tools has called for more knowledge of geometry and more ingenuity of design to solve its unique problems' (Woodbury, 1958). Its development, in many different forms, allowed the solution of one of the major problems of mechanisation, that of regulating the speeds and ensuring accuracy of control of machinery, and it is thus normally considered as a separate type of machine tool of considerable importance.

The technical development of machine tools, 1850–1914

The majority of the tools which have just been described were invented before 1850, several of them, like the lathe, drilling machine and grinding machine, in prehistoric times. The industrial application of these tools to the machining of metal in large quantities was however largely achieved in the second half of the eighteenth century and the first half of the nineteenth century, in response to the demand for accurate machining created by the industrial revolution. The basic form of the major types of machine tool (with the exception of the milling machine, the turret or capstan lathe, some types of grinding machines and the various gear-cutting machines, which were all effectively developed after 1850) thus did not greatly change between 1850 and 1914, and changes in them were confined to relatively minor alterations in size, capacity and method of operation. Although these changes were minor by comparison with the initial development of the machine tools, they made a very considerable difference to the productive potential of machine tools; discussion of them is however complicated by the fact that they were unspectacular and that the changes and improvements which they produced were obtained gradually, often as the result of hundreds of minor modifications.

Apart from these modifications in the tools themselves, the period from 1850 to 1914 was one in which several major changes occurred in cutting tools, and in the methods by which the machine tools were powered. These modifications affected all types of machine tools, and they will therefore be considered first, before the detailed changes in the majority of machine tools, and the development of other types of tool are described.

Cutting tools. As Rolt points out:
  it is obvious that the efficiency of any metal-cutting machine depends
  absolutely upon the ability of the actual cutting tool to do the work
  required of it. Indeed, it would be true to say that the machine is

23

designed round the cutting tool since its proportions, its feeds and speeds are necessarily determined by the tool's cutting ability. (Rolt, 1965, p. 63)

Before the development of special tool steels and the use of metals other than steel in the second half of the nineteenth century, metal working was seriously hampered by the inadequacies of carbon steel cutting tools. Although carbon steel was used successfully in the early machine tools during the industrial revolution, tools made of it required constant sharpening and hardening, since carbon steel was too soft to retain a cutting edge for a long period, particularly as cutting speeds were increased. There was no scientific knowledge of the properties of steel, and none concerning methods of sharpening, so that each user had to develop his own methods. A description of American engineering in the 1860s gives methods for initially hardening, and for rehardening, cutting tools. To harden the tool, the engineer dipped the tool in a mixture of 2 lb pitch, 1 lb whale-oil, and ½ lb tallow, and secondly a mixture of 1 lb of pulverised sal-ammoniac, ⅓ lb tartaric acid, 4 qts water, and 1 pt red wine. To reharden the tool for daily use it was dipped in a further mixture of 1 lb tallow, ¾ lb sal-ammoniac, ¼ lb prussiate of potash, ½ lb black resin, 1 oz pepper, and 1 oz shaving powder (Weissenborn, 1861, p. 25).

Both carbon steel itself, and these various methods of hardening it for use in cutting tools, had evolved without any scientific investigation, virtually by accident. During the second half of the nineteenth century, however, numerous scientific experiments did result in very considerable technical improvements. In 1868 the first improved tool steel, with the extremely important property that it was self-hardening, was produced by Robert Mushet. This tool steel made it possible both to increase the speed of operation of machine tools, and to machine the newly introduced manganese steel produced by the Bessemer and Siemens—Martin processes. The major experiments in this field were however carried out in the United States by Frederick W. Taylor, working with Maunsel White of the Bethlehem Steelworks. Taylor experimented both with different methods of using existing tool steels, and with the development of new materials, and over a period of twenty years greatly altered engineering practice in both these directions. Taylor and White replaced the manganese in Mushet steel with chromium, increased the tungsten content, and finally added silicon.

This new alloy allowed the cutting speed of the tools to be increased from under 30 feet per minute to approximately 80—90 feet per minute. Taylor and White concluded their experiments by adding vanadium to the

24

alloy, further increasing the strength of the tools (Rolt, 1965, pp. 199–200).

The result of these improvements was greatly to increase the speed of feed of the cutting tool, unfortunately far beyond the strength of the existing machine tools, which fell to pieces when run at the new speeds. After the introduction of the new high-speed tool steels, as they were called, from 1900 onwards, all machine tools were therefore gradually redesigned to cope with the higher speeds, and thus the greater strength and stability which was required. This process of redesigning all the machine tools then in existence, and of producing new types of tools, does not seem however to have been as rapid as might have been expected, considering the undoubted cost advantages of the new tools. Rolt recalls that when he served part of his apprenticeship in a British engineering shop in 1929 he still used carbon steel tools on a lathe, having to take them to be tempered by the shop toolsmith (Rolt, 1965, p. 215). He suggests that since to take full advantage of the new high steels would involve a machine tool user in scrapping his entire plant and buying newly designed machine tools, most users preferred simply to buy the new machine tools as their old tools wore out. It is not clear how this affected the machine tool industry itself; the design and retooling costs involved in introducing the new generation of machine tools would have been very heavy, especially if the introduction of new tools did not stimulate increased purchasing by users, but there is very little sign that British machine tool makers were concerned about this, at least before 1914. It seems likely that the introduction of the new machine tools was, in Britain at least, a very gradual process, which did not have a great impact on the industry, largely because of the inertia of many potential customers.

Driving methods. Traditionally machine tools, like other machinery, were driven from a central steam engine in each shop, power being transmitted to individual machines through overhead belting. Changes in speed were achieved by the use of different sizes of pulley-wheels over which the belt, made of leather or canvas, ran. This method had serious deficiencies; the large number of belts required made the shop both dark and dangerous; changes in speed could be made only by changing to other wheels in a series of steps; the whole shop was dependent upon the operation of one steam engine, which at least in the early part of the century often broke down.

Although, as Rolt says, shops of this kind could still be found in Britain in 1930 (Rolt, 1965, p. 215), there were, during the late nineteenth century, a number of important changes in the methods by which machine tools were driven. Change-gears, with which the speed of a machine tool could be varied without stopping the machine, were introduced. The single-pulley belt drive, working with a geared headstock, replaced the system of multiple pulleys in the driving of lathes and other light machine tools. This made it possible to move towards the provision of a single motor, often driven by electricity, for each machine tool, eliminating the use of overhead shafting and pulleys (Steeds, 1969, pp. 118–19).

It is very difficult to assess the effects of the introduction of these new methods, which Steeds dates to the period after 1890. Although these methods affected the design of machine tools, the changes which they made necessary were less spectacular than those produced by the high-speed tool steels. It was also necessary for the machine tool makers to continue to make tools driven by a variety of methods, to suit the power available to their customers. Thus although in the early years of the twentieth century many machine tool makers introduced machine tools incorporating these improvements, as Steeds shows, it is impossible to tell what proportion of tools sold incorporated the new methods or, as with high-speed tools, what the costs of their introduction were.

The changes in tools and in driving methods discussed briefly above were applicable to a wide variety of machine tools. There were also improvements in each type of tool, and new types of machine tools were invented. In the remainder of this chapter, therefore, the more important of these changes will be described.

Lathes

Woodbury concludes his survey of the development of the lathe to 1850 by stating that by that date 'the lathe had developed into an industrial machine tool of precision and high capacity' (Woodbury, 1961, p. 117). The main changes in the lathe during the middle of the nineteenth century were directed towards increasing the size of this machine tool, and widening the range of operations which it could undertake. Lathes were produced with two tool rests, with two headstocks and with various other modifications. But the major development was that of the turret lathe, which Steeds describes as revolutionising machine shop practice in lathe work (Steeds, 1969, p. 55). There is considerable controversy about the exact details of the invention of the turret lathe, but it almost certainly originated in the United States between 1840 and 1850, and was probably first employed in the manufacture of small arms.

As Steeds suggests, the major development of the turret lathe, both in modification of its design and its commercial introduction, came between 1860 and 1890. Essentially, while the traditional lathe was improved in detail and increased in size, the turret lathe was developed as a new type of machine tool, fulfilling distinct functions particularly in mass production of simple components. A further development of this type was the automatic screw machine, developed in the United States and Germany, and introduced into Britain by Greenwood and Batley in the 1880s. This allowed the virtually automatic machining of bar stock which was fed through the chuck of the lathe past a turret containing a number of tools which were brought into position through the use of a cam-shaft. Many British machine tool makers, and their customers, continued however to view the turret as simply a place to store a number of cutting tools, which were swung into position by the operator, rather than as a move to automatic operation as in the screw machine. This situation gradually changed up to 1914, and was combined with the improvement of the traditional type of lathes, and with the development of multi-spindle automatic lathes.

The introduction of those new types of lathes, and the movement which was implied in them towards fully automatic machining, was one of the major sources of dispute between engineering employers and the Amalgamated Society of Engineers which culminated in the engineering strike of 1896. The 'machine question' as it was called, essentially concerned the replacement of skilled workers operating single machines by the new semi-automatic machines which could be operated by semi-skilled operatives under the oversight of a skilled toolsetter. It is unfortunately difficult to know how many of these new machines were imported from the United States. It seems likely that, as with the other changes that have been mentioned, their introduction was gradual and was conditioned by the slow speed of deterioration of the older types of lathes, although the fear of unemployment that these new machines aroused among engineering workers was certainly very real (Jefferys, 1946, ch. VI).

Boring and drilling machines

There were no major developments in boring machines between 1850 and 1914, but particularly after 1890 a number of machine tools were introduced which combined boring with other functions of machine tools. Lathes had previously been used for boring, and turning, boring and drilling was combined in one machine tool in 1892. Multi-spindle boring machines were also developed to be used in mass production.

The major change in the drilling machine in the early part of the period was the introduction and development of the radial drilling machine. In the early types of drilling machines the drill head was fixed, only vertical motion being possible, so that the work-piece had to be repositioned for each hole to be drilled. With the radial drill both vertical and horizontal, and eventually angular, movement of the drill was possible, the head being attached to an arm from a column or from the wall, so that the work-piece could remain clamped in one place while the drill moved above it. The usefulness of the drilling machine was also greatly increased by the introduction of twist drills after 1861, when Joseph R. Brown invented the universal milling machine to make them. Previously the drill had been simply a pointed piece of metal, with no cutting edge, and the introduction of the double-edged twist drill greatly increased the capacity of the drilling machine.

After the introduction of the twist drill, which was at first fiercely resisted, particularly in Britain, few changes were made in the design of drilling machines before 1914, although there was considerable development, as with boring machines, of multiple spindle machines to meet the needs of mass production.

Planing machines

There were no major changes in the design of planing machines between 1850 and 1914, apart from the introduction, early in the period, of the wall or side planer; these tools were particularly useful in machining large and heavy work-pieces, since the work-piece is static, being clamped on the floor while the cutting tool travels along it, supported on ways built into the side of the building. Otherwise there were improvements in the reversing mechanism, always a source of difficulty in design, but in general the modifications in design were much as with the other machine tools, increasing the size of the tools and making them more versatile and easier to operate.

Slotting machines

Slotting machines were invented in the 1830s, and remained almost unchanged throughout the period to 1914, although there were some changes in size, and experiments in combining them with drilling machines.

Shaping machines

Shaping machines, which date from about the same period as slotting machines, also underwent virtually no significant changes in design before 1914.

Milling machines

The milling machine, on the other hand, was largely developed during the period from 1850 to 1914, although some types of milling machine were in use before 1850 in the United States, and Nasmyth is said to have invented a form of milling machine in England (Woodbury, 1960). Before 1861 the major type in use in the United States, although it was also exported, was the Lincoln miller, described by Woodbury as the first production milling machine. In 1861, however, Joseph R. Brown invented the universal milling machine, which although it was designed initially for the manufacture of twist drills, was soon used for a variety of tasks. This invention was combined with improvements in the design and manufacture of milling cutters, which had been one of the major difficulties of the earlier machines. Numerous modifications of the basic milling machine were introduced during the rest of the period, and as Steeds states:

the milling machine developed from a machine that was built by firms for their own use, usually for a particular type of job, until it became of equal or greater importance than the planing, slotting and shaping machines and was being built for sale by numerous firms in most countries that had any machine tool industry. (Steeds, 1969, p. 102)

It is again difficult to estimate the direct impact of the milling machine on British industry in general or the machine tool industry in particular. The impact of the twist drills which it made cheaply and efficiently was considerable, after some delay, and milling machines themselves were certainly introduced quickly into England, particularly into arms factories. They were among American tools bought when the Enfield Small Arms Factory was equipped, and Greenwood and Batley were making and selling them to arms makers from the 1860s onwards. Their use must have improved the productivity of industries using them, since they not only made machining easier and quicker but also replaced a number of other machine tools, but it is impossible unfortunately to quantify this impact in any way

29

Gear-cutting machines

The development of gear-cutting machines largely took place during the period from 1850 to 1914, although clock-makers had used wheel-cutting and dividing engines for centuries. The major changes were that the size of the machines was greatly increased, so that industrial gearing could be produced, that gear-cutting machines were designed to work automatically, simply following a pre-cut pattern, and finally and probably most importantly, that machines were designed to generate gear patterns, rather than to copy them. Together with these developments was a considerable amount of investigation into the capacities and uses of different shapes of gears, and a considerable increase in accuracy.

Grinding machines

The last major type of machine tool, which was largely developed as a production tool after 1850, is the grinding machine. The major developments came between 1860 and 1890, cylindrical and surface grinders being developed simultaneously, and both were facilitated by the development of new types of abrasive wheels. One of the major difficulties with the early types of grinding machines was the poor quality of the abrasive wheel, particularly since the early wheels had a tendency to burst when being operated. The first really successful artificial grinding wheel was developed in 1877, and, as Rolt says, this made precision grinding possible (Rolt, 1965, p. 179). The precision grinding machine was developed in the United States by Brown and Sharpe and numerous modifications and new types of grinding machines were introduced, together with investigations of the optimum speeds and methods of working by Charles H. Norton, much on the model of Frederick W. Taylor's investigations of the cutting tools. New materials were developed for the abrasive wheel, notably silicon carbide and alundum, and Norton's work allowed the specification of correct speeds and methods of feed, and greatly increased the accuracy and capacity of grinding machines. Norton also was responsible for the major change in usage of grinding machines, from machines for finishing work started on other machine tools to machines which would carry out the whole process from the rough casting to the finished smooth stage.

This survey of the technical development of machine tools between 1850 and 1914 has been necessarily short and in many ways incomplete. It is so, partly because it is designed as an introduction and an explanation of the various terms which have to be used in a study of the machine tool industry, and partly because the information on the process of innovation is so inadequate. The books of Woodbury, Steeds, Roe and Rolt, which have been referred to in writing this chapter, concentrate very largely on the process of invention, although both Woodbury and Rolt show themselves to be aware of the importance of assessing the actual use of the inventions they describe. Neither can in fact provide much information of this kind, and without a careful study of catalogues, technical publications and the sales records of many firms, it is difficult to say where the information for such a study could in fact be found. Furthermore, even in the case of Greenwood and Batley, where catalogues, photographs of the machines, and sales records, are available, no very definite conclusions can be drawn, because of the multiplicity of machine tools which were made, about 500 differently named tools between 1856 and 1900.

The major conclusions which can however be drawn from the short survey of technical development given above is that, for the majority of the major types of machine tool, change during the period 1850 to 1914 was essentially a series of minor adaptations and improvements, which over the period as a whole markedly increased the capabilities and the ease of operation of the tools, but did not change their basic forms, except through the introduction of different sizes of tools. New types were introduced, notably milling, grinding and gear-cutting machines, but with these also, once the initial invention was made, the basic design of the machine tool changed little before 1914. Increases in cutting speeds, and much greater accuracy and precision, were the result of improvements in tool steels and in driving mechanisms, and these were applied throughout the field, but their adoption was, at least in Britain, slow and steady rather than spectacular.

3. The machine tool industry: structure and explanation

The fluidity and complexity of the engineering industries as a whole is fully reflected in the machine tool industry, and can be similarly documented from the evidence of the directories. The smaller number of firms in the machine tool industry makes it possible, however, to examine that complexity in more detail than was possible in the first chapter, and to bring to bear additional evidence. In this chapter, therefore, the growth of the machine tool industry will be outlined and examined, on the basis of the aggregative evidence from the directories and similar sources, and on the basis of the scattered information which we possess about the firms in the industry. It is important to emphasise, at the outset, how flawed the evidence is; we have no information on the total output of the industry except at the time of the first Census of Production, and the evidence concerning the operation of individual firms comes primarily from the large and successful firms.

Nevertheless, Kelly's directories make it possible for us to establish, as a first step, the size of the industry in terms of numbers of firms, for the bulk of the period from 1870 to 1914. Table 3.1 presents the results of a number of possible computations of this; the different figures result from different assumptions about the accuracy of the directory material, and from different treatment of firms who appear only once, or who disappear for only a short period. The exact assumptions and methods used, and their rationale, are discussed in the notes to the table. If we take them, for the moment, as giving orders of magnitude, the figures demonstrate firstly that there was relatively slow growth in the industry over the forty-year period as a whole; between 200 and 250 firms formed the industry in the 1870s and 1880s, between 350 and 400 in the early 1900s, before a decline to around 250 between 1910 and 1913. On the other hand, the number of machine tool producers was highly volatile in the short term, and there were significant changes in numbers even from year to year.

Taking the long-term change first, the rise in the number of machine tool firms clearly reflects the growth in the engineering industries as a whole which was established in the first chapter; moreover, numbers of

Table 3.1   *Number of firms in the machine tool industry*

	1	2	3 (1−2)	4	5	6 (4−5)	7 (1−5)
1870	195	67	128	195	64	131	131
1874	227	33	194	230	21	209	206
1877	214	44	170	240	41	188	173
1878	271	60	211	281	35	246	236
1882	275	94	181	311	35	276	240
1883	222	42	180	294	14	280	208
1884	309	122	187	339	39	300	270
1886	231	60	171	293	35	258	196
1887	254	17	237	264	10	254	244
1888	254	20	234	266	5	261	249
1890	227	87	140	302	74	228	153
1891	225	29	196	241	11	230	214
1892	246	12	234	254	4	250	242
1893	273	17	256	288	12	276	261
1894	374	104	270	388	71	316	303
1895	284	14	270	316	3	313	281
1896	306	11	295	322	7	315	299
1897	400	83	317	402	64	338	336
1898	320	8	312	340	6	334	314
1899	311	11	300	322	4	318	307
1900	303	11	292	322	9	313	294
1901	416	60	356	418	47	371	369
1902	358	5	353	373	5	368	353
1903	387	15	372	387	5	382	382
1904	354	5	349	378	5	373	349
1905	447	88	359	449	68	381	379
1906	346	3	343	357	2	355	344
1907	348	8	340	349	4	345	344
1908	345	5	341	352	5	345	341
1909	453	102	351	454	95	359	358
1910	275	21	254	285	21	264	254
1911	247	5	242	250	3	257	244
1912	243	3	240	251	3	248	240
1913	406	174	232	417	166	251	240

Notes

This table represents a number of computations of the number of firms in the machine tool industry at the dates given, derived from the information in Kelly's directories for those years.

Col. 1. The number of firms listed as machine tool makers.

Col. 2. The number of firms who, though listed as machine tool makers at the date given, do not appear in the directories under that heading in the subsequent directory. For example, a firm listed in 1870, but not in 1874, would appear among the 67 firms in col. 2 for 1877.

Col. 3. Col. 1 minus col. 2.

Col. 4. The number of firms listed as machine tool makers or listed as machine tool makers in the preceding and subsequent directories. For example, a firm listed in

1877 would appear among the 240 firms in col. 4 for 1877. Also included among the 240 firms would be a firm which, although not listed in 1877, had been listed in 1874 and would be listed again in 1878.

Col. 5. The number of firms who, although listed as machine tool makers at the date given, do not appear in the directories under that heading either in the preceding directory or in the first or second succeeding directories. For example, a firm would be counted among the 41 firms in column 5 in 1877 if it was listed in 1877, but not in 1874, 1878 or 1882.

Col. 6. Col. 4 minus col. 5.

Col. 7. Col. 1 minus col. 5.

Cols. 2 and 5, and cols. 3, 6 and 7 which are based on them, are intended to allow for possible errors in compilation, either by including firms erroneously as machine tool makers, or by excluding them erroneously. If it is assumed that such errors are likely to be corrected in the subsequent directory, then col. 6 gives the best estimate that can be made of the number of firms in the industry at the dates given.

firms in the machine tool industry continued to rise between 1892 and 1907, in contrast to the slight decline documented for the engineering industry as a whole. This growth in numbers of machine tool firms occurred during a period at which we can assume that the output of the machine tool industry as a whole was rising, although the size of that output, and its rate of growth, remain unknown. The assumption of growth in output is reasonable, however, on two grounds. Firstly, estimates of the output of the engineering industries, made by A. K. Cairncross and more recently by C. H. Feinstein, show rising output; although both series are said by their authors to be dubious in detail, the rising trends are obvious in figure 3.1 which shows them graphed. Although it is not a necessary corollary of the growth of engineering output that the machine tool sector should also have grown, since the increasing productivity of machine tools, and increasing imports of the tools, both have to be taken into account, machine tools are so vital a part of engineering production of all kinds that the assumption of a connection seems justified. Secondly, at a non-aggregative level, there is substantial evidence of a growth in the value of output of a number of individual firms in the industry, presented in table 3.2. It can be seen that the growth in output is rapid, particularly after the 1890s. Again, the growth of output of a number of leading firms in the industry does not, of itself, demonstrate that output of the industry as a whole rose; it is conceivable that these leading firms were simply gaining an increased share of the market, at the expense of other firms. Although it is likely that some increased market did result from the acknowledged technical excellence of these firms, in particular Alfred Herbert, it seems unlikely that all the growth in demand from the engineering and other customer industries could have been catered for in this way. Although

35

Figure 3.1. Output of the engineering industries

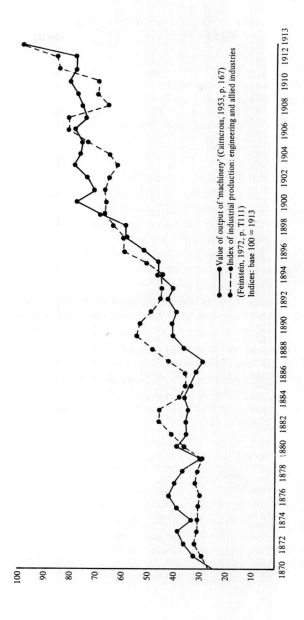

● Value of output of 'machinery' (Cairncross, 1953, p. 167)
– – ● Index of industrial production: engineering and allied industries
(Feinstein, 1972, p. T111)
Indices: base 100 = 1913

Table 3.2   *The output of a number of leading machine tool firms*

Date	Total output (£)	No. of firms included	Total output excluding Alfred Herbert (£)
1857	3,138	1	
1858	5,568	1	
1859	5,234	1	
1860	14,998	1	
1861	21,739	1	
1862	7,939	1	
1863	8,922	1	
1864	3,405	1	
1865	16,875	1	
1866	15,533	1	
1867	10,752	1	
1868	26,920	2	
1869	32,800	3	
1870	32,238	3	
1871	55,981	3	
1872	61,173	3	
1873	66,910	3	
1874	57,889	2	
1875	53,593	2	
1876	39,536	3	
1877	40,100	3	
1878	124,472	3	
1879	39,038	3	
1880	37,414	3	
1881	41,676	3	
1882	47,342	2	
1883	57,760	3	
1884	65,686	3	
1885	65,375	3	
1886	121,039	4	
1887	134,837	4	
1888	133,194	8	127,949
1889	171,690	8	167,904
1890	227,481	9	219,532
1891	237,828	9	228,261
1892	189,427	9	180,761
1893	180,551	9	170,822
1894	134,659	8	120,668
1895	149,359	8	131,372
1896	224,851	8	183,502
1897	258,526	8	195,965
1898	308,211	8	222,049
1899	413,744	8	315,046
1900	497,648	8	379,994
1901	428,011	7	311,479
1902	389,201	7	258,308
1903	440,095	8	284,504

Table 3.2   *Continued*

Date	Total output (£)	No. of firms included	Total output excluding Alfred Herbert (£)
1904	498,553	9	335,021
1905	600,510	9	388,248
1906	689,442	9	426,966
1907	836,730	9	512,853
1908	591,660	9	402,480
1909	553,194	9	320,563
1910	796,354	9	464,531
1911	952,182	9	523,796
1912	1,094,524	9	575,640
1913	1,219,878	9	693,925

Notes:
  (a) All prices are current.
  (b) The firms covered were: Muir (1868–93), Lang (1876–1913 excluding 1882 and 1887), Craven (1869–73 and 1886–1913), Ward (1896–1913), Richards (1888–95 and 1904–13), Archdale (1890–1913), Butler (1887–1913), Asquith (1903–13), Parkinson (1888–1913), Herbert (1888–1913), Greenwood and Batley (1857–1913). Output figures for all these firms, apart from Greenwood and Batley, were taken from records of the firms by Professor Saul. I am very grateful to him for allowing me to make use of them.
  (c) It is not possible to be entirely certain that other goods are not included within these output figures, which should therefore be treated as rough approximations.

these firms were large and growing, their total output in 1907 was only £836,730, 28% of the Census of Production estimate for the total output of the industry. It seems reasonable to assume, therefore, that these firms were partially at least sharing in a general increase in demand for machine tools. This growth was steady, but not spectacular; the output of the engineering industries as a whole rose by 2.8% per annum between 1870 and 1913, while the output of the leading firms in the machine tool industry rose by 7.2% per annum. It seems reasonable to assume that the growth of output of the machine tool industry lay somewhere between these two figures. Neither growth in output, nor change in numbers of firms, shows, therefore, any spectacular aspect.

By contrast, the directory material shows that there were considerable short-term changes in the numbers of firms engaged in making machine tools, while the sole evidence which we have for output, the figures for the leading firms, also shows marked fluctuations in the short run. Taking the numbers of firms first, the changes in this measure of the size of the industry were of two kinds, firstly changes in the total numbers of firms, and secondly changes in the composition of the industry within that total number, that is, changes in the age of firms. As table 3.3 shows, it is possible to partition the changes from year to year or from directory to directory, distinguishing between changes produced by the exit of firms from the industry, by the re-appearance of firms which had earlier formed part of the industry, and by the entry of new firms. It is also possible, as table 3.4 shows, to form at least a rough impression of the average 'age' of firms in the industry at various periods. All these measures reveal that there was considerable movement into and out of the industry, greater than would be revealed simply by study of the numbers of firms in the industry, although that figure itself reveals considerable fluctuations.

In addition, the geographical location of the machine tool industry shifted significantly between 1870 and 1913, although naturally these shifts were slower than those in the numbers of firms. Table 3.5 shows these changes, and it can be seen that the major increase in firms was in the industrial Midlands, while other areas did not show a very significant decrease; only in London, one of the traditional centres of the industry, was the decline substantial, a decline which parallelled the well-known flight of the metal-working industries from the capital in the second half of the nineteenth century.

To explain this pattern of growth, fluctuations and relocation in the machine tool industry is naturally a complicated task. Broadly, it is necessary to explain five phenomena;

a.   the slow growth and eventual decline in the number of firms in the industry.
b.   the short-run volatility in the numbers of firms in the industry.
c.   the existence of firms which left and re-entered the industry.
d.   the persistence of small firms in the industry, and the failure of the leading firms to capture a greater proportion of the market.
e.   the long-run changes in the geographical location of the industry.

In the remainder of this chapter, it will be suggested that these phenomena, and the pattern of growth, fluctuation and relocation which they produce, can be explained in terms of interaction of three characteristics of the industry. These were:

a.   the nature of entry conditions for firms.
b.   the nature of demand for machine tools.
c.   the cycle of demand for machine tools.

38

Table 3.3   *Movement of firms into and out of the machine tool industry*

Year	1 No. entering	2 No. re-entering	3 No. leaving permanently	4 No. leaving temporarily	5 No. in industry
1874	99	0	53	11	230
1877	48	0	35	3	240
1878	91	2	44	8	281
1882	94	3	52	15	311
1883	34	2	40	13	294
1884	65	13	24	9	339
1886	41	6	76	17	293
1887	40	10	32	47	264
1888	12	9	9	10	266
1890	49	48	39	22	302
1891	16	13	30	60	241
1892	33	11	22	9	254
1893	34	21	15	6	288
1894	62	67	22	7	388
1895	24	6	55	47	316
1896	17	7	12	6	322
1897	57	59	30	6	402
1898	29	4	51	44	340
1899	22	8	34	14	322
1900	16	9	23	2	322
1901	67	64	25	10	418
1902	16	8	31	38	373
1903	22	6	11	3	387
1904	14	3	21	5	378
1905	52	52	33	0	449
1906	11	5	58	50	357
1907	13	5	18	8	349
1908	16	5	18	0	352
1909	59	66	23	0	454
1910	24	19	212	0	285
1911	12	0	47	0	250
1912	11	6	16	0	251

Notes:

All figures in this table are compiled on the basis used to compile col. 4 of Table 3.1. That is, if for example a firm is listed in 1877, 1878 and 1882, omitted in 1883, listed in 1884, 1886 and 1887, omitted in 1888 and 1890, listed in 1891, 1892 and 1893, and omitted thereafter, it is treated as follows: entered in 1877 (col. 1), left temporarily in 1887 (col. 4), re-entered in 1891 (col. 2), left permanently in 1893 (col. 3). Thus temporary omission in 1883, for only one directory, is ignored.

Source: Kelly's directories for the years given.

Entry conditions

Firms setting out to begin the production of machine tools were of two types; either they were new firms, entering directly into the industry, or

Table 3.4   *Mean 'age' of firms in the machine tool industry*

Year	No. of 'deaths'	Mean 'age' at death	No. of 'survivors'	Mean 'age' of 'survivors'
1877	11	5.2	181	5.4
1878	32	5.4	156	5.8
1882	18	6.5	196	8.8
1883	19	8.8	239	7.6
1884	54	4.9	207	8.8
1886	44	9.2	202	9.5
1887	9	3.2	205	10.2
1888	56	6.3	189	10.5
1890	16	12.1	189	11.6
1891	20	8.3	192	11.7
1892	17	6.7	193	12.1
1893	17	4.4	216	11.6
1894	31	9.3	228	10.8
1895	15	7.7	271	9.8
1896	29	7.7	269	10.1
1897	31	6.1	255	11.0
1898	42	5.5	265	10.9
1899	21	8.0	271	11.1
1900	26	4.0	271	11.8
1901	22	10.1	265	12.4
1902	9	4.8	340	10.5
1903	21	5.4	338	11.2
1904	28	8.9	333	11.8
1905	40	9.1	305	11.8
1906	24	7.1	317	12.9
1907	14	13.1	317	13.4
1908	18	5.3	313	14.3
1909	117	12.8	212	15.6
1910	26	14.1	216	14.7
1911	13	3.3	225	15.0
1912	8	4.4	226	15.8
1913			240	15.9

Notes:

(a)   This table is compiled on the same basis as col. 6 of Table 3.1. That is, a single omission from a directory is ignored, and similarly a single appearance is ignored.

(b)   Col. 1. The number of deaths is the number of firms who appeared at the date given for the last time.

(c)   Col. 3. The number of survivors is the number of firms who appeared at the date given and in the subsequent directory.

(d)   It should be noted that a firm which, for example, appeared in 1877, 1878 and 1882, was omitted in 1883 and 1884 and reappeared in 1886 and subsequently would be treated as if it 'died' in 1882 at an age of five years and was 'reborn' in 1886, thus achieving, by 1913, an age of 27 (1913–1886) *not* 36 (1913–1877).

(e)   Since a number of firms existed before 1870, while the mean ages used in this table are calculated only *from* 1870, the figures given understate the true mean ages.

Table 3.5   *The geographical location of the machine tool industry*

	1	2	3	4	Area 5	6	7	8	9
1870	1	36	100	12	2	27	1	0	16
1871	1	51	102	19	7	33	0	0	14
1872	3	51	83	33	8	13	2	0	21
1873	8	69	97	24	8	41	1	1	22
1882	4	68	106	27	8	37	0	1	24
1883	5	62	75	23	6	29	0	1	21
1884	10	65	116	38	11	36	0	1	33
1886	3	66	83	21	7	28	0	1	21
1887	4	64	107	25	6	22	0	1	25
1888	5	71	113	26	7	23	0	1	10
1890	2	67	86	22	5	21	0	1	21
1891	4	62	91	25	3	20	0	1	20
1892	4	61	96	35	5	20	0	1	23
1893	3	65	107	42	6	23	1	1	31
1894	6	100	129	53	9	39	1	1	30
1895	2	71	121	42	4	21	0	1	26
1896	4	70	122	49	4	30	0	1	28
1897	12	96	141	64	8	43	2	1	31
1898	9	74	115	58	6	29	1	1	23
1899	7	77	126	57	4	19	1	1	19
1900	6	73	126	53	6	17	1	1	23
1901	13	88	150	65	11	51	2	2	35
1902	9	73	128	57	11	45	1	1	32
1903	10	74	141	64	11	52	1	1	32
1904	9	70	134	56	11	45	1	1	31
1905	12	84	148	75	16	63	2	1	45
1906	8	69	128	52	8	45	1	1	34
1907	8	67	130	54	10	44	1	1	33
1908	6	69	128	54	9	44	1	1	37
1909	9	85	152	76	16	62	2	1	44
1910	4	54	85	43	10	43	1	0	35
1911	4	47	73	41	8	42	1	0	32
1912	6	45	74	40	9	38	1	0	38
1913	9	75	127	64	16	59	2	1	41

Notes:
   (a) This table is compiled on the same basis as col. 1 of Table 3.1. That is, it makes no allowance for accidental omission or inclusion.
   (b) The areas are: 1. northern England, 2. north-west England, 3. north-east England, 4. Midlands industrial, 5. Midlands agricultural, 6. London and south-east England, 7. south-west and southern England, 8. south Wales, 9. Scotland.

they were firms, already in existence but engaged in some other activity, who began to make machine tools in conjunction with, or as substitutes for, their products. Because of the historical development of a largely undifferentiated engineering industry in the early nineteenth century, many of the older machine tool firms in existence in the later nineteenth

century had developed from general engineering firms, gradually specialising to a greater or lesser extent in machine tools. Although there are, in
the later part of the century, many examples of the foundation of firms
specifically to manufacture machine tools, this route into the industry
never became universal; there remained many firms who followed the traditional path from other sectors of the engineering industry. Some came to
produce only machine tools, but many retained their links with other
branches of engineering, and continued to produce other types of machinery. It was in fact normal for machine tools to be made in conjunction
with at least one other engineering product. It was particularly common
for machine tools to be made together with other types of tools, and it is
possible to distinguish, along the lines described in the first chapter, a 'tool-
making group' of engineering firms, making machine tools, lathes and tools,
edge tools, joiners tools, rail and mine tools, hand tools and general tools,
to use the categories employed by Kelly's directories. (Appendix 1.2 shows
the numbers of firms listed under these headings in 1877, 1892 and 1907,
while, as appendix 1.3 shows, there were strong inter-connections between
the manufacture of these products.) It can be seen that the links between
the manufacture of machine tools and the manufacture of these related
products were strong, and were strengthening over the period; there is very
little evidence of increasing specialisation in machine tool production alone.

The frequency with which machine tools were made in conjunction
with other products suggests that entry into the machine tool industry
must have been relatively easy for firms already established in other
branches of the engineering industry, at least in the sense that most engineering firms would be technically competent to produce machine tools,
even if they did not have particular commercial or design knowledge of the
problems of machine tool production. This was particularly so because all
engineering firms use machine tools, and thus acquire a familiarity with
them and with adapting them to their own uses. Clearly, the decision, on
the part of an engineering firm, to begin to manufacture machine tools,
would not be costless; there would be tooling costs, costs of mistakes,
costs of selling, but many engineering firms were in a sense potential producers of machine tools. If trade conditions changed, if their branch of
engineering became temporarily depressed, if machine tool production
promised higher profits, if they developed for their own use a machine tool
which could be sold to others — in all these conditions such firms might
enter machine tool production. Some of the most successful of machine
tool producers entered the industry in this way.

Thomas Ryder and Sons, for instance, a leading machine tool firm which still survives, was founded in 1865. Until the death of George Ryder, the son of the founder, in 1893, the firm made machinery for the textile industry. In 1893, however:

> The peak of development of the textile machinery industry had already passed, and his sons Tom and George, both of whom were minors, were faced with a very difficult situation when they succeeded their father. An obvious alternative line of business was the building of machine tools, since the firm had always made those required in the works, and had supplied a limited number to other companies . . . The machine tool building side of the business was therefore expanded, and a range of lathes . . . was introduced. (Sidders, 1961a, pp. 1485, 1492)

The firm of J. Parkinson and Son of Shipley came to machine tool manufacture because of the need of a special-purpose machine tool to produce sewing machines, which were the original products of the company when it was founded by Joseph Parkinson in 1867. No money could be spared to buy the special-purpose milling machine which was needed, so a machine was designed and built on the works by Parkinson and one of his foremen, based on the latter's memories of a Brown and Sharpe universal milling machine. The company also made lathes for amateur turners, and machine tool production came gradually to take up the major part of the work of the company (Sidders, 1965, pp. 351, 353).

Alfred Herbert Ltd, the largest British machine tool producer, grew out of a steam engine building firm, and came into machine tool production by accident when Alfred Herbert secured the agency for a French patent of great value in the manufacture of tubes for the fast expanding cycle trade in Coventry. On the basis of his profits from this patent the company began to make machine tools for the cycle trade.[1]

Firms could, as these case-histories demonstrate, enter the field of machine tool production quite easily. The material from Kelly's directories suggests that they could also leave the industry temporarily to engage presumably in the manufacture of some other product, returning to machine tools at a later time. Such movements away from and back to the industry are less often recorded in the written histories of firms. One example, however, is the firm of Fraser, of Arbroath. The firm had been founded in 1832 to make sailcloth, but by 1870:

> As the demand for sailcloth declined, with the increasing use of steam power for ship propulsion, some members of this generation of Frasers developed new textile manufacturing processes . . . The general engineering activities of the Fraser company stem from the early interest and wide experience in the design, development and construction of textile

plant. Starting as an extension of the mechanics' shop, normally associated with the larger canvas factories of the late 19th century, the engineering works has continuously developed. Among early products were industrial steam engines for use in coal mines and vertical drilling machines. (Sidders, 1964)

The firm however turned away from machine tools early in this century to the manufacture of machinery for processing jute, returning to machine tools at the beginning of the war (Sidders, 1964). Whitworth's were said in 1874 to be completely occupied with arms machinery, although they almost certainly returned later to the manufacture of machine tools.[2] It is also difficult to demonstrate conclusively why firms left the industry for good, since so many of those who did so disappeared completely; one that did not was the Wolseley Company, which had come into the machine tool industry from the manufacture of sheep-shearing equipment. In 1901 they employed 400 men in the manufacture of motor cars and machine tools, but by 1910, it was said 'The machine tool business had been practically dropped' (Anon., 1910a, p. 1357).

It can therefore be demonstrated that many of the machine tool firms entered the field from other branches of the engineering industry. It can be seen that such entry, and conversely their exit if demand failed, could be rapid, especially if the company already made machine tools for its own use and was setting out, in response to demand, to sell some of them. Such firms were in a position of strength, since they could at any time decide which was more profitable, to use the machines in their own works, or to sell them to others in the industry. It is interesting that in the examples which have been quoted, the switch was not normally total; the firms made a few tools at first, sold some of them, and gradually moved to specialising in machine tools, but in many cases retained some of their production in the old field. Thus the firms continue to appear in the trade directories in both categories, specialising in one or the other as market conditions suggested. It is also clear from the material in the trade directories that many firms made more than one other product, so hedging their bets even further, and giving themselves the ability to concentrate their attention, their labour force and their machinery on any one of a number of fields.

This evidence suggests that entry into the machine and tool industry was normally possible, and often easy, at least for firms already established in other parts of the engineering industries.

It appears also that entry was easy for firms starting from scratch. If one examines the requirements for entry, either by an established, or by a new firm, it is clear that the potential entrant needed, in general terms, sufficient capital to rent or build his workshop and to buy the machine tools which he would need to make further machine tools, sufficient technical ability to produce workable and attractive products, and sufficient skilled labour to help him to do so.

For the established firm, both workshop and machine tools would be available, since any engineering firm would possess the machine tools needed to make further machine tools. Some retooling might be needed, but since few specialised or automatic machine tools were in use until the twentieth century, the cost of such changes was small. For the new entrant, capital requirements were apparently small; the foundation of Willson Lathes of Halifax shows how small they could be. The three founders, having been given £100 each by a Halifax charity, equipped themselves with a lathe, a hand drilling rig, and various hand tools. They began by making a horizontal borer and a planing machine, and with these and their original equipment began to make the lathes which the company was set up to produce. No new premises were needed, the workshop being in a cellar underneath a warehouse (Green, 1964, p. 1263). This experience may be untypical, at least at as late a date as 1897, but it was certainly normal earlier in the century. James Nasmyth, the most famous of early nineteenth-century machine tool makers, set up his own firm in 1831. He had hitherto worked for Joshua Field, the partner of Henry Maudslay, who allowed him to obtain castings of 'one of the best turning lathes in the workshops'. Taking the castings back to his home in Edinburgh, Nasmyth rented a small piece of land 24 feet by 16 feet, and erected a temporary workshop, in which, with the aid of his father's foot-lathe, he erected his lathe. With the lathe, Nasmyth then made a planing machine and then 'Armed with these two most important and generally useful tools, and by some special additions, such as boring machines and drilling machines, I soon had a progeny of legitimate descendents crowded about my little workshop, so that I often did not know which way to turn.' All this took several months, and was financed by the manufacture of a steam engine for an amateur inventor, but Nasmyth finally set out for Liverpool and Manchester, where he had decided to start his firm:

I felt assured that in either Liverpool or Manchester — the centres of commercial and manipulative energy — I could settle down with my limited capital and tools, and in course of time contrive to get on, helped by energy, self-reliance and determination. I also found that the demand for machine-making tools was considerable, and that their production would soon become an important department of business. It might be carried on with little expenditure of capital, as the risks were small and the returns were quick. I resolved to cultivate that moderate and safe class of mechanical business, at all events at the outset. (Smiles, 1885, p. 182)

Nasmyth's capital on arrival in Manchester was £63 in cash. He found a workshop in an old cotton-mill 'now let out in flats for manufacturing purposes. Power was supplied to each flat from a shaft connected with a large mill up the street, the owner of which had power to spare. The flat shown to me was 130′ long by 27′ wide, and the rent was only £50 a year' (Smiles, 1885, p. 185).

While it is possible that Samuel Smiles has exaggerated the ease with which Nasmyth set up his Manchester factory, the experience was paralleled by others, particularly in starting on a small scale in a rented workshop. James Archdale, for example, founded his firm in 1868: 'His first works were at Oozells Street, Birmingham, and he and two boys formed the original staff. As the business expanded, larger premises were taken at Tindall Street, which later also proved inadequate, and a site was then acquired in Ledsam Street, where building started in 1879' (Sidders, 1962c, p. 937).

Nasmyth, similarly if more dramatically, had been forced to move in 1836, after an engine-beam under construction crashed through the floor of the flat, and the owner begged Nasmyth 'in the kindest manner . . . to remove from the premises as soon as I could, otherwise the whole building might be brought to the ground with the weight of . . . machinery' (Smiles, 1885, p. 202).

In order to enter the field of machine tool production in the same way as Nasmyth or the founders of Willson Lathes, the entrepreneurs had of course to be technically competent, both to make their own machinery and to attract orders from others. Technical competence was so important that it is, in fact, the one common feature of the machine tool entrepreneurs, who were otherwise drawn from a variety of backgrounds. Most of them, for whom evidence is available, received an initial formal education suitable to the social class of their parents. William Muir, for instance, the son of a farmer and building contractor, received an ordinary middle class education.

Richard Peacock, the son of a lead miner and engineer, attended Leeds Grammar School (Anon., 1889, p. 187). Joseph Whitworth Hulse, son of Whitworth's nephew and manager, W. W. Hulse, was educated at Uppingham (Anon., 1898b, p. 315), while Alfred Herbert, the son of a prosperous Leicestershire farmer, was educated first at a private school and

then at Stoneygate School in Leicester. On the other hand, many of the
machine tool entrepreneurs, particularly those from poor families, seem to
have received little or no formal education. James Archdale entered a coal
mine at the age of seven, James Butler began work very young as an office
boy in the offices of the Halifax *Courier* and then worked in a chemist's
shop (Anon. 1917). Only one of the machine tool entrepreneurs, Henry
Ward Kearns, the son of a professional violinist, received any form of
higher education; Kearns read chemistry at London University (Sidders,
1962b, p. 9).

Although they came from such disparate educational backgrounds, the
machine tool entrepreneurs had, almost without exception, one common
characteristic, that they had 'served five years' time' as an apprentice
mechanical engineer. Some like Archdale, Butler, James Smith of Dean,
Smith and Grace, William Asquith, Samson Fox of Smith, Beacock and
Tannett, appear to have financed their apprenticeship period themselves,
perhaps from previous earnings or, as in Smith's case, from working in the
evenings (Grierson, n.d.; Sidders, 1961b, p. 1195; Anon., 1903b, p. 919).
Others were premium apprentices, financed by their families, or served
apprenticeships in firms owned or managed by their relations. Herbert was
a premium apprentice with Joseph Jessop of Leicester, Charles Scriven was
apprenticed to his uncle's firm, Woodhead, Scriven and Holdsworth, Alfred
Muir was apprenticed in his father's works (Herbert, n.d.; Anon., 1909, p.
309; Anon., 1902a). But, however, they were financed, all the major entrepreneurs in the field of machine tools whose origins are known, with the
sole exception of Kearns, were apprenticed as mechanical engineers.

It is at the apprenticeship stage, and even more at the stage when these
men took their first jobs as trained engineers, that one of the most significant features of the training of these entrepreneurs becomes apparent. It is
clear that the range of firms within which apprenticeships were served,
and early jobs taken, was very small. Both Herbert and Frederick Pollard
were apprentices at Joseph Jessops (Sidders, 1962a, p. 827). Archdale was
an apprentice with Greenwood and Batley, and then worked for Kitson's,
Walker's and Fowler's in Leeds before moving to Manchester to work for
Hetherington and then for Tangye. Thomas Craven worked for Sharp,
Roberts, while Henry Bates, Thomas Elliott and Joseph Whitworth Hulse
both worked for the successor firm of Sharp, Stewart (Green, 1965, p.
237; Anon., 1903a, p. 351; Anon., 1899b, p. 127; Anon., 1898b). Elliott,
John Stirk, John Shepherd, and Thomas Craven all worked at one time for
one of the Fairbairn companies (Anon., 1938; Anon., 1902b, p. 1039).
Some men also worked for what seems to be an extraordinary number of

47

different firms before setting up on their own. Whitworth worked for Crighton, Marsden, Walker and other firms between 1821 and 1825 in Manchester, then moved to London where in eight years he worked for Maudslay, Holtzappfel, Wright and Clements (Anon., 1887, p. 152). William Muir worked between 1829 and 1840 successively for the Catrine Cotton Co., for Henry Houldsworth, for the Hayle Foundry Company in Cornwall, for Maudslay and Field, for Bramah and Robinson, and for Whitworth. John Stirk was apprenticed to Joseph March of Leeds, and then worked for Fairbairn, Shepherd Hill, Smith Beacock and Tannett, Darling and Sellers, Buck and Watkin, and Scott Brothers, before founding his own business in 1866, when he was still only twenty-eight.

The explanation for this apparent concentration of experience on the part of machine tool entrepreneurs lies of course in the small number of mechanical engineering firms in existence in the early part of the period, and in particular in the even smaller number of reputable firms who could be guaranteed to provide good training. It is unclear why some of these engineers should have worked for so many firms, although it may have been that a good mechanic could best improve his income by accepting offers from successive firms, rather than waiting to be promoted within one firm. Muir, for instance, was foreman at Maudslay and field assistant and representative at Holtzappfel, foreman at Bramah, and then manager at Whitworth's.

A characteristic of successful machine tool entrepreneurs thus appears to be that they were technically trained. The importance of this is presumably related to the speed of innovation, and the importance of the invention of new machine tools; a firm could not be successful unless it could produce a stream of new ideas, new machine tools, or modifications to old tools, and this demanded technical expertise and training on the part of the managers of the firms. Technical training was obviously far more important, and regarded as such, than commercial or financial expertise. James Archdale, who by 1896 was employing about 450 people and selling machine tools all over the world, was taught to read and write only in his fifties, that is somewhere between 1889 and 1899, and as has already been described, some other successful machine tool makers had little formal education.

Technical training did not, of course, necessarily equip an engineer to run a business, but, like so many pioneers in the industrial revolution, machine tool makers sometimes solved this difficulty by taking partners with other qualifications, often solving a problem of lack of capital at the same time. This appears often to have occurred some time after the foundation of the firm, particularly when it was necessary to finance expansion of the firm or its premises.

Archdale had a partner called James Arnot, who took his capital on retirement, and Archdale then, to finance expansion of the works, entered into partnership with two tube drawers, John Earl and George Born, later buying them out. James Butler financed extensions to the factory after 1887 with a partnership entered into in that year. The best documented instance of a firm obtaining capital in this way is provided by John Holroyd; Holroyd had started as a manufacturer and supplier of sewing machines, but at the end of the 1880s was in difficulties after the cancellation of an order for 100,000 child's sewing machines. He was introduced by a local copper merchant to a Mr Liebert, a Manchester export merchant, whose son Henry had been apprenticed at Beyer Peacock and had then worked as an engineer in Finland and Russia. Apparently in order to attract Henry Liebert home, Mr Liebert agreed to put capital into Holroyd's business, and a new company was formed, with Liebert as chairman, and Holroyd, Henry Liebert and another man as directors. With this change, the manufacture of special machine tools, which had been allied with the sewing machine business, was greatly expanded. Another example of a partnership between an engineer and a man trained in finance was that between Thomas Greenwood and John Batley.

The third requirement of entry into the machine tool business was the availability of skilled manpower. Again, the fact that the skills required in machine tool production were those acquired by every engineering apprentice made it possible to draw on a reasonably large number of men qualified in this way, and others not so qualified could be trained to take charge of machine tools.

There is no evidence that labour supply impeded any of the machine tool firms. Even as early as the 1830s, Nasmyth was able to break a strike in his works, directed at forcing him to employ only men who had served an apprenticeship, by importing sixty-four Scottish mechanics and he remarked that 'we might easily have obtained three times the number'. In addition, Nasmyth recruited from his labourers 'the most effective men to take charge of the largest and most powerful machine tools', causing the strike by such actions but at the same time turning out satisfactory work. Again, Nasmyth and Smiles, both of whom had no liking for trade unions, may have exaggerated, but no other machine tool maker appears to have had difficulties in securing labour, or, indeed, as Greenwood and Batley's experiences show, in dismissing it when times were bad, in the confident expectation that the men could be re-employed if trade improved. It must

49

also be remembered that, as Professor Saul has shown, the majority of British machine tool firms, even as late as 1914, employed only a few hundred workers.

It is probable that entry into the machine tool industry became more difficult towards the end of the nineteenth century, as the technology of machine tool-making became more complex and the tools more expensive. As S. F. Walker wrote in 1907:

The conditions are very different in the engineering world today from what they were thirty or sixty years ago, when the men who are pointed out as examples started for themselves. The development in manufacturing processes that was initiated in America, but which all the world have now adopted, is against the small manufacturer. When fitting was done almost entirely by hand, right from the casting, and not too well done then in many cases, things were made in small numbers, and small manufacturers, especially those who could be relied upon for good fitting, had a good chance, and earned good money. Now all that is changed. The fitting, or assembling as it is more properly called, forms only a small part of the work; the major work is done by machines, and it is nearly always a necessity of the case that a large number shall be made, because the machine costs a good deal to buy and to prepare for each separate article. (Walker, 1907a, pp. 613–14)

A major difficulty was the cost of financing the work between the time of receiving the order and its completion, since many machine tools would take some months to build, and it would also often be difficult to secure payment until some time after the tools had been delivered. As S. F. Walker pointed out, 'If he is fortunate, the young business man may get his money in in less than twelve months, but it is not wise to rely upon it' (1907b, pp. 712–13), and to him the difficulty of keeping the works supplied with orders was one of the main reasons for an engineering firm accepting all the work that was offered to it, rather than specialising.

At the same time, machine tool firms remained relatively small, and it was possible, as the directory evidence shows, for firms to enter the industry right up to the first war. Even if capital requirements were greater, the other requirements of skill on the part of the entrepreneur, and a skilled labour force, could still be supplied.

The nature of demand for machine tools

Once in the machine tool industry, the firm had to decide what to produce, and therefore how to use its particular set of capital, labour and experience and to react to the pattern of demand for machine tools established by the technical characteristics of engineering production and by the preferences of customers. As the discussion of specialisation in the engineering industries in the first chapter has suggested, firms reacted in many different ways. In particular, the range of solutions to the question of whether to adopt some form of specialised production was large. This topic has received a considerable amount of attention from economic historians, principally because an alleged failure to specialise, and thereby attain economies of mass production, has been seen as a cause of British economic decline at the end of the nineteenth century. Not all historians have accepted this view, and some have stressed the benefits of 'spin-off' which could accrue to a non-specialised firm. In general, however, there has been insufficient discussion of the meaning of such terms as 'specialisation' in practice, or of the possible or likely economic consequences of different types of specialisation or non-specialisation. Added confusion has been caused by the implicit identification by some historians of specialisation with mass production, leading to the fallacious view that economies of mass production could not be attained by unspecialised firms. It is useful therefore to begin by setting out schematically the various production possibilities open to machine tool firms (and by analogy to firms in many other industries) and this is done in table 3.6. It should be stressed firstly that all these types of production can be shown to have been undertaken in the late nineteenth century. It is by no means obvious that one particular combination of types of production was more or less profitable than any other combination: only detailed empirical observation can suggest why a firm should have adopted a particular combination, given its resources and the market situation which it faced. Nevertheless, it is possible on the basis of scattered evidence to construct some hypotheses to explain the particular choices made by firms.

To take first the degree of specialisation (section 1 of table 3.6): the preceding section was devoted to a description of the possibilities of linking the manufacture of machine tools with the manufacture of other engineering goods, and it was argued that this was often a rational and responsive reaction to market opportunities and to technical and commercial expertise. The range of responses varied from such firms as Greenwood and Batley, listed in Kelly's directories as making at least sixteen engineering products, to firms who made only one or two types. The willingness of British engineering firms to make large numbers of products was often mentioned by contemporary observers, sometimes approvingly and sometimes not. In 1902, for example, J. R. Richardson told the Institution of

51

Table 3.6   *The possible dimensions of machine tool production*

1. Degree of specialisation
   a. The manufacture of engineering products of all or several types.
   b. The manufacture of machine tools:
      (1) of a large number of types
      (2) of a small number of types
      (3) of use to a particular set of customers:
          (a)   with particular technical requirements
          (b)   with a particular geographical location
      (4) of a particular quality and price.

2. Scale of production
   a. The manufacture of a large number of tools of different types.
   b. The manufacture of a large number of a restricted range of types of tools.
   c. The manufacture of a small number of each of a large number of types of tools (possibly with the use of parts interchangeable between types).
   d. The manufacture of a small number of a restricted range of types of tools.

3. Production possibilities of the machine tool produced
   a. Use of tool for generalised mass production purposes.
   b. Use of tool for specialised mass production purposes.
   c. Use of tool for generalised small-scale purposes.

Mechanical Engineers that:

> Not only was it necessary to have on his catalogue 500 different types and sizes of steam engines, but an infinite variety of mining and general machinery; and in addition his firm was expected to do anything required and had to do it even if it only had to be done once. (Anon., 1902c, p. 57)

It appears from the context that it was necessary to do this in order to maintain good relations with customers. Other firms were forced to make large numbers of different types of machinery by their advertised willingness to construct complete factories, particularly for overseas customers. Craven Brothers, the machine tool firm, for example, made a wide range of machinery, and in 1894 'The Craven catalogues included almost every type and size of machine tool then known, together with large numbers of special machines' (Green, 1965, p. 239), while one of their many activities was 'supervision of the building and supply of complete machine tool installations for a number of railway workshops'. Greenwood and Batley undertook similar work, equipping several foreign mints and arsenals with complete sets of machine tools and other engineering equipment. There were, clearly, considerable advantages to be gained by such work, principally in foreign markets where buyers were less technically educated, or less able to compare the merits of different machinery from different companies. The American trade paper, *Engineering Magazine*, ascribed the 'peculiar state of the European tool-maker' in 1898 partly to 'their large export trade, and the fact that they undertake to produce every article called for by foreign enquiries or indents, where complete plants were required' (Orcutt, 1899, p. 55). In effect, the large engineering firms who made many products in this way were acting as consulting engineers or designers, and it seems likely from the Greenwood and Batley accounts discussed below that this was a profitable activity. There is, therefore, no reason to think that, in itself, failure to specialise on one type of engineering production was an irrational or unprofitable act.

Nevertheless, it has often been argued that failure to specialise could be inefficient, particularly in that effort and technical initiative were dispersed, and that costs were increased by the failure to take advantage of economies of scale and mass production. In theory, this is clearly a persuasive argument; in practice, in considering the machine tool industry, it is necessary to take account of some complications. These are shown by section 1 b of table 3.6, which indicates that it was possible to adopt a number of different types of specialisation, of which the decision to make only one or a few types of machine was only one.

Firstly, it was possible for firms to make a large number of tools, or a small number. Alfred Herbert described the choices clearly, as he made it when he began to manufacture machine tools; it should be remembered that he was regarded as one of the most advanced engineers in the country, whose firm 'follow American methods of manufacture perhaps more closely than any other machine tool makers in this country' (Anon, 1899a, pp. 586–7). He wrote in his autobiography that:

Although our first machine tool efforts were directed mainly towards the requirements of the bicycle business, we soon began to supply machines to the much wider field of general engineering . . . It has often been suggested to me that we should have done better if we had specialised more intensively on a limited range of machines. There is no doubt much force in this contention, but in the early days I doubt very much whether there was scope for a growing business, which confined itself to the production of only one or two machines. Rightly, or wrongly, I was more attracted by the idea of covering a fairly wide field. The cycle business, which was our principal customer, required in those days a variety of machines and not many of them of one kind. (Herbert, n.d., ch. 'Alfred Herbert Ltd')

It should be stressed, however, that Alfred Herbert did not make all

types of machine tools. Instead, as he indicates, he confined his production
to those tools, mainly the medium machine tools, which were most in
demand from the cycle industry. It seems clear that this was a normal
method of specialisation, particularly sensible since customer firms requiring particular types of tools were often also geographically close. As the
History of the Ministry of Munitions put it, describing the industry in
1914:

> Machine tool manufacture in Great Britain was, broadly speaking,
> grouped in four districts, where the demand for machine tools was great
> on account of the industries of which these districts were the centre.
> Lancashire was the early home of the machine tool trade, and at one
> time had the reputation of producing the best quality tools. Yorkshire
> competed closely in quality of output, but the machinery was, with
> some exceptions, of a lower grade, being simpler in design and produced
> by a number of small makers who had not the organisation and the up-
> to-date methods of the larger trades. The Midlands produced, on the
> whole, large numbers of machines of the type required for repetition
> work and suitable for use in the small arms, motor and cycle trades,
> while the shipbuilding and marine engineering industries of the Clyde
> had resulted in the development of a flourishing industry in machine
> tools of the heavier type in the immediate neighbourhood. (Anon.,
> 1921, vol. VIII, part III, p. 38)

It is also clear that this type of specialisation was not a recent development, provoked, for example, by foreign competition, since in 1867 a
writer in *Engineering* commented that:

> It is generally known that engineer's tools made in Scotland are some-
> what different in their style and design from the tools made in the
> neighbourhood in Manchester and Leeds, the two great centres of
> machine construction in England. Tool makers in Scotland, who have
> principally to supply the extensive demands of marine engineers and
> shipbuilders in their own locality, are, by the nature of the heavy work
> for which their machines are intended, induced to look to great weights,
> massive framings and very large castings in shape of foundations or base
> plates, rather than to that elegance of form and that economy of
> material which gives to the modern tools of the first toolmakers in
> Manchester and Leeds their style and characteristic appearance. (Anon.,
> 1867, p. 379)

Even general engineering firms such as Greenwood and Batley were tied
in this way to the industries of their own area; it is noticeable that (as is
described in more detail in chapter 7) most of the firm's sales of machine

tools were either to foreign countries or to the north-east, around its factory in Leeds.

There is, lastly, some evidence that machine tool makers specialised in the production of tools of a particular quality and price. This evidence is scanty, perhaps because nobody was willing to admit that their tools were cheap and nasty, but some areas of machine tool production certainly had a reputation for producing cheap tools.

It is thus clear that machine tool manufacturers adopted a variety of possible solutions to the problem of determining the range of their products. In addition, they were faced with two further sets of decisions, shown in sections 2 and 3 of table 3.6. These sections emphasise the essential distinction which has to be made in considering questions of specialisation and mass production in the engineering industry, between the potential use of the machine tool by the customer, and the method by which it was produced. It was quite possible for a machine tool to be designed and manufactured once only, to service a particular purpose which was the mass production of one article; conversely, machine tools could be produced in large numbers, for one-off production of some other article. The other possibilities were all the other combinations of the divisions of sections 2 and 3.

Discussion of the economic causes and implications of these different production possibilities, all of which appear to have been undertaken in Britain, is complicated by the contrasts which are often drawn, and were drawn in the late nineteenth century, between British and American practice. Furthermore, the fact that such contrasts were contentious at the time, and have been thought since to be possible causes of declining British competitiveness at this period, means that not all statements and descriptions of the situation in the two countries can be taken at face value; protagonists on both sides have been guilty, for example, of contrasting 'best-practice' techniques on one side of the Atlantic with 'average' techniques on the other. Nevertheless, it appears to have been broadly true that American engineering practice was characterised by the manufacture, by a particular firm, of a large number of restricted range of tools, primarily intended for generalised mass production, that is choices 2b and 3a. For example, both Brown and Sharpe and Bullard's, two American machine tool makers, produced very restricted ranges of tools; in Brown and Sharpe's case most of their production was of milling machines, grinding machines and gear-cutting machines (though in addition they continued throughout this period to be a major manufacturer of sewing machines). Furthermore, it was an important characteristic of American machine tool makers that many of the parts used in the tools were mass produced by standardised methods and were thus interchangeable, facilitating cheap production, quick assembly and easy replacement of damaged parts; indeed, the 'American system of manufactures' was often used as a synonym for such standardised mass production of interchangeable parts, particularly in gun making.

By contrast, the stereotype of British engineering was that of the firm producing a large number of different types of tools, some for mass production but most for general machine shop purposes, choices 2a and 3b or c. It is undoubtedly true that some British firms adopted choice 3c, making a general range of rather indifferent tools intended for general machinery shops, for which there was always a large demand. On the other hand, it is clear that the decision to make many different types of highly specialised tools was taken by many of the leading British machine tool firms, for clearly stated reasons and apparently with commercial success. For example, Al red Herbert, the firm often held up as an example of the use of American techniques, rejected the idea that the firm should specialise in a few types of machinery, arguing that:

> The cycle business, which was our principle customer, required in those days a variety of machines, and not many of them of one kind. Besides the hand lathes . . . we made specialised machines for turning, boring, drilling, tapping and lapping hubs, for bedding rims, for drilling rims, for sharpening cutters, and were able to keep ourselves well employed. (Herbert, n.d.)

The contrast between British and American practice is perhaps nowhere better stated than in a report in the *Colliery Guardian* of a meeting of the Manchester Association of Engineers in 1896, at which it was said that English customers were to blame for 'insisting upon makers constructing machines, specially designed according to the purchaser's ideas, for every little operation, instead of accepting the standard pattern, thus giving makers much inconvenience and needless trouble'.

On the other hand, English practice was defended because, it was said, particularly with heavy machinery, 'they had to make the machine according to the particular object for which it was intended; they could not make them by the gross' (Anon., 1896, p. 655).

It therefore seems clear, since such discussion of the differences between American and British practice were common in the late nineteenth century, that a real difference did exist, even if individual firms were often exceptions to any generalisation. The search for a satisfactory explanation of this difference has been a major pre-occupation of economic historians since the publication by H. J. Habakkuk of *American and British Technology in the Nineteenth Century*, and most of the debate has been within the framework of neo-classical analysis, with a particular emphasis on differences in factor costs facing manufacturers in the two countries. Ideally, the machine tool industry should provide an interesting framework against which to test the various hypotheses which have been advanced, but in practice this is impossible, principally because of the lack of detailed, quantitative evidence on the behaviour of the American industry and on the work of the majority of British firms. In these circumstances, discussion of the differences between American and British machine tool practice has to be based on impressions and on qualitative evidence, and is to that extent unsatisfactory. In addition, there are several special features of the machine tool industry which differentiate it from the bulk of manufacturing industry.

In practice, it is not clear, despite many assertions to the contrary, which method is likely to be more efficient. Machine tools are, of course, intermediate capital goods, and the efficiency and cost with which they are produced thus has to be considered in relation not only to the operations of the machine tool maker but in relation to the operations of the ultimate user. Broadly, the 'British' system was for the machine tool maker and the purchaser to design, in collaboration, a machine tool particularly adapted to do one task, often as part of a sequence of operations designed to mass produce a finished article. The design function was thus largely carried out by the machine tool maker, who could use his acquired knowledge of machine tools designed for other purposes to design the most efficient machine tool to suit a particular job. The purchaser would receive a machine tool tailored to the job which he wished to do, either a newly designed machine or one adapted by the machine tool maker to that particular purpose, and would need to make few, if any, modifications to the machine tool when it was erected in his factory. By contrast, the 'American' system was for the machine tool maker to produce a range of standard machine tools, designed to perform particular operations but not specifically designed to meet the needs of any one customer. The customer, having bought the standard, multi-purpose tool, was then expected to adapt the machine tool in his own factory and his own time to suit it to whatever machining task he wanted to carry out.

The advantage of the British system lay, for the ultimate user, in the knowledge that the tool had been adapted or designed to suit his needs. Naturally, a tool designed in such a way would be more expensive, as it might be a one-off design task, but the cost is likely to have been reduced by the fact that the machine tool maker would be in the best position to use his accumulated knowledge of design, and of similar problems, to simplify the design task. The machine tool maker, in fact, is in the best position to benefit from the economies of learning-by-doing, and may often be able to adapt existing designs, previously sold to other customers, at relatively little additional cost. By contrast, in the American system the purchaser and ultimate user of the machine tool receives the machine at a relatively low cost, but has to bear himself the costs of adaptation. Since the purchaser will not normally be an expert in machine design, and will not have the benefit of the experience accumulated by a professional designer, these costs of adaptation may be high, and will certainly be higher than those of minor adjustments to a machine made on the British system.

Whether the British or American system was less costly or less efficient, taking the entire process of design, manufacture and adaptation of the machine tool as one, is an empirical question which cannot, at the moment, be answered. It is clear, however, that there are cogent arguments for the view that the British method is not necessarily less efficient than the American, when the object is to reduce the final unit cost of whatever is to be produced by the machine tool in the hands of the customer. Unfortunately, there does not appear to have been much contemporary discussion of this issue in these terms.

In general, it seems that British customers for machine tools preferred to buy specialised tools, even if the capital cost was greater. As H. F. Frevert put it in 1906, 'The average buyer, if convinced that a certain machine is superior or is better adapted for doing his class of work, will not let the matter of price stand in the way of obtaining it' (p. 243).

This discussion has, however, continued in the machine tool industry, and in 1960 an expert committee reported

> In manufacturing costs the price of the machine tool is only one element in comparison with the other elements of overall cost. A study we have made of this indicates that in typical large jobbing engineering factories even as large a reduction as 25% in machine tool prices would result of itself in a reduction of only between 1% and 2% of overall manufacturing costs. To an ever growing extent overall production costs are reduced by the use of high performance tools in spite of their higher price. (Board of Trade, 1960, p. 8)

As the expert committee argued, for an advanced industrial country, the problem of mass produced machine tools is precisely that they are standard and mass produced, and suited to a wide variety of tasks. They therefore require constant adaptation to fit a particular job by the customer, after he has bought the machine. This is often uneconomic, because of

the concentration of production in the machine tool using industries into larger production units. This trend, coupled with rising labour costs, results in a growing demand for complex, high performance, specialised machine tools, the output of any one type of which is small and unit cost high. They are the antithesis of the mass produced machine tools. (Board of Trade, 1960, p. 9)

In other words, the greater the degree of mass production capability required by the customer, the greater the amount of special purpose machinery required of the machine tool maker.

Both conditions may not, of course, have existed in the late nineteenth century and these remarks may therefore not be relevant to that period. On the other hand, a number of mass production industries were being developed before 1914, and it seems likely that they produced much the same pressures as their counterparts in the 1960s. Indeed, H. D. Wagoner, in his history of the machine tool industry in the United States since 1900, suggests that such pressures were turning the industry towards specialised production:

Prior to World War I, the use of special machine tools was increasing rapidly. This was particularly true in automobile manufacturing. Special machines were efficient and economical where a large number of identical parts of unusual size or shape were to be produced. (Wagoner, 1968, p. 20)

It is, however, still possible that American manufacturers were able to produce their machine tools at a lower unit cost than were the British, and that, in the conditions of the late nineteenth century, the difference in costs could have been substantial. It is normally argued that American makers were more efficient than the British because they made more of a given machine, and were thus able to take advantage of the use of mass produced or interchangeable parts; the British, by contrast, are thought to have made each machine individually. Even today, however, it does not seem possible to achieve very substantial reductions in unit costs by increasing the size of batches, that is by increasing the number of machines of a particular type which are produced. C. F. Pratten quotes examples of the effect of increasing batch sizes, and these are reproduced as table 3.7. Moreover, much of the unit cost reduction for higher levels of output comes from the machining costs in the production of parts, and is the result of the employment of automatic machinery. Although some automatic or semi-automatic machinery was being introduced in the late nine-

59

Table 3.7   *Economies of large batch production in the machine tool industry*

Size of batch for assembly (monthly)	1	2	5	10	25	50	100
Index of assembly cost per unit	150	110	100	95	90	87	85
Size of batch for machining (quarterly)	3	6	15	30	75	150	
Index of machining costs, inc. materials	135	115	100	90	85	82	
Combined index	140	113	100	92	87	84	

Source: C.F. Pratten *Economies of Scale in Manufacturing Industry* (Cambridge, 1971) p. 172.

teenth century, in particular with the use of turret lathes and some types of milling machines, the effect of these machines is likely to have been much less than the effects of unit costs on numerically controlled tools today. In addition, it seems unlikely that batch size in the American industry was sufficiently large to enable many scale economies to be captured. Very little direct information on this point exists, but some rough guesswork can be applied to the output of Brown and Sharpe, one of the largest and most famous American machine tool firms. In 1891, for example, Brown and Sharpe produced 500 machine tools, of at least nine different types (probably more, since there were nine types exported to England in that year); average production, on this basis, would be about fifty machine tools of a particular type per year, but this is almost certainly an overstatement, since by 'types of tool' is meant such very general descriptions as 'milling machine' or 'grinding machine', of which probably many different variations and sizes were made. In addition, production was spread over one year. All in all, it seems unlikely that Brown and Sharpe made their machine tools in batches of more than ten or at most twenty, so that economies of large batch production are likely to have been small. In addition, at least one heavily diversified British machine tool firm, Greenwood and Batley, commonly made machine tools in batches of five or more in the 1890s. Although the expansion of Brown and Sharpe production to nearly 2000 tools per annum by 1900 is likely to have increased batch production, expansion and the increased use of semi-automatic machinery after the engineering strike of 1897 is likely to have had the same effect in Britain.

It seems difficult, therefore, to argue that the differences between British and American practice in this period are at all clear-cut, at least in their effects on cost-efficiency. There were differences in practice, perhaps explained by differences in historical development and in market situation.

On the other hand, the differences were not so great as to preclude competition between British and American machine tools in neutral markets, and what may have happened is that the two methods moved towards each other – that British manufacturers began to specialise on fewer tools, and American manufacturers to make more specialised tools, so that probably by 1914 and certainly by the inter-war period the two industries were very much alike. This convergence has been documented, on the British side, by Professor Saul and by L. T. C. Rolt. In America, machine tool firms began to make more specialised tools, and Wagoner also states that the Americans were adopting another British practice which they had earlier criticised, that is of installing their own foundries. American firms had previously relied on outside foundries to supply rough castings, but 'There was a trend, during the first decades of the twentieth century, among the larger tool builders to acquire or establish their own foundries and thereby free themselves from dependence on the not always very reliable services of the custom foundries' (Wagoner, 1968, p. 56).

As the 'Habakkuk' debate on American and British technology has shown, simplistic generalisation from casual observation of different methods in use in Britain and America is dangerous. It cannot be claimed therefore that it has been shown the British were, or were not, more efficient than the Americans in the manufacture and use of machine tools. On the other hand, it has been shown that the simple assumption either that 'mass production is always best' or that 'specialisation is always best', can be extremely misleading.

The cycle of demand for machine tools

Identification of the cyclical and irregular fluctuations around the upward secular trend in machine tool production is complicated by the nature of the evidence; the only evidence on which discussion can be based is the value of the output of ten leading firms which was discussed earlier in the chapter, together with a scattered amount of qualitative contemporary comment. There is, of course, no reason why fluctuations in the output series, based as it is on so small a proportion of firms in the industry, should be representative of fluctuations in output of the industry as a whole. Several of the firms represented, for example, Greenwood and Batley, Ward and Archdale, were heavily involved in making machine tools for armaments production, the demand for which was both highly irregular and different in timing from normal industrial demand for machine tools; the demand for armaments machinery is discussed at greater length below.

Nevertheless, comparison of the fluctuations in the output of the ten leading firms, firstly with the Feinstein series for engineering production, and
secondly with production in the economy as a whole, suggests that machine
tool production followed a pattern akin to that of the aggregate business
cycle. Table 3.8 makes such a comparison in terms of the dates of the
peaks and troughs in the three series. Although precise dating is impossible,
it seems from this comparison that machine tool output peaked slightly
after the rest of the economy, and that the trough came distinctly later; in
other words, the machine tool industry seems to have experienced longer
downswings and shorter upswings than other sectors of the economy.
In addition, the magnitude of the fluctuations in the machine tool series is
considerably greater than in either of the more aggregated series; although
one might normally expect such a contrast, as the process of aggregation
necessarily irons out the most extreme values in separate series, this does
not affect the serious consequences which severe falls in demand must have
had for machine tool producers; between 1891 and 1894, for example,
output of the ten firms fell by 42%, and between 1907 and 1909 the fall
was of 36%.

Table 3.8   *Cycles in output of machine tools*

Gross domestic product		Engineering output		Machine tool output	
Peak	Trough	Peak	Trough	Peak	Trough
1882		1882			
	1885		1886		1885
1890		1889		1890/1	
	1892/3		1893		1894
1900		1899/ 1900		1900	
	1901				1902
1902					
	1903/4		1903		
1907		1906/7		1907	
	1908		1908		1909
1913		1913		1913	

Note:
  It should be stressed that these turning points are approximate.

  Source: Based on series for gross domestic product and engineering output from
Feinstein (1972), pp. 16 and T114, and for machine tool output from Table 3.2
above.

Study of the engineering trade journals also reveals considerable variations in demand in the short run, together with regional differences, presumably related to the fortunes of the predominant industries in the areas

in which the machine tool firms were situated. In addition, as chapter 6 below shows, the influence of patterns of demand from individual industries, such as government orders for arms machinery, could produce violent fluctuations in demand even in short periods.

It appears that the response of many of the established machine tool firms to this volatility of demand was to attempt to build up a regular trade with reliable customers, and to disdain casual orders, even if this meant foregoing orders in times of expansion of demand. In 1900, for example, the *Engineer* commented in an editorial that

there is not a single machine tool works of the higher class in this country which is not as stable as any similar American works. Why? Because the majority of our makers work at large profits in a close market; they know their customers of old, and their customers know them and their work. The American making less profit on his manufactures, and working in a market which may desert him for a rival at any moment, is evidently in a weak position . . . The machine tool makers of Manchester will tell you . . . they make for established customers, and find enough employment from them and a certain number of casual clients without hysterical endeavours to attract new customers. (Anon., 1900, p. 215)

However rational this attitude may have been (the experiences of Greenwood and Batley detailed below certainly show the dangers of excessive expansion in a volatile market) for the individual producer, it must have produced shortages of supply during the upswing in the cycle. This was particularly important because of a characteristic of machine tool demand which has been commented upon by a number of writers, both in the nineteenth century and more recently. Broadly, it is argued that as demand in general in the economy rises in the upswing of the cycle, firms initially satisfy that demand either from surplus capacity, or, slightly later in the cycle, from extending working hours; only when firms are convinced that the rise in demand will be sustained, and will therefore justify expansion in capacity, do they begin to order new capital equipment for that purpose. At the same time, expenditure on replacement rises as firms are forced to replace machinery which cannot stand the strain of harder working. The result is a rapid increase in demand for machinery, accompanied by a desire to acquire the machinery rapidly, either because it is needed to replace old machinery, or to take advantage of rising demand for manufactures. In such circumstances, customers would turn to any firm which could supply suitable tools quickly. As H. F. L. Orcutt put it 'It is one of the vexations of the machine tool business that customers put off ordering until the last minute. Having once decided, however, time of delivery determines where the order is to be placed' (1899, p. 16).

In such circumstances, the demand for machine tools seems to have been filled partly through imports, particularly in the 1890s and thereafter, but principally from the entry into the industry of new firms able to offer both shorter delivery times and the type of personal design service to which British customers were used.

The established firms were not able, of course, to remain impervious to changes in demand, and it is clear that they did expand and contract production in response to demand, as the output series indicates. They were able to do this partly at least because they do not seem to have experienced major difficulties in acquiring labour which, as the Greenwood and Batley evidence shows, was a major factor in machine tool production. There is very little evidence of any firm having difficulty in finding workers, in spite of the high skills required for engineering employees, and Greenwood and Batley apparently frequently took advantage of the Leeds custom that men could be hired or fired at any meal-break. In addition, the rapid development of automatic machinery towards the end of the nineteenth century reduced the skill requirement for engineering workers, particularly after the defeat of the Amalgamated Society of Engineers on this issue in the strike of 1897; although it is likely that this change had more effect on the customers for machine tools than on the machine tool industry itself, where the work remained highly specialised and skilled.

The reaction of many of the leading machine tool firms to the volatility of demand was thus to play safe by refusing to over-expand in times of rising demand, and to cope with unexpected falls in demand by reductions in the labour force. That this was not confined to Greenwood and Batley can be inferred from the scattered evidence on the size of the labour force in different firms, which shows marked year to year fluctuations. There is very little evidence that any firms adopted one obvious technique for avoiding the worst effects of fluctuating demand; building for stock was not common in the industry, although there are some signs in the Greenwood and Batley records that the firm was holding increasingly large stocks of sectional parts.

The size of the machine tool industry in the late nineteenth century, and its shape in terms of the distribution of firms among different specialisms and across the country, was thus a response to a large number of factors, many of which must remain merely hypotheses in the present state of the evidence. Nor can the relative influence of the different factors easily be calculated, since no technique exists which could make such a calculation. Some indication of the importance of one factor, the total demand for machine tools, on the number of firms in the industry, can be gained through a regression analysis, although the evidence is less than perfect. As has already been stated, the evidence as to numbers of firms in the industry is likely to be incorrect or incomplete in detail, although correct in its indication of broad movements and orders of magnitude. Secondly, no index exists of total demand for machine tools in the economy; the best proxy measures are series for output of engineering goods. These are likely to be imperfect as indicators of demand for machine tools, firstly because machine tools are, as has been shown, a relatively small part of the various inputs into engineering production, and secondly because the pattern of orders for machine tools is known to differ somewhat from the pattern of output, as has been argued above. Thirdly, all the series for engineering output in the late nineteenth century are, according to their authors, highly speculative, being based not on output itself but on weighted averages of the cost of labour and of the most important material, iron and steel.

The relationship between numbers of firms and demand was explored by regressing numbers of firms, both total numbers and numbers entering, leaving temporarily, re-entering and leaving permanently, on demand measured by the Feinstein index of engineering output. Lagged values of output were also used as the independent variable. Initial analysis suggested the presence of autocorrelation in the residuals, and since it seemed reasonable on a priori grounds to assume that proportionate change in output might be reflected in proportionate change in demand, the regressions were re-run using the logarithms of the original values. The hypothesis was therefore that

$$Y = aX^b$$

where Y is the dependent variable, numbers of firms and X the independent variable, the demand index. The estimating equation was therefore

$$\log Y = \log a + b \log X$$

and this equation was fitted by ordinary least squares regression.

Table 3.9 shows the results of these regression calculations. It can be seen that total numbers of firms is positively, and significantly in terms of the value of the F-statistics, related to demand lagged by one year. In addition, numbers of firms entering the industry is negatively related to demand lagged by one year. All other measures of movement into or out of the industry show non-significant relationships with output measures. As is shown by the value of the Durbin–Watson statistic, the hypothesis of autocorrelation in the residuals can, with these log values be rejected. It should be said that both output and the various measures of numbers of firms and of entry into the industry are highly correlated with the time trend, and regressions utilising the first differences of these variables produce non-significant results. To this extent, the relationships shown in table 3.9 may be spurious, although the size of the Durbin–Watson statistic gives some grounds for arguing that they are not.

Table 3.9   *Regression estimates of the relationship between demand and the number of machine tool firms*

Dependent variable	Independent variable	Constant	b (S.E.)	R	F	D–W d
N.Blank	$Output_{t-1}$	3.8679	0.4534 (0.0998)	+0.6260	20.6213	1.5273
Blanks Enter	$Output_t$	9.2949	−1.4419 (0.3017)	−0.6454	22.8395	2.4050
Blanks Enter	$Output_{t-1}$	9.5957	−1.5244 (0.3121)	−0.6536	23.8609	2.3101
Blanks Enter	$Output_{t-1}$	8.8743	−1.35434 (0.3298)	−0.5875	16.8691	2.3015

Notes:
   (a)   N.Blank = Total no. of firms in the industry, as shown in col. 1 of Table 3.1.
   (b)   Blanks Enter = No. of firms entering the industry in a given year on the basis of col. 4 of Table 3.1.
   (c)   Output = Index of Production of the Mechanical and Electrical Engineering Industries (Feinstein, 1972, p. T114).
   (d)   Significance points of the Durbin–Watson distribution are $D_L = 1.39$, $D_u = 1.51$. In all other estimates, d was less than D_u.

As they stand, however, the results of table 3.9 suggest that the total number of firms broadly followed the course of the cycle of demand for engineering goods. More surprising is the inverse relationship between entry and demand, indicating that it was normal for firms to enter the industry not at the peak but rather at or after the trough of the cycle, when demand was depressed. This could be explained by what might be called a 'shake-out' effect, by which a decline in demand led to the disappearance of marginal firms from the industry, and allowed for their replacement by new and hopeful firms, perhaps in some cases inheriting the stock and capital goods of the defunct firms. This is difficult to demonstrate, both because departures from the industry do not appear to have a consistent relationship with demand, and because there is very little contemporary evidence about such transactions or about the secondhand market for machine tools.

The fact that no significant relationship exists between output and the return of firms to the industry could be reconciled with the 'shake-out' hypothesis, in that such firms, established in another branch of engineering, would be unlikely to choose a period of depression as one in which to return to machine tool making. Testing this hypothesis of a shake-out effect would, of course, require more data about individual firms than are, or are likely to be, available, and it is also clear from the regression results that at most only about 40% of the variance in firms or in firms entering the industry can be explained as a reaction to changes in demand; even these results may be spurious, because of the pervasive influence of the time trend and of the fact that the scatter diagrams do not show a strong linear relationship.

Factors other than the overall growth of demand were therefore clearly important in determining the growth and shape of the machine tool industry, although it would be interesting to know whether the simple regression results are paralleled by similar results from other nineteenth century industries. Broadly, the impression which emerges from the disparate hypotheses and evidence discussed in this chapter is of a fluid industry, responsive to demand both in the output of individual firms and in the number of firms, and containing within it firms specialising in a wide variety of types of production; any impression of the industry at this period as hide-bound or conservative, clinging to inefficient methods of production, is clearly incorrect.

4. International trade in machine tools

In 1851 the British superiority over all other nations was in machine tools, as in many other products, unchallenged.

> At the Great Exhibition of 1851 it [Britain] may be said to have been without a rival; the display of machine tools then made by some English houses took the world by surprise. The French and German, and even the American engineers were not prepared for such refinement of form combined with solidity of construction, the several fittings having a degree of precision never seen before, and yet constructed with such severe simplicity of arrangement in every detail, which by general consent placed England above comparison with the rest of the world. (P.P., 1867–8, p. 341)

This technical superiority, which was coupled with the commercial superiority of firms like Whitworth and Nasmyth, was eroded by foreign competition during the next seventy years, and it is the purpose of this chapter to describe this erosion, to estimate its effect on British sales of machine tools both at home and abroad, and to suggest some explanation.

The sources for a study of international trade in machine tools are limited, and those that exist are deficient in a number of ways. Statistical evidence on the trade is very scarce, at least until the early twentieth century, largely because the trade appears to have been small, at least in comparison with other engineering products. Some statistical evidence is available from the records of the machine tool producers, and that from Greenwood and Batley of Leeds, and the American company Brown and Sharpe, will be used below, but the extraction of such information is extremely cumbersome, and is possible only when the detailed order-books of the firm are available; the financial records of the companies, balance sheets and similar material do not, in the British companies whose records have been examined, normally distinguish home and export sales.

Qualitative evidence is fuller than is the statistical evidence, partly because of the conviction which was held at the end of the nineteenth century that Britain was falling behind in competition with other nations, but since in most cases the information, at least on aggregate trade, was as scanty for contemporary writers as it is for an historian, the value of the qualitative statements has continually to be questioned. It has always to be remembered, for instance, that depreciating statements about the British export effort could stem either from a real failure of British commercial effort or, as is the case with many of the consular reports, from a desire to spur British exporters on to further effort. They can therefore not be taken to be entirely objective summaries of the true competitive position of the British manufacturer.

Secondly, the qualitative evidence is deficient because much of it related to technical rather than to commercial success, to the appearance of new technical refinements rather than to the volume of sales. This is particularly true of the reports of the major international exhibitions, valuable though they are as a source of evidence, and it is true of much of the comment in the trade press. A biased picture may also emerge from the comments in the trade press because of the variety of products made by the machine tool industry; success in the field of heavy, multi-purpose machine tools by British manufacturers was, as will be argued later, often obscured by failure in the lighter, single-purpose mass production machine tools which were newer, changing more quickly in design, and thus attracted most attention from technical commentators.

In spite of these deficiencies, it is possible to construct a picture of the British position in the international trade in machine tools. The first section of this chapter will therefore attempt to use this evidence to describe the chronology of the loss of British pre-eminence in machine tools.

The chronology of the loss of British pre-eminence

To John Anderson, a leading British engineer, the beginnings of the loss of British pre-eminence in machine tools could be traced directly to the display of that pre-eminence at the Great Exhibition of 1851. As he put it:

The effect of that display immediately told, not only upon the machinists of other countries, but likewise on our own of second and third degree, and by the arrival of the Paris Exhibition of 1855 it was at once perceptible that a great change had taken place. (P.P., 1867–8, p. 702)

The example set at that exhibition by Whitworth, Nasmyth, Fairbairn, Sharp and the other British machine tool-makers whose tools were displayed stimulated the emergence of native machine tool industries in France, Germany and the United States. At the Paris Exhibition of 1867 it was clear to both British and foreign observers that Britain no longer had a commanding lead. To Anderson, although the French and Germans displayed a large number of tools in 1867, they did not show evidence of technical originality, but the American machine tools were a more serious threat; in America, he wrote, the student of machine tools will find something new; not only exquisite workmanship of the highest class, but new combinations even in connection with such a stereotyped article as a turning lathe or a planing machine, and without the loss of any of the essential points secured by English models. (P.P., 1867–8, p. 702)

An American observer in 1867 described the change

The principal nations exhibiting were France, England, Prussia and America. At the former exhibitions of 1851, 1855 and 1862 the English were almost without rivals. On the present occasion they made but a small display, and were vastly outnumbered by France and Prussia, while in point of novelty of form and excellence of workmanship America was admitted to be on a par with any nation. (Blake, 1870, p. 178)

The decline in the British lead in machine tools, as demonstrated in the reports on the international exhibitions, continued during the next decade. Anderson, reporting on the Philadelphia Exhibition of 1876, was very critical of the British display, which

contained so little of freshness, and was of so stereotyped a character, as to give encouragement to some of our foreign competitors to express openly in their printed reports, that we are losing our former leadership, and that it is passing to the Americans. (P.P., 1877, p. 306)

To the American observer, at Vienna in 1873, R. H. Thurston, the competition was severe, at least between America and Britain, 'as it should be expected to be between what are really divisions of the same nation' (Thurston, 1876, p. 241). Both British and American observers agreed that the majority of the French and German tools displayed were copies, in general inferior, of British or American designs, although these were interested comments; a French observer, perhaps from similar motives, commented that all the German and Austrian machine tools at Vienna were copied from tools made in Britain, the U.S.A. and France (Fontaine, 1874, p. 128).

After the Philadelphia Exhibition of 1876, however, the criticisms of the British effort weaken. There are, in fact, fewer comparisons of the type quoted above made in the exhibition reports, and those that are made are not hostile to Britain. In 1878 the British observer commented that at Paris the British display was 'highly satisfactory and maintained our reputation' (P.P., 1880, p. 38) while, to the American observer, the British tools were 'in point of workmanship . . . in advance of all others', although he also made the comment, slightly eccentric by this date, that British makers, unlike others, 'were thoroughly well acquainted with the uses of the fundamental tool of the machine shop of today — the planing machine' (Porter, 1880, p. 391). The American commissioners to the Paris Exhibition of 1889, although referring to the tributes to American mechanical skill 'frequently expressed by both British and Continental Engineers', reported that the 'grandest single machine in this class at the Exposition was, without doubt, the large lathe just built for Schneider and Co.' by Greenwood and Batley of Leeds (Barr, 1893, pp. 317, 352). In Brussels in 1910, *The Times* Engineering Supplement reported that 'about half-a-dozen firms worthily upheld the reputation of British machine tools for excellence of workmanship and solidity of design' (Anon., 1910b) and the same newspaper praised the British effort even more highly in reports of the Olympia engineering exhibitions of 1910 and 1912. In 1910 they commented that 'The exhibits . . . as a whole illustrate the reasons why many English makers are so successful in holding their own against foreign competitors in this department' (Anon., 1910c). In 1912 the exhibition 'vividly illustrates the forward step which has been taken by British manufacturers within the last few years', the industry having organised itself, begun to specialise, reduced its costs, adhered to delivery dates, and fought off the danger that it would succumb to foreign competition (Anon., 1912).

The evidence of the reports on the major exhibitions of the period from 1850 to 1914 thus suggests a chronology of British competitiveness in the international market in machine tools in which the British lead is eroded between 1850 and, approximately, 1870 to 1880. From that time commentators seem to cease to comment on Britain's lost leadership, and instead concentrate on the advantages of particular British tools or types of tools, thus treating Britain as one among equal competitors. This is particularly true in relation to American competition; British tools are still usually referred to, at least by British and American commentators, as being superior to the general run of tools from European countries, largely France, Germany, Switzerland, Belgium and Austria.

The evidence of the miscellaneous other commentators on the relative status of Britain in the international production of machine tools confirms this chronology, and also provides information on the competition between Britain and other countries in the period after the erosion of the British lead. In the earlier period, before the 1870s, although competition is fierce, the British tools are in general described as the best in the world. In 1868 a correspondent of the *Scientific American*, for instance, wrote that although American tools had 'the greatest amount of originality . . . it is not always easy to assert that their designs are decided improvements on the usual British types of machines', and he concluded that, 'If there is any one branch of engineering in which the English particularly excel, it is in the construction of machine tools' (Brown, 1868, p. 293). At the same time, it was said in a series of articles in the *Standard* that in machine tools 'The Belgians challenge us [Britain] for cheapness; we challenge them and all the world for quality' (Brown, 1868, p. 299), while 'The reputation of England as the first machinist in the world should not be permitted to be lowered. The Prussians and Saxons are the best of our competitors, but they do not equal England as represented by her best tool-makers' (Brown, 1868, p. 302). An American writer, in general hostile to British engineering, Charles T. Porter, thought that at least in 1868, British tool-making was superior:

> At that time, toolmaking in this country [U.S.A.] which has since become so magnificently developed, was in many important respects in a primitive condition, and I proposed to introduce into my shop every best tool and method, adapted to my requirements, that I could find in England . . . I found also the remarkable fact that I could obtain these tools, duty and freight paid, decidedly cheaper than corresponding inferior tools could then be got from American makers. (Porter, 1908, p. 169)

In the later part of the century, the competition of American and German machine tool producers, both in the British home market and abroad, became much more severe. This was particularly true in the field of light mass-production tools, suitable for the sewing machine and cycle industries. According to a Mr Henry Webb, addressing the Manchester Association of Engineers in 1898, 'The bulk of the tools in the cycle works at Coventry came from America', since the American manufacturers excelled the British in the manufacture of automatic screwing machines and turret lathes, suitable for cycle manufacture (Webb, 1898, p. 66). Bertold Buxbaum, while commenting that 'Um das jahr 1850 begannen die Staaten von New England ihre Werkzeugmaschinen auch nach England auszufuhren', dated the main penetration of the British market to the development of the turret lathe between 1890 and 1900 (Buxbaum, 1960, pp. 128, 144). Further impetus to the American sales of machine tools in Britain came it was said as a result of the British engineering strike of 1897 (Cox, 1903, p. 331), coinciding with the bicycle boom and with a domestic slump in the United States in 1895–6 (Anon., 1899c, p. 627). These statements give the impression of a sudden penetration of the market, but one of the major importers of American machine tools to Britain, Charles Churchill, wrote, on a number of occasions, that the growth had been slow and steady:

> The introduction of American machinery has not been simply a matter

of two or three years. It has been a steadily growing demand for many
years past. It was boomed a little through the bicycle trade, but the
present time shows every evidence that trade in American tools throughout Great Britain will steadily increase in the future. (Churchill, 1899,
p. 265)

He repeated in 1902 that:

As we look back upon the work now we see that steady progress has
been made; a curious feature of the growth of the business being that, if
we disregard the 'hump' in the curve of our progress caused by the
bicycle boom of 1896–7, the curve is generally regular and steadily
upward. (Churchill, 1902, p. 1621)

On the other hand, it is certainly true that the 'hump' was spectacular. The
American Machinist reported in February 1895 that Churchill's sales were
up by 20% over 1893–4, 'at a time when the general trade in Great Britain
has been extremely quiet' (Anon., 1895, p. 104), in 1896 a dividend of
230% was declared on the share capital of £5500 (Anon., 1965a, p. 109)
and in 1897 the recent growth of the firm was described as 'phenomenal',
sales in a recent period of six months in London and Birmingham having
been worth $625,000 (Miller, 1897, p. 371).

Whether the growth of demand for American tools was slow and steady,
or the result of a chance conjunction of the bicycle boom and the engineers' strike in 1896–7, there can be little doubt but that American tools
were well established in Britain and in other European countries by the
beginning of the twentieth century, and that in many cases they had sup-
planted British tools. In 1898 the President of a large American machine
tool firm (Davis and Egan) referred to the large exports of machine tools
in recent years to Germany, heavy sales to the French government, and to
Belgium. (Dans, 1898). G. L. Carden, the American who toured European
engineering works on behalf of the American government in 1909–10,
comments several times that only the older tools in various factories are of
British origin, the more modern having been bought in America, or in one
or two cases, from the native machine tool industry or from Germany
(Carden, 1909–10, pp. 73, 74, 78, 174).

There are, however, some signs that the effect of American competition,
and the backwardness of the British industry, were over-rated by contemporaries.

In the period after 1900 there was undoubtedly a revival in the British
machine tool industry. Thus Dr Shadwell, writing in 1908, admitted that
'in the modern development of machine tools . . . British makers have not
played a prominent part . . . Our people had been asleep for some time . . .

They had got into a comfortable groove and had stayed there', but he thought that there were now some signs of recovery. In 1906 a British engineer argued that the difference between British and American practice was not very great: 'In most respects an up-to-date American shop does not differ greatly from an English one engaged on similar work' (Foster, 1906, p. 14), and the United States consul in Birmingham reported in 1907:

the great headway made by British makers of machine tools . . . the long delay of American manufacturers in executing orders is leading British engineers to buy their tools elsewhere, and . . . British tool-makers are seizing the opportunity to make and push tools made on American models. (Anon., 1907, p. 18)

Carden commented on a number of British firms who offered strong competition to American and other makers. Foremost was Alfred Herbert of Coventry, of whom Carden said that 'There is no denying that the Herbert machine tools, and in particular the turret lathe of this firm, are strong competitors of the best work turned out from American shops' (1909–10, p. 225). But he also praised Lang's and Darling and Sellers (ibid., pp. 213–44). On the other hand, in spite of this revival, it is clear that there continued to be considerable imports of machine tools into Britain; as the Balfour Committee of 1918 reported:

Throughout the evidence we were confronted with large purchases before the war from the United States of machine tools, in which their manufacturers specialised, such as automatics, grinding, milling and drilling machines, presses, lathes and gear cutting machines, measuring instruments and other small engineers tools, whilst, as a rule, special tools only were brought from Germany. (P.P., 1918)

Contemporary comment on the position of Britain in the international market in machine tools is certainly confused, and is biased by the various standpoints of the commentators. It is however possible to discern, so far, a certain chronology in the decline of British pre-eminence, which had been demonstrated in 1851. It would appear that French, German and American tool-makers began to compete seriously with the British makers in the 1860s and that by the 1870s the British lead, at least in technical terms, had been eroded. The major penetration of the European markets, including Britain, by the United States, can be dated in the middle of the 1890s, at which time the British makers were not offering any serious competition to this invasion of their markets. Lastly, during the period 1900 to the first world war there were signs of a British revival, in both the technical and the commercial field, but the revival was not sufficient to win back fully the position which Britain had earlier held.

This chronology, vague as it necessarily is, especially in the imprecision of the distinction between technical and commercial superiority, which is particularly important, can only be checked by statistical evidence on the actual volume of machine tools entering international trade during this period. Unfortunately, as has already been made clear, the sources for such evidence are very few. The British trade statistics do not distinguish machine tools from other engineering products, while the German trade statistics, although they do distinguish machine tools from other engineering products, do not provide information on the country of origin of the tools, but record imports by the frontier post through which they entered the country; there is therefore no way of distinguishing countries of origin, since an import through, for instance, Hamburg, might well have come from either Britain or the United States. The Belgium trade statistics do distinguish imports by country of origin, but make no distinction until very late in the period between machine tools and small tools. The only major industrial country in this period which did distinguish imports of machine tools from other products, and which listed imports by country of origin, was France, and the French trade statistics are therefore used below. As to private sources, the only business records available are those of two American manufacturers, Brown and Sharp and the Bullard Machine Company, and of one British manufacturer, Greenwood and Batley.

The French Trade statistics, *Commerce de la France*, insofar as they relate to machine tools, have a number of deficiencies. From 1865, the first year in which machine tools are distinguished from other machinery, until 1880, machine tools are listed in a category headed 'Machines-outils et machines non denommées', and the distinction between these two categories is not made clear in the printed returns. From 1881 a second category of 'Machines non denommées' disappears; machine tools are still listed under 'Machines-outils et machines non denommées'. From 1892 to 1914 a separate category of 'Machines-outils' is used, and a category of 'Mecanique generale' is introduced. The first problem in using the statistics is therefore to estimate how seriously the change in categories, and the possible inclusion of an indefinite amount of miscellaneous machinery in the machine tool category from 1865 to 1891, affects their value. It is clear that the other categories under the general heading of this section of the Trade statistics, 'Machines autre qu'à vapeur' were designed to distinguish separately as many types of machinery as possible, so that the number of possible 'Machines non denommées', the residual category, is likely to be small.

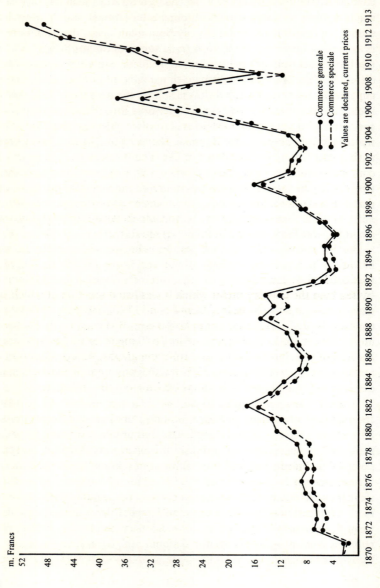

Figure 4.1. French imports of machine tools

Secondly, it is possible to examine the statistics themselves to see whether there is any marked change or break in trend in either 1881 or 1892, which might be the result of a change in categories rather than a real change in imports of machine tools. As figure 4.1, French imports of machine tools (or categories including machine tools), shows, there is no sign of a change in trend between 1880 and 1881; machine tool imports rise, as would be expected if all miscellaneous machinery was added, but the trend does not alter markedly. For 1892 the situation is somewhat different; there is a marked change apparent in the statistics, imports apparently dropping by approximately 50%. It seems likely that this was in fact at least partially the result of separating the 'Machines-outils' category from that for 'Mecanique generale', and that, when absolute import figures are being considered, it is wise to regard the series as being broken at that point, and to remember that the figures certainly for 1881 to 1891 contain machinery other than machine tools. It is however clear from figure 4.2, percentages of total imports from the major countries of origin, that these market shares do not alter in any marked direction in either 1881 or 1892; it seems therefore reasonable to regard these shares, which are in fact the main point of interest, as reliable.

A second difficulty with the statistics, which relates only to the period before 1870, is that up to that date the item imported was attributed to its true country of ultimate origin only if it reached France by land; if it came by sea then the country under which it was listed was that at which the ship bringing it had last called. In and from 1870, however, the true country of origin was asked for in both cases. It is possible that some imports from the United States before 1870 might be under-enumerated because of this, but as can be seen from the graphs, American imports remained very small long after 1870, so that any under-enumeration cannot seriously affect any conclusions drawn from the statistics.

Thirdly, the statistics distinguish two categories of imports, 'commerce speciale' and 'commerce generale'. Broadly, 'commerce generale', was total imports into France, including items that would subsequently be re-exported, or which were transhipped in French ports, while 'commerce speciale' included all items destined for use or consumption in France itself. 'Commerce speciale' was therefore imports net of re-exports. Fourthly, the imports were recorded by volume and value, but only volume figures are given for individual countries. Since no information is available on the weight–price ratios for imports from different countries, it is impossible to know how seriously this method of recording affects any attempt to look at the value of international trade in machine tools. For instance, if

American tools were in general more expensive per tonne than British tools, the French trade statistics would under-rate the relative amount of American machine tool exports to France, as compared with British tools. The real value per tonne of machine tools was probably rising over the period from 1865 to 1914, but the reasons for this are not entirely clear, and it is impossible to know whether the trends in price per unit of weight differed markedly from country to country.

Within these deficiencies, which should be borne in mind in interpreting the statistics given below, it is possible to examine the French trade returns to see whether they support the chronology of the loss of British pre-eminence in this field which has been suggested above on the basis of the qualitative evidence.

Figure 4.2 shows the proportions of total French imports of machine tools net of re-exports originating in the six countries from which imports largely originated. (Machine tools is used here and hereafter as a shorthand for the various categories including machine tools which were discussed above.) Imports from other countries were quantitively insignificant compared with those from England, Germany, U.S.A., Belgium, Italy and Switzerland, which are those graphed. The major trend which can at once be observed is the decline of British exports to France, from a peak of 69.5% of French imports in 1865 to a low point of 7.1% in 1909. This decline accords with the evidence given by contemporary observers, and it is clear that the chronology of the decline shown in figure 4.2, also accords with that gathered from contemporary evidence. Britain is still in a strong position in 1865, but is losing her predominance, in the face of competition from, in particular, Germany and Belgium. The British share of the market is first exceeded by Germany in 1873, although from 1874 to 1882 Britain regains her lead, to lose it to Belgium in 1883. From this period it is clear that the British pre-eminence has been lost, and that, in the competition for exports to France, Germany, Belgium and Britain rank together, each with approximately 30% of the market.

The major change in this pattern of parity between Britain, Belgium and Germany in the French market can be dated to the 1890s, and particularly to the rise in imports from the United States in 1897, 1898 and 1899. This rise can be ascribed partially to the bicycle boom, which affected France as well as Britain in this period, but it is also clear that at this period the United States effectively captured approximately half the share of the French market previously held by Britain. Germany from the same period captured an increased share, perhaps at the expense of Belgium, whose share dropped from 30% in 1895 to 4% in 1901. (It is of course imposs-

79

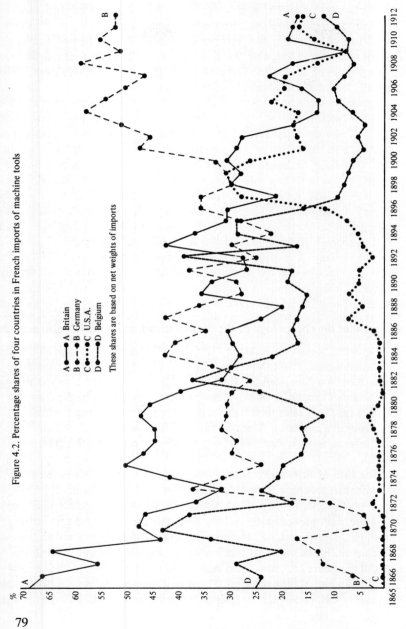

Figure 4.2. Percentage shares of four countries in French imports of machine tools

A ●——● A Britain
B ●——● B Germany
C ●····● C U.S.A.
D ●——● D Belgium

These shares are based on net weights of imports

ible to know whether in fact the shares of Belgium and Britain were divided in exactly this way.) There is no sign thereafter of any British recovery in the field of French imports, but it is interesting to observe that, after the initial loss of approximately half her share in the 1890s, Britain retains a parity, at a lower level, with the American imports; British sales to France exceed those of the United States in 1900, 1901, 1902, 1907, 1908, 1910 and 1912, and equal them in 1909 and 1911.

The most surprising feature of the French statistics on the import of machine tools, when they are considered in the light of contemporary comment, is the long delay before the effects are felt of American technical excellence in the design of machine tools. It will be recalled that it was in 1867 that John Anderson described American machine tools as a more serious threat to Britain than those of France and Germany, and in 1876 that he said that 'we are losing our former leadership, and that it is passing to the Americans'. In the light of these and similar comments, it seems surprising that the American technical advantage was not translated into commercial success in France until 1896 and thereafter, though there is a short spurt, in which 7% of the market was achieved, in the period from 1886 to 1891. In other words, the American penetration of the French market was delayed for anything up to twenty years from the time when a British expert regarded American tools as superior to those of any European competitor; these same European competitors were, at the same time, selling vastly more machine tools to France than was the United States.

Confirmation of the relatively late penetration of the European market by American manufacturers of machine tools can be obtained from the records of two American machine tool makers. Information on the Brown and Sharpe Company's sales to Europe were obtained from the company records (as far as sales to Britain were concerned), and from Professor MacDougall's article on 'Machine tool output, 1861–1910', which also gave information on shipments by the Bullard Company (MacDougall, 1966).

The firm of Brown and Sharpe was founded in 1833, but began to manufacture machine tools only during the Civil War (Woodbury, 1959, pp. 59–60; Rolt, 1965, p. 171). Milling machines and grinding machines were the main preoccupation of the firm, but they also sold gear-cutting machines, screw machines, lathes, polishing and finishing machines, screw-slotting machines, chucking machines and tapping machines, as well as special machines for armaments manufacture (MacDougall, 1966, p. 504 and Brown and Sharpe records). The firm pioneered the production of new machine tools, principally milling and grinding machines. Brown's universal milling machine, invented in 1861, is described by Woodbury as 'epoch-making', and as embodying 'nearly all the basic features of milling machines to this day' (Woodbury, 1960, p. 44), while his universal grinding machine, invented in 1875, was similarly the prototype for the modern grinding machine which is 'still basically the universal grinding machine as Joseph R. Brown conceived it' (Woodbury, 1959, p. 66). The Brown and Sharpe Company were therefore in the forefront of the technical development of the two major innovations in machine tool design which took place between 1850 and 1914, and they were able to sell these prototype machines, and those of improved design which they later produced, both at home and abroad (Woodbury, 1959, p. 56 and Brown and Sharpe records). While Brown and Sharpe concentrated on the light, mass-production machine tool which was considered by many observers to be typical of American machine tool production, the Bullard Company, established as the Bridgeport Machine Tool Company in 1880, concentrated on 'the larger type of production machine tool', and sold many tools to railway and other heavy engineering workshops (MacDougall, 1966, pp. 501, 504). Between them the two firms thus span the range of machine tool production during this period.

It is therefore interesting to note that, in the case of both of these firms, sales of machine tools to European, or indeed extra-American customers, were very small before 1895. Table 4.1, reprinted from Professor MacDougall's article, shows foreign shipments of machine tools by the two companies. As MacDougall makes clear, foreign sales were an important part of the output of the companies, making up more than 10% of sales by Brown and Sharpe from 1865 onwards. On the other hand, absolute numbers sold, particularly to Europe, were very small before 1895, when there is a very obvious spurt in demand. Brown and Sharpe sold 1290 machine tools to north-west Europe in the thirty-five years up to 1894, and 2560 in the following five years from 1895–9. The contrast is even clearer with Bullard shipments, 27 between 1881 and 1894, 446 between 1895 and 1899 (MacDougall, 1966, p. 507). The more detailed breakdown of the British sales allows the change to be dated even more precisely to 1896. Only 74 milling machines worth 54,215 dollars were sold by Brown and Sharpe to British customers between 1865 and 1895, but in 1896 alone they sold 61 milling machines worth $38,953, and in 1897 and 1898 a total of 212 machines worth $130,470. A similar expansion took place in sales of grinding machines and gear-cutting machines. Yearly total sales of machine tools to Britain by Brown and Sharpe did not rise above $15,000 in any year until 1895, and did not fall below that level again until 1917, having reached a peak of $203,648, in 1904 (Brown and Sharpe records). As MacDougall shows, this pattern of a rapid expansion of sales after 1895 was paralleled in sales by Brown and Sharpe to all major European countries, with the exception of France, where sales peaked from 7 machines in 1880—4 to 352 machines in 1885—9, and then fell to 60 machines in the next quinquennium, before rising again with all other countries after 1895. As MacDougall says, this peak can be explained by heavy sales to French government arsenals, which took nearly 200 tools between 1886 and 1888 (MacDougall, 1966, p. 508).

Table 4.1   *Foreign shipments of machine tools by two American machine tool firms*

Period	North-west Europe	South Europe	Russia and East Europe	Canada	Other	Total
		A. *Brown and Sharpe*				
1861—4	0	0	0	0	0	0
1865—9	27	3	1	16	0	47
1870—4	60	10	5	34	0	109
1875—9	55	0	0	5	3	63
1880—4	84	0	2	29	10	125
1885—9	633	0	2	13	7	655
1890—4	431	6	38	25	22	522
1895—9	2560	43	257	39	41	2940
1900—4	2349	49	127	140	356	3421
		B. *Bullard*				
1881—4	7	0	0	1	1	9
1885—9	13	0	0	0	0	13
1890—4	7	0	0	4	0	11
1895—9	446	0	8	2	1	457
1900—4	394	3	1	30	3	431
1905—9	341	20	9	29	14	413

Notes:
  (a)   South Europe: Italy, Spain, Portugal, Greece, Turkey.
  (b)   East Europe: Poland, Rumania, Bulgaria.

Source: MacDougall, 1966, p. 507. Data extracted by MacDougall from company records.

In the case of these companies, therefore, the same paradox emerges as in the more general consideration of contemporary comment and French imports of machine tools. Both companies were innovators in the machine tool field — Bullard produced 'a significant contribution to the technical progress of the machine tool art with the invention of a small boring mill' in 1883 (MacDougall, 1966, p. 501), and the technical advances made by Brown and Sharpe have been mentioned. The machine tools made by Brown and Sharpe were certainly well known to European customers from

1867, when their tools were exhibited at the Paris Exhibition, and they produced a French catalogue in 1867, and a German catalogue in 1868 (MacDougall, 1966, p. 503). Yet both Brown and Sharpe and Bullard, and American tool-makers in general, as can be seen from the French trade statistics, failed to make a significant impact on the extra-American market for machine tools before 1895–7.

This apparent delay on the part of American tool-makers in exploiting overseas markets was paralleled by American manufacturers in other branches of engineering. Study of the American trade statistics show that it was only in the middle of the 1890s that American engineering goods were exported on a significant scale, and at that time exports expanded to a wide variety of foreign markets. This development, which has been discussed and documented elsewhere, suggests that some general factors were at work determining the expansion of demand for American products in the world market, and that machine tool exports were simply part of this general expansion (Floud, 1974). It is, however, instructive to consider machine tool exports initially as a case study in the possible effects of such factors as differences in commercial method and in the efficiency of salesmanship, before returning later in the chapter to consider the general issue.

The British sales effort in international markets

During the first part of the period 1850 to 1914 British exporters of machine tools seem to have been fortunate in a lack of effective competition from any other country; British tools were superior in every way, and often, as the quotation from Porter given above demonstrates, cheaper than foreign-produced tools even when transport costs were taken into account. With the advent of foreign competition, both commercially and technically, it was necessary for British machine tool makers to seek more actively to make sales abroad, and to cease to rely on the maxim, so often quoted by early tool makers, that a 'good tool sells itself'. British machine tool makers were faced with a number of choices when they sought to sell their tools in foreign countries; they had to choose whether to sell direct or through agents, either in Britain or in the export market, whether to produce catalogues in foreign languages, whether to exhibit at international exhibitions in the hope of attracting interest or orders, whether to employ salesmen, and they had to decide on the payment and credit terms which they were prepared to offer foreign customers. It is apparent from the scattered evidence that is available that all these choices were taken up, at one time or another, by British companies; they will therefore be examined in an effort to understand their advantages and disadvantages, and the effect which they had on the British ability to sell machine tools in the international markets.

One of the most obvious methods of making new machine tools known to a wide audience was to exhibit them at one of the many international exhibitions, held at various times in most of the industrialised countries of Europe and America. It was therefore often a criticism of British machine tool-makers at the time that many did not exhibit at exhibitions, and that Britain was under-represented compared to her competitors. In Paris in 1867 the British exhibits were described as 'but a small display' by the American commissioner, while John Anderson commented that Britain was 'lethargic . . . and, but for the circumstance that a few of the best makers have come forward, Great Britain would have been unrepresented' (Blake, 1870, p. 178; P.P., 1867–8, p. 702). Anderson's report on the Vienna Exhibition of 1873 commented that 'many of our best houses were not represented at Vienna by even so much as a single specimen; hence the general poverty' (P.P., 1874a, p. 12), while the technical reports on the same exhibition by W. H. Maw and James Dredge were prefaced by the comment that:

> Altogether the collection of machine tools in the British department but very poorly represented the progress of this branch of engineering in England, and to all who were familiar with the numerous admirable special tools to be found in our leading engineering factories, the British exhibits of this class at Vienna could not fail to be most disappointing. (P.P., 1874b, p. 771)

This catalogue of British failure was continued at a number of other exhibitions. The international judges at the Philadelphia Exhibition of 1876 regretted that:

> Great Britain, which stands so high in this class of machinery, was not better represented. The exhibit of that country was conspicuous by the absence of all the well known names with which the world has been familiar. (P.P., 1877, p. 782)

At Paris in 1889 most of the leading British engineering manufacturers were not represented, and those that were, were criticised by the French official report for failure to show off their exhibits:

> L'impression de monotonie que nous ressentions tout a l'heure s'est accrue d'une manière sensible. Tous ces employes, hommes ou femmes, assis au debout derniere leurs utrines, semblent dormir les yeux ouverts. Il ya a la comme une vie automatique en suspens, qui se reveille de temps en temps à autre par mouvements saccades. (Anon., 1890b, p. 103)

In the report on the Paris Exhibition of 1900 the British juror commented on the small number of British firms exhibiting, and listed six firms as 'conspicuous by their absence' (P.P., 1901, p. 368). Before the St Louis Exhibition of 1904 the British government tried to encourage British firms to exhibit, but:

> The replies showed that no engineering firms were prepared to take part in the exhibition, even to the extent of furnishing engines or dynamos for the motive power plant, for which the Administration of the Exhibition were willing to pay all expenses. (P.P., 1906, p. 459)

while the report of the British Commissioners on the exhibitions at Brussels, Rome and Turin in 1910 and 1911 commented that the machine tool section contained the work of only seven British firms:

> whose products were of high excellence, design, build and finish, comparing very favourably with those of foreign competitors, but not sufficiently numerous as compared with the latter to give an adequate idea of the enormous importance and leading position of the machine tool industry in Great Britain (P.P., 1912–13a, p. 233).

Proof that the failure of British manufacturers to exhibit at these exhibitions was the result of lethargy or failure of enterprise would throw considerable light on the failure of British machine tool makers to maintain their predominant position. It is clear, however, that British machine tool makers could have sound commercial reasons for failing to send their tools to exhibitions, even if they were taking a short-sighted view of commercial considerations. The reasons given by the makers for dislike of international exhibitions were that exhibiting was expensive, that it did not produce an adequate return in terms of additional machines sold, and that it diverted attention from manufacture of machines which had already been ordered. In 1867 Anderson admitted that one of the reasons for the poor British display was that 'the majority of houses were tired of the unremunerative expense of former exhibitions' (P.P., 1867–8, p. 702). Both the British and the American observers at Vienna in 1873 recognised that a rise in demand for machine tools made it difficult for British makers to spare the time to make tools for exhibition (P.P., 1874b, p. 771; Anon., 1876, p. 244), and much later in the period, the British commissioners at Brussels, Rome and Turin, discussing the failure of British firms to exhibit, said that the firms relied on their long-established reputations to sell their tools, and saw little advantage and much expense in sending machines to exhibitions (P.P., 1912–13a, p. 235).

It is difficult to know how well-founded these objections or excuses were, especially because, even when detailed sales records are available, sales as a result of exhibitions cannot easily be distinguished from sales which would have been achieved anyway. Greenwood and Batley sent machine tools to the Melbourne Exhibition in 1880, but sold only ten machine tools in Australia, in the next twenty years, one in 1886, eight in 1889, and one in 1899; it seems unlikely that any of these sales resulted from the exhibition. Although the firm did send machine tools to a number of exhibitions, the attitude of the firm was made clear in 1889, when the large engine lathe, praised by commentators, was sent to the Paris Exhibition; the Minutes of the Board of Directors recorded that 'After a great deal of trouble and at considerable expense, the large lathe had been erected and was now working in the Paris exhibition, where it formed one of the chief attractions' (Greenwood and Batley Board, 12 July 1889). It was largely because the Machine Tool and Engineering Association, formed in 1911, promised to control the number of exhibitions, that Greenwood and Batley joined the Association as a founder member, it being recorded in the Board Minutes that 'The object of the Association . . . [is] . . . to prevent the holding of a large number of Engineering Exhibitions, and to promote the sale of Machine Tools of English Manufacture'; the order in which the objects are stated is surely significant (Greenwood and Batley Board, 19 January 1911). It was apparently felt that a large amount of effort and expense was being wasted by the holding of a large number of exhibitions, and the new Association undertook to organise national exhibitions to be held every three years, the first being held at Olympia in 1912.

The attitude of Greenwood and Batley, and the other British firms, is understandable if it is remembered that the expense of sending a machine tool for exhibition could be considerable; in addition to the shipping costs of the tool itself, men would have to be sent with it to erect it and to work it at the exhibitions where the machinery was displayed in action, and, for firms where machinery was made only to order rather than to stock, the investment in a new machine could be entirely wasted if no customer could ultimately be found whose needs it suited. Even if the machine itself was sold, unless its display generated several further orders it was unlikely that a profit would be made on the venture as a whole, particularly in view of the profit margins under which firms like Greenwood and Batley were operating. Thus, while it is possible to view the comments of manufacturers hostile to exhibitions as lethargy or lack of enterprise, it is also possible that they had reasonable grounds for their scepticism; as has already been mentioned, Brown and Sharpe received high praise for their exhibit of a universal milling machine in Paris in 1867, but their total sales to France in the quinquennium 1865–9 were only twelve machine tools of all types, and sales in the next quinquennium were only one machine (MacDougall, 1966, p. 508).

Perhaps a more fundamental choice which had to be made by British tool makers in this period was concerned with the methods of selling abroad, and particularly whether the firm should sell its machines through agents or should attempt to sell direct, either through its own salesmen or through the dispatch of catalogues to potential customers. It is apparent that most British firms sold abroad by both methods; Greenwood and Batley, for instance, sold through twenty-two agents in foreign countries, as well as seventy-seven at home, many of whom, from their names, or the ultimate destination of the machinery, were acting as forwarding agents for foreign countries. Greenwood and Batley had agents in Belgium, Holland, France, Spain, Austria, Turkey, Russia, Canada, Italy and South Africa and in addition sold to Japanese and German agents who had offices in London. However, it is also clear that the directors of the firm spent long periods abroad in search of orders. On 10 April 1889 the Board were told that a director, George Greenwood, had been to Vienna to get an order for rifle barrel drilling machines from a Mr Werndl, who was described as 'a gun-maker having large contracts with the Austrian and German governments', while the Chairman and one of the managers had been in Berlin to get an order for cartridge-making machinery. Later in the year one of the managers was reported to be returning from the Melbourne Exhibition by way of New Zealand, Java and Batavia in search of business, and in November George Greenwood was sent to Russia in search of contracts. Visits by directors to possible foreign customers in Hungary, Russia and other countries were also reported to the Board in later years (Greenwood and Batley Board 10 April 1889; 12 July 1889; 4 November 1889; 29 May 1890; 22 June 1895). Foreign purchasers were also encouraged to visit the factory in Leeds to discuss further purchases. Several British firms also established offices abroad, sometimes acting as agents for other, non-competing British engineering firms. In 1874 Thomas Turton and Sons of Sheffield, who made machine tools amongst other machinery, had offices in Paris and New York.

Alfred Herbert's also sold either directly or through foreign agents, a fact which G. L. Carden saw as related to their success:

I think it is safe to say that I found more Herbert machine tools on the Continent than from any other single English firm. There is no denying that the Herbert machine tools, and in particular the turret lathe of this firm, are strong competitors of the best work turned out from American shops. From several months' observation in Europe I am convinced not only of the excellence of Herbert material but the efficiency of the commercial branch of this firm. It is noteworthy that Herbert is selling his own goods, and so far as I know his agents are under his direct control. (Carden, 1909–10, p. 225)

Herbert's began by selling through agents:

We had made some contacts with Continental Cycle Manufacturers and this led us to explore the export field. Our first foreign agent was Adolf Yansen of Paris and Brussels, who at one time had an extensive connection among machine tool buyers. We then opened a branch of our own in Paris, which afterwards became Societe Anonyme Alfred Herbert, to be followed by similar enterprises in Belgium and Italy, and by a branch in Japan and then by subsidiary companies in India, Australia and the Argentine, and agencies in Berlin and Frankfurt. None of these business [*sic*] was manufacturing but only distributive; they widened the market for our pioducts and encouraged the extension of the Coventry Works. (Herbert, n.d.)

Greenwood and Batley also set up a subsidiary company, The Phoenix Engineering Works Co., in Russia, although this had the object of protecting their large trade with Russia from the effects of Russian government measures against imports of machinery (Greenwood and Batley Board, 28 May 1897).

The British machine tool trade with foreign countries was thus conducted, at least as far as the leading firms were concerned, through a variety of channels, suggesting that the companies were looking for business wherever and however they could get it. Again, as far as the leading firms were concerned, they were prepared to produce catalogues of their machine tools in the languages of the countries to which they hoped to sell. Greenwood and Batley produced a number of catalogues in French and German; Herbert's produced catalogues in Italian. The British consul in Kharkov emphasised the importance of this in his report for 1909, adding that the giving of dimensions in metric terms was also essential, although it is doubtful how many firms took his advice (Board of Trade, 1910b, p. 328). It is of course impossible to know how the majority of British firms sold abroad, if they did so. There are a number of comments from British representatives abroad suggesting that sales methods were not very intense, and that British manufacturers did not exercise enough care in choosing foreign agents, sometimes choosing foreign firms who made competing machine tools:

The engineering and weaving industries (in Lyons) use British machine tools and looms, which are at present imported through local agents, many of whom are themselves constructors. A direct trade in these goods might possibly be established between producer and consumer. (Board of Trade, 1910a, p. 370)

A South African engineer commented that many South African agencies for British machinery were little better than ironmongers, and could give no service to potential customers (Morgan, 1902, p. 150). It is also likely that a number of manufacturers shared the attitude of the firm of Dean, Smith and Grace of Keighley, who, formed in 1865, did not appoint their first traveller or salesman until 1886, James Smith believing that 'no amount of office organisation can sell a bad machine, but good machines sell themselves' (Anon., 1965b, p. 230).

In general, it would seem that the distinction between 'best practice' firms and the rest can be drawn with reference to commercial as well as to technical ability. Herbert's seem to have been exceptional in the care which they took. Carden reported on their contacts with the Budapest Locomotive Works that:

Mr. Kanitzer (the manager) told me that Herbert's engineers paid periodical visits to Budapest and personally instructed the locomotive workmen in the management of Herbert machines. An inspector from Coventry comes to Budapest at varied intervals, and personally takes notice of the running of the tools. Herbert has gone further and induced the locomotive works authorities to send over to Coventry five of the leading workmen from the Budapest shops. These men will be instructed at Coventry and will undoubtedly learn much regarding the varied lines of machines as manufactured for modern-day requirements (Carden, 1909–10, p. 39)

Greenwood and Batley also sent their workmen to superintend erection of their plant in foreign factories, a director, George Greenwood, spending much of his time between 1860 and 1890 in charge of such work. However, in general it seems likely that this type of after-sales service must have been confined to such sales as those of complete sets of factory equipment, and that the majority of firms did not undertake to do more than sell the machine. This discussion of the sales methods of British machine tool firms must therefore remain somewhat inconclusive. Some firms undoubtedly tried hard to sell their products abroad, others, at least if the image of the British manufacturer uninterested in exporting has any foundation, did not.

A further criticism which was levelled at British exporters in this period, as today, and which was regarded as one of the factors responsible for poor export performance, was that they were unwilling to grant generous credit terms, and demanded payment at an earlier stage in the progress of the work than did their competitors. In 1907 the commercial attaché in Madrid commented that British firms often found it difficult to sell in Spain because of the requirements which they laid down for payment:

Theoretically the usual terms are one-third with order, one-third on leaving works, or on arrival, and the remaining one-third three months later; but, in practice, one would be fortunate to get normal terms of this kind, buyers liking to pay as much as possible from the profits derived from the machine purchased. The custom of long credits has been introduced within the last eight years by Continental firms, and it is now common to give one, and sometimes up to two years. Under these circumstances it can be readily understood that 'cash with order' which is often asked by British houses, is not very acceptable in Spain.

(Board of Trade, 1907, p. 408)

The catalogues of British machine tool firms show the type of conditions which were laid down; Henry Berry of Leeds, who made hydraulic machine tools, listed the conditions of sale in their catalogue of 1890. Terms were cash in one month, less 2½% discount for cash. Foreign orders must be accompanied by a remittance of one-third, and credit arranged in England. Packing cases were charged extra, but two-thirds was allowed for them if they were returned free and in good condition. The 1905 catalogue of J. Butler and Co. of Halifax stipulated that references had to be given with first orders, and that in the case of foreign orders the order should either be accompanied by full payment or arrangements should be made to pay in England in presentation of bills of lading or invoices. Because of their large foreign business, Greenwood and Batley were obliged to accept payment in foreign currencies, although they made efforts to obtain at least some of the money in England. A large contract with the Russian government in 1890 was the subject of considerable discussion by the full Board of Directors, demonstrating the importance of terms of payment to both customer and producer. One of the company's engineers, who had been sent to Russia to discuss the contract, had sent a telegram to enquire 'whether the Company would accept payment in roubles instead of in pounds sterling. As the value of the rouble might fluctuate, payment in roubles had been declined' the Board was told. The conditions of the contract, as proposed by the Russians, were that 25% should be paid on signature of the contract, 40% on the machinery arriving in Russia, 15% on arrival at Tula (the site of the factory), and the last 20% four weeks after verification by the government engineer. The Russians also required a bank guarantee of repayment of the 25% deposit if the contract was not completed. One of the directors reported that this condition was normal, adding that many foreign governments required caution money to be paid by contractors, rather than giving an advance. The Russians also wanted to pay to Greenwood and Batley's agents in Russia, but the Board decided to try to obtain payment in London (Greenwood and Batley Board, 30 December 1890).

The importance of payment terms was of course that, particularly with the larger machine tools which might take over a year to build, to allow payment to be deferred until the completion of the order could have a serious effect on the liquidity of the producing firm. The managing directors of Greenwood and Batley, for instance, reported in 1902 that 'An order had been received from the Indian Government for Cartridge Machinery amounting to about £5,000 on which a good deal of money would be spent this year, whilst the profit would not come in until next year' (Greenwood and Batley Board, 31 January 1902), but the company was forced to accept the order because of the depressed state of its order-book. When in addition it was doubtful whether the customer would eventually pay for the work, it can be seen why British firms were dubious about accepting foreign orders without substantial guarantees, but naturally the foreign customer was, in his turn, not anxious to tie up his capital in advance payments. All that can be said in conclusion on this point is that the difficulties in the way of easing terms of payment were increased by the low level of capital resources available to British machine tool firms. Had the firms been larger, and had larger reserves, it would have been possible for them to have given easier terms for payment, without, as Greenwood and Batley were forced to do, incurring a large overdraft essentially to finance current expenditure.

There is no firm evidence, however, that the commercial methods of Britain's competitors in the field of machine tools differed very markedly from those of British manufacturers. Many of the American machine tools which were imported into Britain were sold through British firms acting as agents, the largest of these being Charles Churchill and Co. This firm was established in 1865, its founder having come over to England from the United States to install machinery for covering wire with braid, an early stage in the manufacture of crinolines. He is said to have realised that there were a large number of machines available in the United States which were not known in this country, and to have seen the potential of importing these machines. It is clear that machine tools were, at first, only one of the types of machinery which the company imported, others being agricultural implements, small tools, pumps and domestic machinery, but the company did act as the British agent for many of the leading American firms, principally Pratt and Whitney, Brown and Sharpe, Warner and Swasey and the Cincinatti Milling Machine Company (Anon., 1965a, p. 109). Charles Churchill himself argued that the growth in demand for machine tools was steady, but there is no doubt that the main expansion of the agency came after 1890, with the bicycle boom. As a result of the expansion in demand, branch offices were set up in Birmingham, Glasgow, Manchester and Newcastle. It is however clear that the expansion in demand placed severe strains on the resources of the company. In 1888 a new partner had been introduced, and in the following year the partnership had been dissolved and a limited company formed, and in 1901 it was decided that the company would have to begin to build tools itself, 'because of the large amount of capital that could become tied up in stocking American machines and slow delivery of certain types of machine tools'. The decision to make grinding machines lost Churchill's agency for Brown and Sharpe, illustrating the difficulties of conflicts of interest between maker and agent. Another British firm, Sharp, Stewart and Co., of Manchester, made American tools designed by the Sellers Company under licence at least as early as 1873, unlike Churchill's who only began to do this in 1906 (Spon, 1873, pp. 2329, 2338), and there were certainly other agents for American tools, among them Buck and Hickman, who were apparently in competition with Churchill's as agents for Brown and Sharpe and Pratt and Witney. It was said in 1897 that there were six agents for American machinery in London alone, and that 'If a machine does not happen to be in stock, it can generally be delivered from America in from three weeks to a month' (Horner, 1897, p. 969).

In spite of this developed agency system for American machine tools in Britain, some dissatisfaction was expressed at the system as a whole, and it was argued that direct selling, or the establishment of branch factories, would be more satisfactory, although there was certainly no agreement on this among commentators. The reasons for dissatisfaction with agencies were expressed in an article on 'How machine tools are sold'; although this appears to refer to sales within America, it probably reflects conditions abroad also. The writer, a Mr Frevert, argued that:

> The dealer, especially in the smaller cities, may have the agency for two or more manufacturers of the same kind of tools, and in that case one or the other manufacturer is sure to feel that he is not getting the amount of business he feels he is entitled to, and there is no doubt that the machine having the greatest number of talking points, or the one

that is advertised the most, or that is sold for the least money, is the
one that is easiest to sell and has the greatest sale, for the salesman
invariably takes the line of least resistance, and will sell the machine for
which his customer shows a preference, and the average salesman is not
slow to note and fall in with the views of the buyer. The very fact that
the machinery dealers are required to sell a great variety of tools pre-
vents them or their salesmen from being familiar with all the working
details and the advantages of certain parts of the different machines and
it is no doubt true that there are many tools sold daily that are not the
best for the kind of work for which they are purchased. (Frevert, 1906,
p. 243)

In view of these difficulties, it was argued that American manufacturers
should:

follow the methods of securing business abroad that they so successfully
employ at home. I mean the establishment and maintenance of branch
houses, managed by engineers who work solely in the interest of their
own companies, understand advanced methods of manufacturing, and
can make an application of their knowledge to the European situation.
(Orcutt, 1899, p. 273)

The United States consul in Birmingham also argued for this course in
1899, although for slightly different reasons:

The system adopted by one of the leading American firms of having a
branch in this district where all tools are made for the English trade, is
an excellent one, and should be employed by other American concerns
building machines for similar work. Not only is there a saving of several
weeks' time in the delivery of a machine by having a place to fit it up
here, but it also gives the opportunity to a possible customer to see
machines in actual operation, and is the very best advertisement possible.
As screw machines are usually fitted with special tools made to fit
models furnished by the customer, it is necessary, of course, where
there is no branch shop here, to forward the models to the home shop
in America, and the time elapsing until the machine is returned is necessarily of considerable length. (U.S. Consular Reports, 1899, p. 252)

It is clear that there was as little uniformity in selling practices, and as
little agreement about correct methods, among American as among British
machine tool-makers. Some advocated agency agreements, some branch
offices, some branch factories; to some the important factor was for a
member of the firm to visit customers. Orcutt praises 'representatives of
more than twenty prominent machine tool makers who, for some time,
have been visiting European countries once or twice a year' (Orcutt, 1899,

93

p. 272). But to Consul Halstead this same practice was to be deplored:

> They [representatives of American engineering firms] claim that the
> heads of even the big machinery concerns consider the export business
> as the place for the exercise of a little personal vanity, and take it into
> their special care, with the result that, having other multitudinous
> duties, much is neglected. (U.S. Consular Reports, 1899, p. 248)

Aside, therefore, from Orcutt's remark that:

> In their methods of securing business, the American manufacturers of
> machinery have as little veneration for time worn customs as respect for
> old fashioned machinery. The best of them advertise their wares in the
> leading technical journals in a manner which many European machine
> tool makers would not think it possible to do without sacrifice of their
> so called 'respectability'. (Orcutt, 1899, p. 17)

there is very little concrete evidence that American selling practices in the
field of machine tools varied very greatly from those of British makers, or
from those of other European countries. German and French producers of
machine tools operated in very much the same way, through a mixture of
agencies, direct selling, exhibiting their machinery, and the other methods
which have been described.

American 'hard-sell' methods could have mixed results, as W. G. Riddell,
a British machine engineer, described:

> While Mr. Murdoch [his employer] was making a clean sweep of his
> machinery, many other engineers were installing new plant and there
> was a boom in the machine tool trade. A number of salesmen from
> America arrived to push their wares. They were usually amusing fellows
> who had possibly been selling patent medicines in the past, for they
> made very extravagant claims. They sold quite a number of machines,
> many of which were quite unsuitable and they did a lot of harm to their
> employers. I got the impression that American machines were rubbish,
> and it was several years before I discovered how good many of them
> really were. Even Mr. Murdoch was impressed, and he sometimes sent
> for me to look at their catalogues, which were really a great advance on
> anything our more modest tool makers published, and they were
> beautifully illustrated. (Riddell, 1948, p. 196)

It would therefore seem unlikely that, in the field of machine tools,
Britain's early predominance was lost primarily as a result of inadequate
methods of advertising or selling the tools. It was perhaps short-sighted to
refuse to take part in international exhibitions, but there is no real evidence
that these exhibitions led to commercial success, as distinct from praise
from the juries or the technical journals; in all other ways, the British

makers publicised and sold their wares in much the same ways as their competitors.

Other influences on international trade in machine tools

Three other factors could have affected the international trade in machine tools during the period from 1850 to 1914: transport costs, tariffs, and other government measures to encourage or protect home industries.

Assessment of the effects of differential transport costs on the export performance of the machine tool manufacturers seems impossible because of the complete lack of evidence on the subject. All that can really be said is based on negative evidence, that the question of direct transport costs is not mentioned by contemporaries as affecting decisions by customers on purchases of machine tools. There were apparently some differences in practice between different countries, British firms normally selling free on board, while some American firms sold c.i.f., but these differences do not seem to have been at all important. Indirect transport costs, principally the time involved in getting delivery from a foreign producer, were apparently of some importance, as has been suggested in the previous section, and many of the agency agreements which have been described were attempts to reduce the waiting times for imported tools, and to provide a quicker and more effective service for spare parts. It is very difficult to see that any one country had any great advantage in transport costs over any other, particularly with the fall in Atlantic shipping rates during the period, and it therefore seems unlikely that transport costs can provide an explanation of the trends in international trade in machine tools which have been described.

Tariffs, on the other hand, were definitely thought to have a serious effect on international competition in machine tools. Garanger quotes, for instance, from the report by a French manufacturer, Emile Chouanard, on the St Louis Exhibition of 1904:

> Dans ce document, ce constructeur montre l'écart considérable qui sépare les industries mécaniques françaises et americaines, fait ressortir l'impossibilité pour le matériel européen de pénétrer dans ce vaste marché beneficiant de droits de douane 'presque prohibitifs' et demande que le tarif douanier français soit triple.
> Ce tarif, en effet, elaboré en 1892, correspondait à une protection de 3 à 6% (suivant le poid des machines) contre 45% aux Etats-Unis.
> (Garanger, 1961, p. 33)

An assessment of the effects of tariffs on the trade in machine tools is

Table 4.2   *Rates of duty levied on British exports of machine tools*

Country	1868–9	1876	1880	1882	1884–5	1890
Russia	2/11d	2/11½d	2/11½d	8/10d	11/10d	13/10d
Sweden	nil	nil	nil	nil	nil	nil
Norway	nil	nil	nil	nil	nil	nil
Germany (Z.V.)						
Cast iron	1/6¼d	1/0¼d	1/6¼d	1/6¼d	1/6¼d	1/6¼d
Wrought iron and steel	2/6½d	1/0¼d	2/6½d	2/6½d	2/6½d	2/6½d
Other metals	4/10½d	1/0¼d	4/10½d	4/10½d	4/10½d	4/10½d
Holland	1% ad. val.	1% ad. val.	nil	nil	nil	nil
Belgium						
Cast iron	9¾d	9¾d	9¾d	9¾d	9¾d	9¾d
Wrought iron and steel	1/7½d	1/7½d	1/7½d	1/7½d	1/7½d	1/7½d
Other metals	4/10½d	4/10½d	4/10½d	4/10½d	4/10½d	4/10½d
France						
>75% cast iron	2/5¼d	2/5¼d	2/5¼d	2/5¼d	2/5¼d	2/5¼d
50–75% cast iron	4/0¾d	4/0¾d	4/0¾d	4/0¾d	4/0¾d	4/0¾d
<50% cast iron	6/1d	6/1d	6/1d	6/1d	6/1d	6/1d
Portugal	5½d	5½d	5¾d	6d	6d	3/5d
Spain	6% ad. val. + 1¼d per cwt	6% ad. val.	3/8d	3/8d	3/8d	3/3d
Italy	9¾d	1/7½d	2/5¼d	2/5¼d	2/5¼d	3/8d
Switzerland	1/7½d	1/7½d	1/7½d	1/7½d	1/7½d	1/7½d
Austria						
Cast iron	2/8½d	2/8½d	2/9d	not iron 10/2d	10/2d	15/3d
Wrought iron and steel	4/0¾d	4/0¾d	4/0¾d	75% cast 5/1d	5/1d	
Other metals	8/2d	8/2d	8/2d	other 6/1d	6/1d	
U.S.A.	45% ad. val.	45% ad. val.	Iron 35% ad. val. Steel 45% ad. val.	35%	45%	45%

Notes:
Specific rates given are per cwt, of net weight unless otherwise indicated.
Sources: Returns 'of the rates of import duty levied by the existing tariffs of European countries and of the United States upon the produce and manufactures of the United Kingdom'. 1868–9: P.P., 1868–9,

International trade in machine tools

1893–4	1897	1901	1903	1908	
15/1d	13/10d	13/9½d	13/9½d	£1-7-7d	
10% ad. val.	10% ad. val.	10% ad. val.	10% ad. val.	10% ad. val.	
nil	nil	nil	nil	10% ad. val.	
1/6¼d	1/6¼d	1/6¼d	1/6¼d	<250kg	6/-
2/6½d	2/6½d	2/6½d	2/6½d	250–1000kg	4/-
				1000–3000kg	3/-
4/10½d	4/10½d	4/10½d	4/10½d	3000–10000kg	2/6d
				>10000kg	2/-
nil	nil	nil	nil	nil	
9¾d	9¾d	9¾d	9¾d	9¾d	
1/7½d	1/7½d	1/7½d	1/7½d	1/7½d	
4/10½d	4/10½d	4/10½d	4/10½d	4/10½d	
<250kg 20/4d	20/4d	20/4d	20/4d	20/4d	
250–1000kg 6/6d	6/6d	6/6d	6/6d	6/6d	
>1000kg 4/0¾d	4/0¾d	4/0¾d	4/0¾d	4/0¾d	
>50kg 13/9d	13/9d	13/9d	13/9d	13/9d	
50–100kg 11/5d	11/5d	11/5d	11/5d	11/5d	
100–500g 9/2d	9/2d	9/2d	9/2d	9/2d	
500–1000kg 6/10d	6/10d	6/10d	6/10d	6/10d	
>1000kg 4/7d	4/7d	4/7d	4/7d	4/7d	
8/2d	7/6¼d	7/6¼d	7/6¼d	<500kg	10/2d
				>501kg	8/1½d
>300kg 3/8d	3/8d	3/8d	3/8d	3/8d	
				<100kg	6/6d
				100–500kg	4/10½d
				500–2500kg	3/3d
1/7½d	1/7½d	1/7½d	1/7½d	2500–10000kg	2/10d
				10000–50000kg	2/5½d
				>50000kg	2/-d
<10000kg 12/2d	12/2d	12/2d	12/2d	8/5½d	
>10000kg 5/1d	5/1d	5/1d	5/1d		
45%	45%	45%	45%	45%	

lvi, p. 583; 1876: P.P., 1876, lxviii, p. 145; 1880: P.P., 1880, lxvii, p. 197; 1882: P.P., 1882, lxvi, p. 331; 1884–5: P.P., 1884–5, lxxi, p. 67; 1890: P.P., 1890, lxvii, p. 209; 1893–4: P.P., 1893–4, lxxxi, p. 351; 1897: P.P. 1897, lxxix, p. 257; 1901: P.P., 1901, lxxx, p. 519; 1903: P.P., 1903, lxxi, p. 1; 1908: P.P., 1908, ci, p. 1.

complicated by the multiplicity of different tariffs, by the differences in methods of assessment, and by the frequent changes which were made in tariff-rates during the period. Table 4.2 shows the rates of duty levied at different dates between 1868 and 1908 on British machine tools exported to various countries, as calculated, at the dates given, by the Board of Trade. It is clear that the general trend of duties levied on British goods was upwards. The most spectacular increase in duties on machinery was that on imports to Russia, but particularly from the 1890s onwards duties were raised sharply in France, Portugal, Spain and Austria, and there were later increases in the duties on imports to Germany and to Switzerland. A further difficulty in assessment of the effects of tariffs is that the duties given in table 4.2 applied to British exports, but not necessarily to those of her competitors, because of the operation of reciprocal tariff agreements and the most favoured nation clauses. In 1897 the editor of the *American Machinist*, reporting on a European tour, quoted rates of duty on the import of machine tools which showed variations in rates of duty applicable to British and American tools imported into Austria, France and Spain, although in other countries goods from both these countries carried the same rate of duty. The full table is given below as table 4.3 (Miller, 1897, p. 389)

Table 4.3   *Rates of duty levied on American exports of machine tools, per metric ton ($ U.S.)*

Country of import	From U.S.A.	Great Britain
France (under ¼ ton)	60	40
(over ¼ ton)	36	24
Spain	50	40
Austria–Hungary	42.50	37.50
Germany	7.50	7.50
Belgium	4	4
Switzerland	8	8
Russia	65	65
Denmark	12	12
Italy	24	24
Finland	31	31

Apart from discrimination of this kind against American exports, it is likely that the method of assessment of duty produced differential duties as between Britain and her competitors. The round of new tariffs introduced in the early 1890s, of which the French Meline tariff is the best-known, introduced a system of duties according to the weight of the machinery. By 1908, as can be seen from table 4.2, this system, although with individual variations on the cut-off points between different rates, was in operation in Germany, Portugal, Spain, Italy and Switzerland, as well as in France. In all these cases, the rate of duty lessened as the weight of the machine tool increased, thus discriminating against the lighter machine tools, of which the American tools were the most prominent example.

The tariffs were further complicated by differences in the methods of assessing weight, some countries using the gross weight including packing, other countries using net weight; inexplicably, while Germany in 1908 assessed machine tools on net weight if they weighed less than 1000 kilograms, and on gross weight if they weighed more than 1000 kilograms, Switzerland at the same time used gross weight if the machines weighed less than 10,000 kilograms, and net weight if they weighed more. The effects of such regulations can be seen in the slightly hopeless note appended to an order to Greenwood and Batley. 'Duty in Switzerland being payable on the gross weight, packing is not to be unduly heavy; at the same time it must be sufficiently strong.'

The effective tariff-rate payable thus depended on the country of origin, the weight of the machine tool, and, in the case of a number of countries at some periods, on the metal of which it was made. Calculation of the actual percentage tariff payable is thus extremely difficult. As an example, using the Greenwood and Batley material to arrive at average weights and prices for the machines which they sold, it appears that the highest percentage tariff was that of the United States, at 45%. The other tariffs payable, based on average weight per machine in 1894 of 52 cwt, and an average price of £145, were (to nearest 1%):

Russia	27%	France	7%	Norway	Nil
Austria	21%	Italy	7%	Holland	Nil
Spain	14%	Switzerland	3%		
Sweden	10%	Germany	3%		
Portugal	8%	Belgium	1%		

Had the machinery been of the same price and weight, but made in the United States, based on the figures given by Miller the percentage duties would have been 10% in France, 18% in Spain, and 25% in Austria—Hungary.

It is clear from these figures that the tariffs imposed by America and the European countries — Britain of course remained a free trade country without tariffs — could have made a substantial difference to the price of machine tools; the 45% American tariff in particular must have been effectively a prohibitive tariff, and the Russian tariff must have become so by 1908. The British trade statistics in fact show no British exports of engineering goods to the United States in this period. On the other hand, it is clear that the history of tariff barriers to trade in machine tools can do little to explain the chronology of the development of that trade. As an example, the American export success of the mid-1890s came at a time when tariffs on American imports to Europe were higher than they had ever been before, and moreover were higher in three countries than tariffs on the products of any of their competitors. All that can be said in general terms is that the gradual raising of tariffs which can be seen in this period must have operated to reduce, or slow down the growth in, international trade in machine tools.

The development of trade in machine tools was also affected by the actions of governments in other fields than tariffs. At the same time as raising the duties on machine tools, the Russian government, for instance, tried by other means to encourage the growth of a native machinery industry. The directors of Greenwood and Batley, who sold a large number of machines to Russia, were told in February 1897 that an imperial edict had been published ordering that as much work as possible should be done within Russia, and that the import of engineering machinery should be discouraged. Greenwood and Batley's response to this threat was to set up in Russia the Phoenix Engineering Works, wholly owned by an English subsidiary called the Anglo-Russian Engineering Company, so as to obtain the advantage of Russian protection of home industries. The *American Machinist* ascribed the reasons for this to the policy of the Russian government in favouring its own 'industrial establishments' in placing orders for machinery for the construction of the Trans-Siberian railway, together with high tariff duties and high freight charges on imported heavy machinery:

> The situation has led to a clear perception of the fact that, particularly for heavy tools, a shop located in Russia will have a very great advantage; and a shop in which it is intended to build such tools is now being put up at St. Petersburg, the capital coming partly, or perhaps mainly, from England, and the equipment from the shops of Greenwood and Batley of Leeds.

It was believed that further factories might be established in Russia in this way, 'primarily with a view to government orders' (Anon., 1897, p. 578). It is not clear how successful this enterprise was, since in 1911 the directors were told that 'the outfit and plant were not arranged for producing small tools for which there was a market in Russia, and buyers there preferred to have German or American tools', but the fact that it was thought worthwhile to attempt to get round Russian dislike of imports in this way demonstrates the threat which such government interference could be to the machine tool trade (Greenwood and Batley Board, 12 February 1897; 28 May 1897; 12 October 1911). Similar government intervention can be seen as working to the advantage of British machines, in that they received orders from the crown agents for the colonies, and received the benefits of imperial preference.

An explanation

The major problem which arises in considering the international trade in machine tools in the late nineteenth century is to explain why the entry of the United States machine tool industry into the European market was so long delayed, why it came in the middle of the 1890s, and why it was so immediately successful. There are a number of possible solutions to this problem, of which two, a possible failure in British sales effort, and the effects of tariffs and other artificial barriers to United States exports, have been discussed and provisionally rejected as possible explanations. There are, however, three more complex possible solutions, which need to be explored in more detail. They are:

1. That before the mid 1890s, American and British (or European) machine tools were not homogeneous products, and therefore did not compete in world markets. In other words, America and Britain were making use of a different machine tool technology. In the 1890s, however, there occurred either a change in the character of American machine tools which made them competitive with British machine tools, or a market for American machine tools developed in Britain and Europe.
2. That American and British machine tools were homogeneous, so that the two countries were making use of the same technology, but that either:
   a. the structure of British relative costs made it unprofitable to make use of American machine tools before the 1890s, or
   b. it would have been profitable for the British to have made use of American machine tools, since American machine tools had a lower real cost than British tools, but this was not realised due to prejudice or ignorance. (The phrase *lower real cost* is intended to include the theory that American tools were in some way superior to British machine tools of an equivalent price.)
3. That American and British machine tools were homogeneous, but that the American supply curve for machine tools before the 1890s was above the British supply curve. The American industry before 1890 is

thus treated as an infant industry protected by the 45% American tariff, whose products were uncompetitive on the world market before the 1890s.

These possible solutions will now be considered in turn, although it is not always entirely possible to make neat distinctions between them or the evidence relevant to them.

1. The first explanation, which essentially is that for a good part of the period, American machine tools were different from British or European machine tools, has considerable attractions but also a number of disadvantages. In theory, there is no reason why the demands of the American economy, and the supply of factors available in that economy, should not have produced the supply of capital goods such as machine tools which were unsuitable for use under different demand conditions and different factor cost structures. There is some evidence that there were differences of this kind between American and British machine tools in the late nineteenth century, although the evidence is often impressionistic and difficult to interpret. The major differences which were observed by contemporaries were in the physical characteristics of the tools, and in the degree of specialisation of function which they embodied.

The alleged lightness, lack of durability and shoddiness of manufacture of American machine tools was a favourite theme of commentators on machine tools, the American machine tools being contrasted with the well-built, solid and long-lasting British tools. There is no doubt that, to most British engineers, solidity was in itself a virtue. R. S. Burn, commenting on the London Exhibition of 1862, praised the 'massive' machine tools which were employed, and saw them as the results of 'the requirements of the more recent period [which] appear to have progressed amazingly in the direction of speed, bulk and power' (Burn, 1869, p. 198), while an American praised British tools at the Paris Exhibition of 1867 as 'models of solidity and excellence of workmanship' (Brown, 1868). In 1890 S. Dixon, an English engineer, reporting on a trip to the United States, commented that American machinery was much lighter than British, perhaps by 25–30%, and explained that 'We in England had been tending in the direction of solidity and strength in all our machinery, and in America they were gradually changing in the same direction, but they were still some years behind' (Anon., 1890a, p. 476). In the same year the Institution of Mechanical Engineers were told, in a paper by George Addy entitled 'On milling cutters' that 'The milling machines originally imported from America and the Continent were deficient in the solidity and stiffness which constitute the first requirements for the production of good work' (Addy,

1890, p. 535). G. L. Carden admitted in 1909 that there was a difference between American and British tools in solidity; he reported that British tools were preferred at the Dubosc machine tool works in Turin, 'because of their rather heavy proportions. Some American turret lathes do appear a trifle light in close comparison' (Carden, 1909—10, p. 200). It was also argued, although this point was hotly disputed, that English tools had to be made more solid because the English iron which they had to machine was harder than American iron; whatever the truth in this dispute, it is clear that there was observable differences between British and American machine tools.

It is also clear, as the discussion in the last chapter has suggested, that there were observable differences between British and American machine tools based on the different jobs which each were expected to do, the British concentrating on special-purpose and the Americans on general-purpose machine tools. Lastly, the chronology of machine tool inventions and innovations shows that the types of tools made in the two countries differed in the short-run, although by the beginning of this century all the main types of machine tools appear to have been in both countries.

W. Steeds (1969) describes a number of inventions and innovations in machine tool design which took place either in Britain or in the United States, or occasionally in Germany or France, but there is little indication of any pattern in the different developments, or of such sustained differences as might indicate the presence of entirely different technologies.

In spite of these scattered pieces of evidence, it is difficult to sustain the view that American and British machine tools were not homogeneous products of the same technology for most of the late nineteenth century. Most important, there is very little sign of any change in any of the alleged differences between American and British machine tools which occurred either quickly enough or sufficiently widely to produce the American invasion of British markets in the 1890s. Although there probably was a convergence in solidity and durability, and in the degree of specialisation built into the tool, this convergence came too slowly and undramatically to be relevant, while the amount of interchange of ideas and designs across the Atlantic, observable in all the technical journals of the day, is also difficult to reconcile with any hypothesis of different technologies.

2. The second possible explanation is that America and Britain were using the same technology of machine tool production and use, but that either a different structure of factor costs in the two countries, or prejudice and ignorance, retarded the adoption of American machine tools overseas before the 1890s. Much of the so-called 'Habakkuk' debate about the

possible differences between American and British production methods in the nineteenth century has been concerned to explore this theoretical possibility and to illustrate its workings in practice. The simple model used in this discussion normally assumes that since labour was more costly relative to capital in the United States than in Britain, the United States would have had an incentive to adopt techniques which were relatively more capital-intensive than those adopted in Britain. It follows that Britain might have had little incentive to adopt machinery as extensively as in America, and in particular to adopt American machinery designed to take advantage to the full of American relative factor costs, since Britain could use her cheap labour, combined with less sophisticated and less labour-saving machinery, to produce goods at an equally low cost. Figure 4.3 illustrates this possibility in terms of a simple, two-factor model.

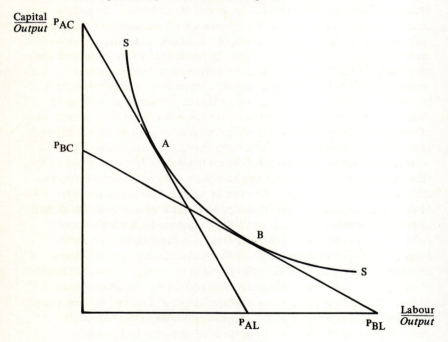

Figure 4.3. A simple model of American and British technical differences

In figure 4.3 the isoquant SS represents the various combinations of factors of production. In this case, capital and labour might be combined to produce a given quantity of engineering goods. On the normal assump-

104

tion of the Habakkuk debate that America had higher labour costs relative to the costs of capital than did Britain, America is shown producing at point A, where its price-line $P_{AC}P_{AL}$ is tangent to the curve; $P_{AC}P_{AL}$ shows the relative costs of capital and labour in the U.S. at a particular moment. By contrast, Britain economises in capital rather than labour, because of its relative costs shown by $P_{BC}P_{BL}$, and produces at B on SS. Since A and B are different points, production at them requires different techniques, and hence, in this case, different or more machine tools. It will also, and interchangeably, require different techniques of production of machine tools, since machine tools are made by machine tools; this is both a complication and a simplification of the argument, possible only with this unique product.

In terms of the simple model, the explanation for the growth of American exports to Britain and Europe in the 1890s would lie either in a shift of British and European factor costs leading them to adopt a more capital-intensive form of production using American machine tools, or in a realisation on the part of British and European purchasers of machine tools that they should have adopted a capital intensive form of production at an earlier point, but had not done so through prejudice or ignorance.

There is some contemporary evidence that American machine tools were thought to be suited to a more labour-saving form of production than British tools, in the particular sense that the use of automatic or semi-automatic machinery economised on skilled labour. Since the machines could be operated by semi-skilled men, their introduction was resisted by the Amalgamated Society of Engineers, representing the skilled trades, until resistance was broken by the defeat of the engineering strike of 1897. Before the strike, according to Fred Miller, editor of *American Machinist*, American machinery was not used in the older engineering trades:

It is explained that our labour-saving machinery has been largely put into the bicycle factories here, and has worked well, because that is a new industry and mostly new men have been put to work in it — men that have few or no preconceived ideas of what amount of work a machine ought to do or how it ought to do it, but simply operated the machines as they were instructed. (Miller, 1897, p. 413)

After the strike, according to an editorial in the *Engineer*,

Manufacturing engineers of all sorts are, since the conclusion of the strike, and in consequence of their improved position with regard to their employees which that strike brought about, removing or not purchasing machines of the old type, but are adopting the new patterns. (Anon., 1898a, p. 543)

105

It is, however, very difficult to fit either contemporary evidence on the differences between British and American practice, or the chronology of the export invasion, into the simple, two-factor, framework which has been set out. This is partly because the model is so simple, and it is therefore possible that other factors may have been significant, and partly because it is difficult to view even those factors which have been included as homogeneous in the way which the model demands. As Ames and Rosenberg (1969) observed in their study of the adoption of machinery by the Enfield Arsenal, it is necessary to take account of far more variables than are comprehended in such a model. At the least, labour has to be split into at least two categories, skilled and semi-skilled, to take account of the apparent cost savings resulting from the use of American automatic machinery which allowed semi-skilled labour to be substituted for skilled craftsmen. The assumption that American machine tools economised, relative to British tools, on skilled labour, is difficult to reconcile with the pattern of British manufacture of special-purpose machine tools which was discussed in the last chapter; presumably the British special-purpose machinery, although made by highly skilled men, could have been operated by less skilled men than could have operated, or adapted to particular purposes, the American general-purpose machine tools. Such disparities could be reconciled, within the framework of the two-factor model, only by postulating different factor costs in different sections of the engineering industry, which is inherently unlikely.

There are, moreover, other difficulties in the way of accepting that British and American factor costs were so different that trade between the two countries could not exist, or could perhaps exist only in special categories of machines, before the 1890s. It is clear that trade did exist, and it also is clear from the pattern of innovation described by Steeds (1969) that machine tools invented or innovated in one country were, with various lags, innovated in the other country, and that similar tools were produced simultaneously in both countries. In the 1890s, for example, although there were other minor differences in lathe design, 'the larger [American] lathes were generally very similar to their English counterparts'. In the field of automatic lathes or screw machines, an American patented a machine to make pointed screws in 1846; in 1854 the Birmingham firm of Nettleford and Chamberlain acquired rights to use the patent, imported some machines from America, and made others in this country. A type of multi-spindle drilling machines, developed by the Scottish firm of Andrew Shanks in the early 1860s, was adopted several years later by an American firm. Steeds gives numerous examples of such trans-Atlantic diffusion of

106

innovations, all of which are difficult to reconcile with an argument based on factor-cost differences so great as to preclude trade in machine tools before the 1890s.

Lastly, for the factor-cost explanation to have any general validity, it would be necessary to show that some change in factor costs occurred in the 1890s so as to make it possible for trade to take place. It is very difficult to demonstrate that such a change took place, and moreover took place so quickly, and in so many countries, as to provide a convincing explanation for the boom in American exports of all types of machinery, including machine tools, which took place in that decade. Even the introduction of automatic machinery after the defeat of the strike of 1897, which could be regarded as being due to a reduction in the real cost of operating such machinery, through the use in conjunction with it of semi-skilled labour, is ambiguous evidence; it is clear that the Amalgamated Society of Engineers had been resisting the change for some time, which implies that the relative costs of the opposed methods had altered some time before 1897, but the effects had been delayed by the monopoly power of the trade union. This peculiarly British circumstance has thus to be seen as coincidentally occurring at the same time as other changes produced demand for American machine tools from other countries. Although this explanation is possible, it is unconvincing.

An alternative hypothesis which might explain the timing of the American export invasion is that, although for some years Americans had been producing superior machine tools to those available from British makers, and although these machines could profitably be used with British factor costs, these tools had not been imported, because of a different pattern of demand. As Professor Saul has put it, rejecting the type of simple two factor explanation which has just been discussed,

> it is almost certainly more important to think of factors determining the development and use of new technologies rather than just shifts in factor proportions. Many of the American innovations in machining techniques, for example, offered immense advantages whatever the cost of labour and system of accountancy. Once these were realised during the 1890's, the engineering industry adopted them with alacrity and the machine tool industry itself moved into a new age. (Saul, 1968a, p. 236)

In other work, Saul has blamed British engineers for failing to see the advantages of the new machine tools, until the 'breakthrough in demand' came with the cycle boom in the 1890s.

At the extreme, this view is analogous to that discussed in the first section of this chapter, the hypothesis that the American industry was operating on a different and superior production function, which it would have been sensible for the British to have adopted 'whatever the cost of labour'. This is shown in figure 4.4 in which the American production function, or technology, is shown as an isoquant closer to the origin at all points than the British isoquant, so that Britain should have moved to the American isoquant, operating on it at a point determined by the British price line.

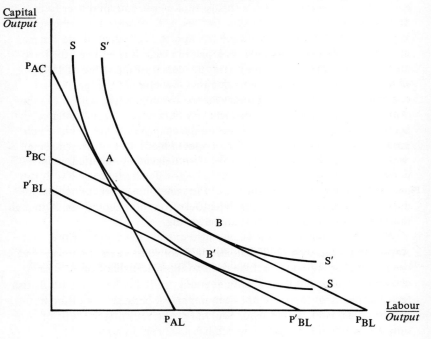

Figure 4.4. A simple model of American and British technological differences

In figure 4.4 the isoquants SS and S'S' represent different production functions; as before, they represent the different combinations of factors (capital and labour) which might be used to produce a given quantity of goods. It is assumed that the amount produced by using technology SS and technology S'S' are equal, but technology SS is therefore superior to technology S'S' since the same amount of goods can be produced for a lesser input of both capital and labour. As before, the American factor prices, $P_{AC}P_{AL}$, together with the technology, determines where production takes place; America, it is assumed, produces using technology SS, at point A.

Britain, on the other hand, combines her price line $P_{BC}P_{BL}$ with her

108

inferior technology S'S' to produce at point B. It can be seen that it will, whatever the British prices, be profitable for Britain to adopt the American technology, which will save both capital and labour. She should do so, and produce at B', the point of tangent of the American technology, S, and the British price line $P'_{BC}P'_{BL}$, drawn parallel to the price line $P_{BC}P_{BL}$, on the assumption that British relative factor prices do not change.

While it is possible to imagine that two countries might use different technologies in this way, if they are in ignorance of each other, or if there is a significant third factor which is ignored by the model, it is difficult to see how Britain and the United States in the late nineteenth century could fit such an hypothesis. Much of the evidence already presented in this chapter has shown mutual knowledge of technical developments in machine tool design, and other examples cited by Steeds show that American inventions were often taken up in Britain, and vice versa, within a few years of the original patent being granted. At the major international exhibitions, engineers could easily discover the state of technology of their competitors, and journals such as *American Machinist, Engineer, Engineering* and the numerous journals of the professional societies of engineers reported all new technological developments. Furthermore, if Britain was really producing, and using, machine tools suitable to an inferior or obsolete technology, it is unclear why she was able to resist American competition at all, either at home or in neutral markets; her failure to export machine tools to the United States could of course be explained in these terms, but it will be argued below that the existence of a 45% ad valorem tariff is an alternative explanation.

Saul has, however, produced an alternative version of this hypothesis, which in essence relies on the existence of a spectrum of customers for machine tools; the best-practice firms were willing to adopt the new methods and new machines, but the bulk of firms remained wedded to the obsolete technology, until the shock of the bicycle boom. It is difficult to disagree with the hypothesis that there is a spectrum of technologies in use at any one time, representing successive stages of improvement of technology which have been diffused over time, and in which the smaller and less efficient firms are operating with less developed technologies than the best-practice firms. Inevitably, also, the differing speeds of innovation in different branches of machine tool technology, combined with the fact that a firm would not constantly scrap all its capital equipment and replace it with the most up-to-date equipment, would mean that almost all firms would be producing somewhat less efficiently than, in theory, they would be able to. What is difficult to accept is that, in spite of the evidence of constant interchange of knowledge and products across the Atlantic, British machine tool-makers, or their customers, could consistently be significantly less efficient than American producers, perhaps for thirty years, catching up only when revelation dawned in the 1890s. For all these reasons, this second hypothesis must be rejected.

3. The third hypothesis implies that the British and American industries were producing at or near the same point on the production isoquant so that trade between them would have been possible for much of the late nineteenth century, but that it did not occur in significant quantities until the 1890s for some reason which has not so far been discussed. In a static, two-product, free trading world one could assume that until the 1890s the United States did not have a comparative advantage in the production of machine tools; in the real, protective, multi-product world the situation was not so simple, and it is useful to begin by setting out the evidence which is available and likely to be relevant, that is evidence on prices, on protection, and on the shape and changes in supply and demand curve in the British and American industries.

The information can be most easily categorised into established facts, controversial deductions from inadequate data, and inferences and suppositions.

A. Established facts

1. For most of the period, the United States tariff imposed a duty of 45% ad valorem on imported products made of iron and steel. The effective rate of protection for the United States machine tool industry is not known, but Hawke has calculated that in 1904 analogous products, all with a similar 45% nominal tariff, enjoyed effective protection of 74% (carriages and wagons), 63% (electrical machinery), 62% (bicycles and tricycles) and 52% (automobiles and parts). In 1899 the only product for which an estimate independent from that for 1904 is available is carriages and wagons, with an effective rate of 88%, while in 1889 agricultural implements had an effective rate of 56% (Hawke, 1975, pp. 90−1).

2. The Annual Statements of Trade of the United Kingdom show no exports of engineering products to the United States in the export class including machine tools between 1870 and 1914. No evidence exists in the records of British machine tool firms which have been examined of any sales of machine tools to the United States.

·3. Exports of two United States machine tool firms, Brown and Sharpe and Bullard, rose rapidly in the 1890s, having been at a low level before that point. Table 4.1 gave this evidence.

Total United States exports in the export class which included machine tools also rose rapidly, as shown in Figure 4.5.

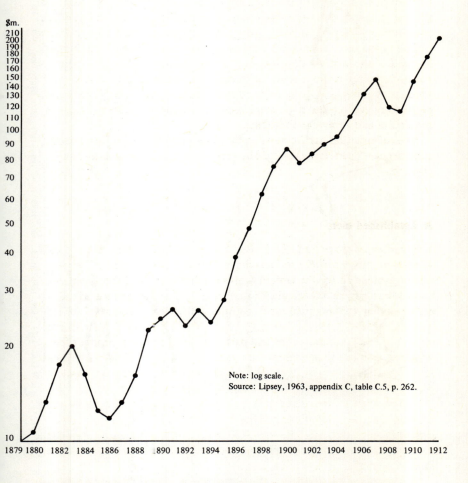

Note: log scale.
Source: Lipsey, 1963, appendix C, table C.5, p. 262.

Figure 4.5. Exports of engineering goods and metal products from the United States

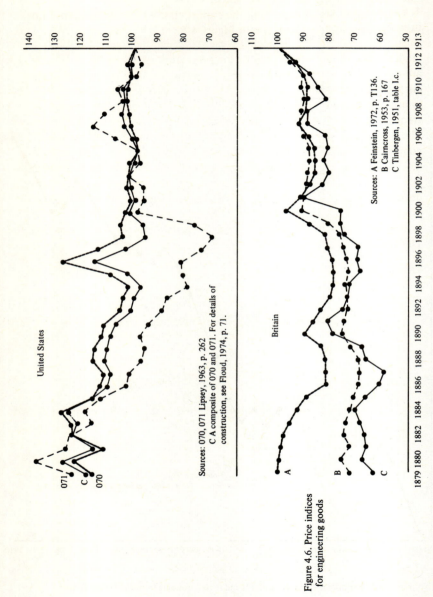

United States

Sources: 070, 071 Lipsey, 1963, p. 262
C A composite of 070 and 071. For details of
construction, see Floud, 1974, p. 71.

Britain

Sources: A Feinstein, 1972, p. T136.
B Cairncross, 1953, p. 167
C Tinbergen, 1951, table I.c.

Figure 4.6. Price indices
for engineering goods

B. Controversial deductions

4. Current prices of British machine tools were either static, or rose slightly, in the 1890s. This statement is based on extremely inadequate evidence. In general, three indices of engineering prices, graphed in figure 4.6, show a gradual upward movement over this period; although these series, which are regarded by their authors as speculative, are based principally on input costs, and it is extremely difficult to make a realistic allowance for improvements in productivity, it seems likely that the general upward trend, or at least the absence of a downward trend, is a correct inference. The only direct evidence on the trend in prices of British machine tools comes from the records of Greenwood and Batley, and is shown in table 4.4. Unfortunately, for reasons which are explained below, the Greenwood and Batley material is likely to exaggerate any upward movement in prices during the 1890s, and is thus of limited use for that period; at the least, however, the evidence does not suggest that prices were falling.

5. Current prices of American tools, f.o.b., were either static or falling. The Lipsey price index for the export class including machine tools is

Table 4.4   *The prices of machine tools produced by Greenwood and Batley*

Year	Mean price	Year	Mean price
1865	89	1881	138
1866	113	1882	91
1867	73	1883	121
1868	67	1884	160
1869	102	1885	130
1870	74	1886	102
1871	69	1887	107
1872	77	1888	74
1873	51	1889	135
1874	69	1890	84
1875	77	1891	69
1876	51	1892	93
1877	98	1893	118
1878	120	1894	153
1879	130	1895	182
1880	98	1896	130
		1897	202
		1898	310
		1899	198
		1900	118

Note: Prices are mean prices, in £ sterling current.

Source: Company records.

113

shown in figure 4.6. The evidence of the Brown and Sharpe records, shown in table 4.5, is as difficult to interpret as the Greenwood and Batley material, but it appears to support the view of a downward trend in prices. Moreover, the raw material prices facing American producers were, on the evidence of the Lipsey price index for semi-manufactured metals, also shown in figure 4.6, falling even more rapidly than the prices of finished metal goods.

Table 4.5   *The prices of machine tools produced by Brown and Sharpe*

Year	Milling machines	Grinding machines	Gear-cutting machines	All machines
1865	450			92
1866				
1867		130		27
1868				
1869				
1870				174
1871	855			174
1872				
1873	855			103
1874				163
1875	800			106
1876				245
1877	966	115		128
1878	700			143
1879	650		650	133
1880	675		650	128
1881	800			163
1882	1038	800		167
1883	1200	650		151
1884		673		116
1885		260		68
1886		950		133
1887				68
1888	683	442	750	103
1889	700	833	750	158
1890	705	534		137
1891	629	594		119
1892	683	385		101
1893	558	394	635	97
1894	649	363	550	105
1895	606	435	638	108
1896	598	369	1164	113
1897	520	434	815	103
1898	653	492	1013	129
1899	627	562	917	130
1900	638	651	1240	145
1901	638	557	1158	131
1902	660	503	920	117
1903	681	500	1020	142

Table 4.5 *Continued*

Year	Milling machines	Grinding machines	Gear-cutting machines	All machines
1904	778	559	1039	148
1905	778	594	1081	149
1906	835	688	1079	157
1907	678	538	1138	135
1908	911	536	1083	146
1909	803	644	1183	150
1910	727	617	1386	146

Notes:
(a) Prices are mean prices for machine tools sold to England by Brown and Sharpe.
(b) Prices for individual machine tools are given in current dollars. Prices for all tools are given as current sterling prices, converted from dollars at $4.90 = £1.

Source: Company records.

6. The mid-1890s were a period of depression in the United States, and of a minor upswing, the 'home boom of the 1890s' in Britain. The direct effect of these cyclical states on the machine tool industry is unknown, but it can be deduced that demand for machine tools and other capital goods followed the general path of the cycle in both countries.

C. Inference and suppositions

7. The machine tool industry was characterised, in both Britain and the United States, by slightly increasing returns to scale, as suggested by the discussion in the last chapter.

8. On the evidence of the last chapter, the industries in both countries exhibited highly elastic supply curves, both because of the ability of firms to expand or contract production quickly and because of the possibilities of rapid entry from or exit to other sectors of the engineering industry.

9. Machine tools had a low price elasticity of demand in Britain. This can be inferred from the evidence presented in the last chapter about the structure of the industry and the nature of costs, and from contemporary evidence. That customers were slow to respond to changes in capital goods prices does not imply, of course, that they were indifferent to costs, but that such factors as suitability for the job and durability were of great importance.

10. Machine tools are a homogeneous product, so that it is reasonable to speak of 'price of', 'demand for' machine tools rather than of individual types or even models of machine tools. This is a very difficult assumption

to justify in practice, since clearly a customer is not indifferent between a planing machine and a lathe, which perform entirely different operations. However, this discussion is concerned with international comparisons, and with aggregates, and unless it can be shown that imported machine tools were of different types from those produced at home, the assumption is justified. The records of Greenwood and Batley and of Brown and Sharpe, two best-practice firms in Britain and America respectively, do not show such a dichotomy, and Steeds gives examples of British and American manufacture of all types of machine tools.

A model of American intervention in international trade which appears to fit these facts, deductions and suppositions is given as figure 4.7. Essentially, the model rests on the assumption that the American machine tool industry was essentially an 'infant industry' unable to produce competitively with industries to other countries, and therefore requiring tariff protection. Its maturity, and its entry into overseas markets, are then seen as occurring mainly in the 1890s, for the following set of reasons:

a. Technical improvements resulting from learning-by-doing and from inventions of new tools and modifications to old tools.

b. Reductions in the cost of raw material inputs, demonstrated by the Lipsey price indices, which show the price of these inputs falling even more rapidly than the price of finished metal goods.

c. The impact of the severe domestic recession in the United States in the early 1890s, leading firms to seek foreign markets more forcefully. Although it is likely, given the existence of economies of scale, that domestic recession would have increased prices, this may have been outweighed by other factors.

d. The expansion of foreign demand, with the boom in many European countries in the mid-1890s. While some of this expansion would have resulted in an expansion of supply (not shown explicitly in figure 4.7) in foreign markets, the rising price of some British machine tools suggests that there was some excess demand, perhaps made greater by the effects of the British engineering strike of 1897. The bicycle boom may also have had some impact.

These conditions led, it is argued, to an initial boom in sales of American machine tools, which then diminished as demand slackened and European and British supply expanded; finally, by the beginning of the first decade of the twentieth century, America settled down to a role as a major competitor in the world market for machine tools. In these circumstances, of course, the American tariff on machine tool imports would have become superfluous, and should, on the basis of infant industry theory, have been

116

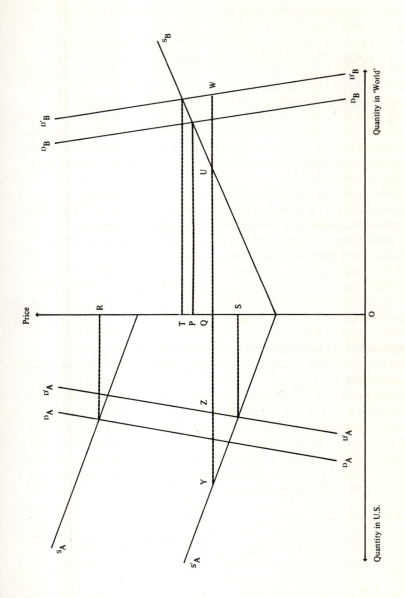

Figure 4.7. A model of American intervention in international trade in machine tools

removed; in practice, American tariffs on goods of all types were maintained and sometimes increased in this period, and the machine tool tariff
simply followed this general pattern.

This hypothesis is shown more formally in figure 4.7, in which the
demand curves are shown as highly inelastic, and the supply curves as
highly elastic, in conformity with the assumptions made above. The inter-
section of D_B and S_B (taken either as the British or the 'World' supply and
demand curves) determines the initial world price OP. America, with her
supply curve S_A cannot compete at this price, since the entire supply curve
lies above P; a tariff, RP, is therefore necessary to allow her to supply the
American market at the protected price, OR. After some time, and due to
the increasing efficiency of her industry, the American supply curve shifts
to a new position, S'_A.

At the same time, American demand is depressed, shown by D'_A as a
new demand curve, intersecting with the new supply curve S'_A to give a
new price OS, below the previous world price, and, therefore, below the
new world price, OT, formed by the outward shift of world demand to
D'_B along the supply curve S_B. Trade then takes place, and the price moves
up in America (from OS) and down in the rest of the world (from OT)
until equilibrium is reached at OQ, where the volume of American exports,
YZ, equals the volume of 'World' imports, UW. American home consumption is then QZ, and 'World' production QU.

Like most models, this figure is an abstraction from reality. The price
changes which are observed and represented by the model were the product
of shifts, and possibly changes in the shape of, both supply and demand
curves, neither of which can be directly observed. In the terminology of
econometrics, the model is under-identified and possibly mis-specified. At
the same time, it is unlikely that even intensive study of the American
machine tool industry, the major area of ignorance, would allow us to proceed very much further in specifying the exact nature of whatever process
was occurring. This model is offered, therefore, as one attempt at a description, which may very well be disproved when further evidence comes to
light, but which appears to capture most of the features of the evidence at
present available.

Seen in this light, the chronology of international trade in machine tools
in the late nineteenth century is clarified; the gradual rise of the American
machine tool industry to efficiency and to prominence in trade can be
explained without resort to explanations of American superiority or to
inferred differences in relative factor costs. Similarly, the response of the
British industry, and of British customers for machine tools, seems neither

irrational nor inefficient, but rather represents a gradual adjustment to changing market conditions and to the introduction of new techniques.

5. Greenwood and Batley: history, records and methods

In the preceding chapters, the English machine tool industry has been treated very much in aggregate terms. With the exception of some consideration of individual firms in chapter 3, the performance of the industry at home and abroad, and its structure, has been treated from aggregate sources, and even the evidence presented from the history of individual firms has been treated as helping to build a general picture of the industry and of its growth over the whole period from 1850 to 1914.

In this and the following chapters, by contrast, attention is concentrated on the experience of a single machine tool producer, the engineering firm of Greenwood and Batley of Leeds. Such a concentration makes it possible to answer many questions about the industry which cannot be answered on an aggregate level, questions of the nature of demand for machine tools facing individual firms, of the methods of production, of accounting methods, entrepreneurial behaviour and relationships with other firms and with customers. For reasons of space, several of these questions can be treated only scantily or not at all; an example of the latter is the history of labour relations and the labour force. Instead, attention is concentrated on the sales made by the firm and on its relationships with customer firms and industries, and, in chapter 7, on its efficiency as a producer. This is preceded, in this chapter, by a short history of the firm and by a discussion of the records which it left, and which make it possible and profitable for it to be studied in such great detail.

A short history

1. Foundation and management. The firm of Greenwood and Batley was founded in 1856, as a partnership between Thomas Greenwood and John Batley. Thomas Greenwood had been apprenticed to his father, a machine-maker in Gildersome, Yorkshire, had then worked in Kirkstall for the firm of Stephen and Joseph Whitham, and had in 1843 become chief draughtsman to Sir Peter Fairbairn at the Wellington Foundry, Leeds (Sellers, 1912, p. 400). John Batley had worked with Greenwood at this period, but nothing is known about his earlier life.

120

The firm continued under the management of Greenwood and Batley until 1873, when Thomas Greenwood died. He was succeeded in the partnership, and in the management of the firm, by his sons, George and Arthur, and by his nephew Henry. A fifth partner, also active in the management of the company, was John Henry Wurtzburg, brother-in-law of both Arthur and George, and of Henry Greenwood. Some division of responsibilities seems to have taken place; Arthur Greenwood and Wurtzburg took control of the day-to-day operations of the firm, Henry Greenwood became head of the drawing-office, although Arthur Greenwood, like his father, was responsible for the invention of much of the machinery made by the company, particularly in the field of machine tools for the manufacture of armaments. George Greenwood spent at least some of his time as foreign salesman for the company, largely in Europe, but also made trips to the Far East and Russia. John Batley appears by this time to be playing little part in the management of the partnership (Anon., 1910d, p. 386).

In 1888 the partnership was dissolved, and the firm became a public limited company. Three outside directors were appointed, and Arthur Greenwood became Chairman and Managing Director. George and Henry Greenwood and Wurtzburg continued as the other managing directors, while John Batley dropped out of the management, and even of the control of the firm; he did not, unlike the Greenwoods, receive part of the purchase price of the new company in the form of shares. The three outside directors were almost certainly appointed because of their knowledge of, and contacts with, the most important single customer of the firm, the British government and its military services. Vice-Admiral Philip Colomb had retired from the navy in 1886, after a distinguished career, particularly in the field of safety at sea and signalling systems (*Who Was Who 1897–1915*, 1920, p. 150). He conducted for Greenwood and Batley negotiations with the Admiralty about the manufacture of Whitehead torpedo, although he does not seem to have been successful in obtaining any orders, as most of the investment of £30,000 was wasted (Greenwood and Batley, Board Minutes (hereafter G & B Board), 11 July 1888). The second outside director was Lieutenant-Colonel Ralph Vivian, who had served in The Scots Guards until his retirement from the army in 1883; he does not seem to have had particular contacts with the army purchasing departments, and he played little part in the control of the firm (*Who Was Who 1916–1928*, 1929, p. 1076). The third director appointed in 1888 was Major-General Edward Micklem, who had been a distinguished Royal Engineer, and had ended his army career in 1887, having been Assistant Adjutant-General of the Engineers. He was also a director of several other companies, at least one of whom lent money to Greenwood and Batley (*Who Was Who 1929–1940*, 1941, p. 937 and G & B Board).

After the formation of the limited company in 1888, few changes took place in the management of the company before 1914, except those caused by the deaths of George Greenwood in 1893, Wurtzburg in 1903 and Arthur Greenwood in 1910. They were replaced as directors by employees of the company about whom little information has survived. Arthur Greenwood was replaced as Chairman by Major-General Micklem.

2. Products of the company. Greenwood and Batley were at their foundation, and remained for much of the period until 1914, general engineers, manufacturing many different types of engineering equipment. In 1908 a writer in *The Times* Engineering Supplement described them as:

> the most famous of all the Leeds firms . . . They make such a bewildering variety of different things – torpedoes, turbines, electrical plant, cartridges, machinery for silk mills, oil mills, boot sewing, woodworking etc. – that the machine tool department is dwarfed; but it is large, extremely varied, and modern. (Shadwell, 1908)

To this list can be added, on the basis of the order-books of the firm and the minutes of the meetings of the Board of Directors, electrical carriages, horseshoes, rifles, and steam engines, and the firm even invested in a number of light railways. Even within the field of machine tools, with which this study is principally concerned, the range of products was very considerable. A list of the machine tools which they manufactured between 1856 and 1900 is given in appendix 5.1.

The principal preoccupation of the firm, in its production of machine tools, was with machine tools suitable for use in the armaments industry. However, since they supplied tools not only for the small-arms trade, with its demands for light, special purpose, machine tools, but also the heavy gun-makers, whose needs were for the largest and heaviest machine tools, the products of the firm spanned the whole range of machine tools produced during this period, either in this country or abroad. They were among the first makers of milling machines in Great Britain, and also pioneered the use of the capstan lathe. Thomas Greenwood was known as the foremost inventor of machine tools for armaments manufacture in this country, and his successors carried on this innovating tradition, working closely with the arms manufacturers in developing new machine tools.[1]

Although Greenwood and Batley continued until 1914 to make a number of different products, there are signs of attempts, common throughout the engineering trade at this period, to standardise and to reduce the number of products made. This was particularly difficult in the machine tool trade, because of the tradition of special-purpose manufacturing and because customers expected their suggestions and needs to be incorporated into the design of their tools, but the firm, in the first decade of this century, began to attempt to produce standard patterns of machine tools, 'so that these could be made to stock and early delivery of them given' (G & B Board, 2 March 1911). During the period up to 1900 however, with which these three chapters are largely concerned, standardisation was limited to a few parts which could be easily interchanged, such as lathe beds, and to a policy of making machines for stock; if an order for one machine of a type was received, perhaps four or six would be made, to save the time and expense involved in retooling.

3. Financial history. Very little is known about the financial history of the company as a whole prior to 1882. Thereafter figures on the profits of the company are given firstly in the share offer prospectus of 1888 and then in the profit and loss accounts, balance sheets, and directors' minutes. It is said that Thomas Greenwood and John Batley invested £10,000 in the partnership in 1856, but this seems an extremely high figure, much higher than the initial capital investment in any other machine tool or engineering company; it is also difficult to explain how two working engineers could have raised such a sum (Glover, 1956, p. 343).

The profits of the firm were given in the documents concerning the share offer as an average of £18,329 per year between 1882 and 1885, and an average of £33,236 for the period 1886 to 1888. In spite of these profits, it appears that the main impetus behind the decision of the partnership to dissolve and form a public company was the need for further capital to finance an expansion of the business. As the prospectus of 1888 stated, the initial capital issue of £300,000 would leave a balance of £35,000 after the payment to the partners of the value of the firm, £265,000; this £35,000 was 'partly required to carry out additions to the Buildings and Plant, which are already commenced, and are being rapidly proceeded with; and partly for increased turnover of the firm'.[2]

The initial share issue, and the £35,000 which it raised, soon proved insufficient to provide for the needs of the company, which was engaged on a major rebuilding of its works, and in 1890 a further £44,000 worth of shares was offered to the existing shareholders, although in the event only 1466 preference shares of £10 and 1252 ordinary shares, also of £10 were applied for. Only £3 of each share was called for in 1890, so that the total capital raised was only £8,154 (G. & B. Board, 6 May 1890; 29 August 1890).

The only remaining changes in the capital structure of the company came in 1893, when £20,000 of debentures were issued to the bank as security for the large overdraft which they had granted to the company (G. & B. Board, 19 May 1893), in 1899 when further calls were authorised on the issue of 1890, and in 1909 when a further £2 was called for on the shares issued in 1890, apparently to meet a need for working capital (G. & B. Board, 9 June 1899; 3 July 1908).

The expansion of the works, and the flotation of the company which the need for finance for expansion demanded, both proved to have been based on incorrect assumptions of the course of future demand for the products of Greenwood and Batley. Figure 5.1 shows the number of orders received by Greenwood and Batley during the period from 1857 to 1914 (it would of course be much more satisfactory to have sales figures, but the labour of compiling such figures from the order-books ruled out such a calculation). In the light of the steady but slow growth in orders up to 1888 it is surprising that such heavy investment should have been undertaken at this period, and it is unclear on what evidence an expectation of the type of future growth for which this expansion could cater was based. The total value of the firm in 1888 was, according to the valuation, £265,000, yet capital expenditure undertaken during the financial years 1888–91 was £104,149, and the burden which this placed on the firm was increased by the dislocation caused in the works by the rebuilding operations, particularly the expensive construction of a link to a nearby railway.[3]

The result, therefore, of the conversion of Greenwood and Batley to a public company, and of the expansion of capacity undertaken at the time, was to provide the new company with a burden of some £310,000 nominal of share capital, on which dividends had to be paid, and a large debt to the company's bankers, who financed the gap between the approximately £40,000 raised by the share issue and the capital expenditure of over £100,000 undertaken by the company. Further, the need for working capital was increased by the extension of capacity both because of an expansion in the clerical and other overhead costs, and also because expansion was concentrated in departments of the works engaged in production of goods, payment for which might be long delayed. The expansion was in fact concentrated in the heavy tool shop, the torpedo plant, and the cartridge department. The first of these branches was engaged in making the larger tools, where manufacture could take a year or more, during

124

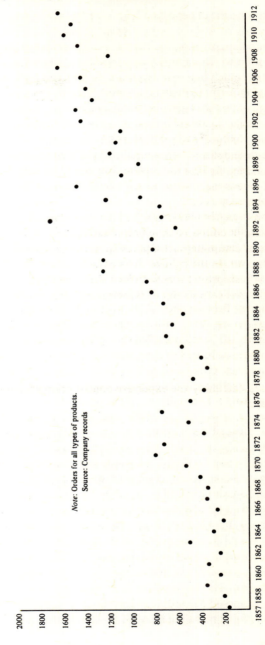

Figure 5.1. Greenwood and Batley: number of orders received, 1857–1912

Note: Orders for all types of products.
Source: Company records

which time the expenditure had to be financed by the firm; there was apparently no system of part-payment before delivery. In the cartridge and torpedo departments, the firm was catering almost entirely for government orders, on which payment was often long delayed, and was in a market situation much like that described by Mr Trebilcock as existing in the cordite industry (Trebilcock, 1966). That is, the government attempted, by placing orders with selected companies, to persuade them to install machinery to make a particular type of arms; once the machinery was installed, and the first order was completed, no further orders would be placed, all peace-time demand being supplied by the government factories, the government reasoning that the private firm would be unwilling to scrap its investment in new machinery, which would therefore be available for use in time of emergency need.

The expansion undertaken by Greenwood and Batley around 1890 appears, therefore, to have been misguided. While in March 1889 the company had a credit balance with their bankers of £30,362, by the following year it owed £12,072, and in 1891 £32,524. The debt continued to increase, and some consols owned by the company were required to be sold; the debt, however, increased to £37,602 by June 1892 (Greenwood and Batley Balance Sheets, 1889–91). In 1893 £20,000 worth of debentures were deposited with the bank as security for the loan into which the overdraft had been converted, but a further overdraft had to be obtained soon afterwards. In this situation, it is clear that two policies were open to the directors, retrenchment and the writing-off of the unproductive investment, or further expansion in the search for some profitable occupation for the works. The managing directors chose the latter course, and during the period from 1893 to 1899 undertook a series of speculative investments, most of them unsuccessful, while trying to pacify the London directors, Micklem, Colomb and Vivian, with minor economies in administration. In 1893 Arthur Greenwood was dissuaded with difficulty from taking up a concession to establish a light railway in Mandalay (G. & B. Board, 10 February 1893). In 1896 'By an arrangement with a coach builder in Leeds a Wagonette has been placed at the company's disposal, and it was intended to see whether an electrical motor car could be made which would be a success' (G. & B. Board, 8 December 1896), a venture which ended in a substantial loss ten years later. In 1898 the company entered a new field, with the formation of the English de Laval Steam Turbine Co. The London directors initially refused to agree to the investment, proposed by Arthur Greenwood, of £30,000,

Bearing in mind the increase of net earnings which would be needed to

render it remunerative, and the fact that the large expenditure on capital
account which was incurred in the early years of the company has not
(so far as we can judge) proportionately increased its earning power,
while, in order to fill the works with remunerative employment a much
larger yearly amount of orders has been rendered necessary.

In spite of this refusal Greenwood and Batley made large advances to the
new de Laval Company, and in 1903 it was necessary for them to return to
Greenwood's initial proposal, and effectively to take over the de Laval
Company as a subsidiary.[4] During the course of these negotiations,
Greenwood and Batley were also investing heavily in a light railway in
Lancashire, another investment producing an extremely low rate of
return.[5]

Apart from these speculative ventures, which have the air of desperate
attempts by the managing directors to regain some of the former prosperity
of the company, the internal financial management of the firm appears to
have been very loosely conducted. Large credits were given to weak customers, particularly those, like the Colonial Ammunition Company, in
which Arthur Greenwood was personally involved (G. & B. Board, 26 June
1900). In 1893 the auditors reported that the financial affairs of the
company were conducted in a way which made it impossible to keep accurate records of sales and purchases, largely because of a long-standing practice of paying for supplies by means of cheques received from customers,
without passing the cheques through Greenwood and Batley's account (G.
& B. Board, 28 June 1893). It was also discovered in 1893 that the managing directors had habitually borrowed from the company in anticipation of
their salaries; no exact sums are given in the minutes of the Board of
Directors, but the Chairman in particular appears to have been a substantial
debtor (G. & B. Board, 28 June 1893; 25 May 1894). In 1894 he transferred to Greenwood and Batley shares in the Chelsea Electricity Company
with a paper value to £2765, to 'reduce his indebtedness' to Greenwood
and Batley, but since the Chelsea Electricity Company was a moribund
concern, the annual general meeting of Greenwood and Batley in 1896
ordered their Chairman to take back the shares and pay cash instead (G. &
B. Board, 9 July 1874; 28 July 1896); Arthur Greenwood and J. H.
Wurtzburg still appeared as debtors of the company in 1899, though for
comparatively small amounts (G. & B. Board, 15 December 1899).

The combined result of the financial mismanagement and unwise investment policies of the company, together with the apparent instability of
demand for their products during the period from 1890 to 1914, is
reflected in the dividend record of the firm, given in table 5.1 below.

Table 5.1   *Dividend payments on the share capital of Greenwood and Batley, 1889–1914, expressed as a percentage of the nominal value of the shares.*

Year	£10 preference shares	£10 ordinary shares
1889	7	10
1890	7	10
1891	7	Nil
1892	7	Nil
1893	7	Nil
1894	Nil	Nil
1895	Nil	Nil
1896	10½	Nil
1897	17½	2½
1898	7	Nil
1899	7	3
1900	7	2½
1901	7	5
1902	7	5
1903	7	4
1904	7	5
1905	7	6
1906	7	5
1907	7	4
1908	7	4
1909	7	Nil
1910	7	Nil
1911	7	Nil
1912	7	Nil
1913	7	Nil
1914	7	5

Further measures of the financial success or failure of the company would be the rate of return on the capital employed, or alternatively the trading profit as a proportion of turnover. In the case of rate of return on capital, complications are introduced into the calculation by the practice employed in allowing for depreciation of the capital stock. In common with many firms of this period, Greenwood and Batley adopted a policy of varying the depreciation allowance according to the trading profit, reducing the amount written off when the trading profit seemed low, as in 1895, when nothing was written off the value of capital equipment. In figure 5.2, therefore, two methods have been adopted of dealing with depreciation. In the first, the result of the calculations being line B on the graph, a figure of 5% per year has been written off, regardless of the depreciation allowed by the firm, while in the second method, line C, the mean of the depreciation allowed by the firm over the whole period has been calculated, and applied to the figures for each year. Thirdly, as a measure of profit-

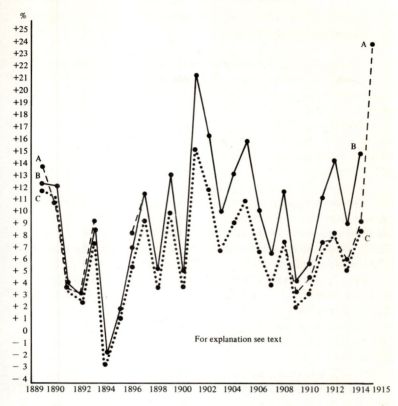

Figure 5.2. Greenwood and Batley: profit levels, 1889–1915

ability, line A shows trading profit as a percentage of turnover. All these measures are extremely crude but together, as shown in figure 5.2, they do give some indication of the profitability and efficiency of the firm. They do at least demonstrate the truth of the comment in the *Financial Mail* of 4 July 1914, that:

> Greenwood and Batley have a splendid name for quality. It is one of the best engineering works in Leeds. Nevertheless, its record as a limited company has been simply disastrous. Over-capitalisation and bad management are probably responsible for the fact that no ordinary dividends have been paid since 4% was distributed in 1908 . . . It seems to the ordinary outsider that Greenwood and Batley with its magnificent reputation should do far better. It was over-capitalised at the start and

129

the finances have never been carefully attended to. None of the securities are satisfactory. (Anon., 1914)

4. The technical standing of Greenwood and Batley in the machine tool industry. Even in an hostile article commenting on two decades of financial ineptitude and failure in the management of Greenwood and Batley, the *Financial Mail* could still describe it as 'one of the best engineering works in Leeds'. This raises the question of the standing of Greenwood and Batley within the engineering industry, and particularly within the machine tool industry. To establish the position of the firm vis-à-vis other makers of machine tools is particularly important in order to assess the value of the analysis of the market situation facing Greenwood and Batley, and of its internal organisation and production, which follows in the succeeding chapters. If Greenwood and Batley can, throughout the period, be considered to be one of the 'best-practice' machine tool plants, then it is possible to utilise the evidence of its organisation and its production as a guide to the experience of other 'best-practice' firms in the industry, and through them, to the speed of innovation and changing methods in the machine tool industry as a whole. The use of evidence from Greenwood and Batley alone is subject to the criticisms, made at length in chapter 3, of the use of evidence from what may be exceptional firms. It is not claimed, however, that Greenwood and Batley is typical of the industry, but rather that the evidence suggests that it held, throughout the period from 1856 to 1900, a place among the leading firms, and was not exceptional either in growing faster than other firms or in falling behind its competitors. Greenwood and Batley, in fact, progressed as did the rest of the industry, and, in some particular respects, can therefore be regarded as representing that progress.

To support this claim is particularly difficult in view of the paucity of quantitative data on the operations of other firms, either 'best-practice' or less advanced in their technical or commercial progress. Greenwood and Batley's experiences can therefore not be compared directly with those of other firms. It is however possible to gain some idea of the place of the firm within the machine tool industry by studying the comments of unbiased observers, particularly those engineers who wrote the official reports on the international exhibitions. Although these observers were largely concerned, as was suggested in the last chapter, with technical rather than commercial competence, their reports can be a guide to the relative standing of the major English machine tool makers who sent tools to these exhibitions.

Greenwood and Batley's first appearance as an exhibitor at a major international exhibition was at the London Exhibition of 1862, at which they showed a machine with circular cutters for machining rifle muskets. They were commended for this machine by D. K. Clark in his extensive work on *The Exhibited Machinery of 1862* (1864, p. 130), and the Jury Reports of the exhibition mentioned the 'great ingenuity and originality of Greenwood and Batley'. At the 1867 Paris Exhibition, at which Britain was generally under-represented in machine tools, owing, according to the British Commissioner, John Anderson, to the fact that 'toolmakers had been busy for many months preceding the opening of the exhibition, and had been unable, frequently, to fill regular orders', Greenwood and Batley did not show any machine tools. This fact was commented on, by John Anderson, who linked their absence with that of Nasmyth, Hulse, Smith, Beacock and Tannett, and Fairbairn, all of them well known makers of machine tools (P.P., 1867—8, xxx, pt. II. pp. 341, 702, 722). The next major exhibition at which Greenwood and Batley exhibited was that in Philadelphia in 1876, at which the firm received an award for a bolt heading machine; this was in fact one of the few British machine tools sent to the exhibition, perhaps reflecting the unwillingness of British manufacturers in general to attempt to sell in protected American markets, (P.P., 1877, xxxiv, p. 310 and P.P., 1877, xxxvi, p. 1).

During the next decade Greenwood and Batley's tools do not seem to have attracted any attention at the international exhibitions, but in 1880 the firm received a silver prize for cartridge-making machinery, and a diploma for twist drill chucks and cutters, at the Melbourne Exhibition of that year (P.P., 1882, xxviii, pp. 471, 476). In 1889 other British makers, Hulse, Selig Sonnenthal and Smith and Coventry, were mentioned by the American Commissioner to the Exhibition in Paris, but most space was given to a description of a large engine lathe made by Greenwood and Batley for Schneider and Co. of Creusot:

These builders [Greenwood and Batley] have made many large tools for the arsenals and other government institutions. They do not confine themselves exclusively to machine tools, but this line of work is the most important of their productions. The grandest machine in this class at the Exhibition was without doubt, the large lathe just built for Schneider and Co., of Creusot, by Greenwood and Batley ... Not the least remarkable thing in connection with this tool is the shortness of the time taken in its design and execution. A consideration of the following statement conveys some idea of the facilities possessed by this house for turning out large work.

There followed a description of the production, and of the dimensions of this machine (Barr, 1893, pp. 352–4).

In 1900, at another Paris Exhibition, Greenwood and Batley was linked with Whitworth, Muir, Hulse, Shanks and Buckton, all well-known tool-makers, as 'conspicuous by their absence' (P.P., 1901, xxxi, p. 368), but by this time both the lure of international exhibitions, and Greenwood and Batley's reputation, was diminishing, and the only other comment on their activities from an impartial observer, writing in 1910, seems to confirm this. In 1909 and 1910 G. L. Carden's consular report on the engineering works of Europe was published by the U.S. government. Greenwood and Batley are mentioned only three times in the reports, although other British firms are prominent. Two mentions concern the Italian government arms works, at Terni, which was fitted out with nearly 900 tools 'in the early eighties' by Greenwood and Batley, where 'much of the . . . equipment is now old', and that at Rome where Carden commented:

Greenwood and Batley of Leeds have supplied several universal spiral gear cutters. This firm, I understand, did considerable business with the Italian Government works in previous years, at a time when the Leeds house was regarded as one of the first in the building of arsenal tools. The Greenwood and Batley tools present are not of recent make. (Carden, 1909–10, pp. 168–9)

These impressions of the standing of Greenwood and Batley, culled from exhibition reports, undoubtedly do not give a very complete picture of the standing of Greenwood and Batley within the machine tool industry. The products of the firm were also mentioned often in the technical journals serving the industry, giving an impression of innovative activity, but no very concrete evidence can be gained from these sources. In general, all that can be said is that Greenwood and Batley were ranked, on a number of occasions which have been quoted, with the acknowledged leaders of the machine tool industry, Whitworth, Nasmyth and their successors. Therefore, the evidence which is available suggests that Greenwood and Batley can, at least for the period before 1900, be regarded as a 'best-practice' firm, although it seems likely that their reputation and standing declined during the early years of this century.

Sources and Method

The sources available on the work of Greenwood and Batley make it possible to reconstruct in considerable detail many aspects of the history of the firm and of its production of machine tools. There are however a number of features of the records, of which a full list is given in appendix 5.2, which affect the nature of the analysis, and it is the object of this section to describe the records which have been used and to indicate the ways in which they can illuminate the history of the firm.

The major sources which have been used in the analysis in the following chapters are the order-books, the cost-books, the directors' minutes, the balance sheets and the profit and loss accounts of the firm. In addition, the letter books, catalogues and press cuttings have been studied, and information from them has been used on a number of occasions. No attempt has been made to use the ledgers relating to particular sections of the works or to the manufacture of sectional parts, nor have the patent specifications, photographs, cash and cheque records, and carriers' delivery records been studied in any detail.

The order-books, for which an unbroken series from 1856 to 1920 are available for study, provide the following information:

1. Order number.
2. Member of the firm who obtained the order.
3. The date on which the order was received.
4. The date on which the order was dispatched to the customer.
5. The name and address of the customer, or of the agent to whom the order was consigned.
6. A description of the machine or machines ordered.
7. The number of machines in the order.
8. The price of the order.
9. The number of the photograph of the machine ordered.
10. The catalogue number of the machine ordered.
11. The number of the order from the dispatch book.

The cost-books, which are available in an unbroken run from 1856 to the present day, give, for each order:

1. The date of starting work on the order.
2. The time worked each day on the order by each of five categories of worker.
3. The wage rate of each of these categories of worker.
4. The total cost of labour on the order.
5. The 'management cost' or overhead cost.
6. The piecework cost.
7. The cost and weight of each metal input.
8. The net and gross weights of the order when dispatched.

133

9. The cost of any sectional parts used in manufacture.
10. The profit or loss on the order.
11. The date of finishing work on the order.

The directors' minutes, available for the period from the foundation of the limited company in 1888, and the balance sheets and profit and loss accounts for the same period, provide information on the financial affairs and the general policy of the firm.

Greenwood and Batley were, from their foundation in 1856, general engineers. The focus of this study is, however, one segment of the engineering industry, the manufacture of machine tools, and in order to utilise the records of Greenwood and Batley for this study it was necessary to extract from the records all information relevant to the production of machine tools. The order and time ledgers were therefore searched, and information on each order for machine tools was recorded over the period from 1856 to 1900. The following pieces of information were recorded for each such order.

1. The order number.
2. The date of receipt of the order.
3. The date of dispatch of the order to the customer.
4. The name and address of the customer.
5. The name and address of the agent, if this was given.
6. The price of the order.
7. The description of the machine ordered.
8. The number of machines comprising the order. (Machines of different types were given, by the firm, separate order numbers. Thus a number larger than one here will indicate an order for more than one machine of the same description.)
9. The date of beginning work on the order.
10. The total cost of labour on the order.
11. The total 'management cost' of the order.
12. The net weight of the completed order.
13. The total cost of the order.
14. The cost of piecework labour for the order.
15/19. The hours of labour on the order by five categories of labourer. (The categories were: boys, planers and borers, turners and fitters, boy joiners, and men joiners.)

It will be apparent that some of the information provided in the order and time ledgers was not recorded, and was therefore not available for use in the analysis. The catalogue and photograph number of the machine was not thought to be of use in an analysis largely concerned with the economic history of the firm. The name of the member of the firm obtaining the order was not given in many cases, and such information did not in any case seem very susceptible of quantitative analysis. The number in the dispatch book was simply an identification number and thus duplicated the order number already recorded. The date of finishing work did not normally differ by more than a few days from the date of dispatch, and was therefore not included. The profit or loss could be calculated from the information recorded, and its inclusion as a separate item was therefore unnecessary. The gross weight of the order, although significant in transport costs and, in some export markets, tariff charges, seemed of less value than the net weight, and was therefore excluded.

Of the remaining items, the cost of metal inputs and inputs of sectional parts can be calculated as a residual when labour, management and piecework expenses are deducted from total cost; although it might have been of interest to have had these pieces of information in more detail, the effort required in recording them, when up to ten different metals and as many sectional parts could be used on one order, would have seriously hampered the data collection, and added little to the final analysis. Note was however taken separately of the cost of the different metals employed. The final omission, that of the hours worked on the order during each day can be justified also on the grounds of the effort involved in recording the information, and the probability that it would add little to the analysis, since the length of the period of manufacture, and the total hours worked, had been recorded for each order.

A further omission was that of information on the period after 1900. It would have been desirable to have carried the analysis of production of Greenwood and Batley up to the terminal date of this study, 1914. During the course of data collection, however, it became clear that during the last decade of the nineteenth century the firm was increasingly adopting a system of bulk manufacturing of sectional parts, in particular for the machines which it built in some numbers. The manufacture of these sectional parts necessarily involved some labour cost and 'management cost' which was included within the 'sectional parts' entry for each order recorded in the time ledger. As the manufacture of sectional parts became more common, therefore, the proportion of final cost attributable to 'sectional parts' rose, producing an apparent reduction in the 'labour cost' element in final cost. This reduction was apparent rather than real, being the result of the system of accounting within the works. It would theoretically be possible, through the use of the sectional parts ledgers, to trace each part used and to add the labour cost element in its production to the labour cost element in the final machine (and similarly with the 'management cost') but this would be so time-consuming as to be impossible within the scope of this analysis. It was therefore decided to conclude the recording of data in 1900, before this source of bias became too great, and additionally before a change in accounting practice in the firm reduced the amount of information given in the time ledgers. The order-books were not affected by these changes, and it would thus have been possible to continue recording the information from them, but it seemed more sensible to keep the final data set consistent in the amount of information it contained, and to conclude the recording of orders in 1900 also.

A number of conventions were established in the course of recording the data from the order- and cost-books of the firm.

Broadly, they are consistent with the attitude that, if the data were ambiguous in some way, it should be treated as missing, rather than recorded with a probability that it would be misleading. Thus in the case where an order was for a number of machines, which were completed and dispatched at different dates, then the date of dispatch would be omitted, unless the dates were very close together. The adoption of conventions of this kind, and the inevitable omissions from the original records, together with the necessary omission of such data as price for a machine made by Greenwood and Batley for its own use, resulted in a large amount of missing data. Data of some kind were found to be misleading in 2526 orders out of a total of 4961 orders which were recorded. The problem of missing data is of course very common in historical studies, and indeed in all studies in which the data are taken over from a source not under the control of the researcher. It is possible to utilise techniques which have been established to deal with such problems, principally by interpolation of results on the basis of mean values found in the data which one does have, sometimes with associated probabilities. Such techniques have not been used in this study, for a number of reasons. Firstly, there is no warrant for assuming that missing values are distributed in the same way as those that are available. Secondly, the sample size of the set of entirely correct records, 2435, is very large by the standards of most economic studies, and it is unlikely that much greater accuracy could be achieved by the interpolation of values in the remaining records, while the effort involved in doing so would be very great. Thirdly, it must be emphasised that, for a number of variables used in the analysis, the number of missing records is much less than 2526, and in some cases there are no missing data; for instance number of machines in the order, and the machine type, are known in every case, and in only two cases are the name and address of the customer or agent omitted. The actual number of cases of missing data for each variable is given in appendix 5.3. Thus for analysis of many of the variables, the problem of missing data is not acute, and can safely be ignored. It should however be noted that, for this reason, the sample sizes quoted in the analysis that follows may differ according to the variables that are being analysed.

The actual method of recording and analysis was to record the data, coding where necessary the information originally in non-numerical form, on data recording sheets. The data were then punched onto paper tape or cards, and a number of checks for accuracy and consistency were applied and the errors thus discovered were eliminated. The corrected data were transferred onto magnetic tape for analysis using a computer. Analysis was carried out largely through specially written programs but partly by the use of statistical routines supplied by the Social Research Centre at the University of Michigan, and by the Biomedical (BMD) and Statistical Package for the Social Sciences (SPSS) Program packages.

One further methodological point is of considerable importance to the analysis that follows, and must be considered at some length. The method of data collection was to extract from the records of Greenwood and Batley all information relevant to the production of machine tools. It may be argued that this is unjustifiable, because the work of an industrial firm is an integrated process, and that it can make no sense to abstract from that integrated process one sector for separate analysis. Furthermore, to do so is to discard a great deal of material, and to make it impossible to see the direction in which the firm as a whole is moving; factors in the production of some other segment of the production of the firm may affect its organisation and policy in ways which rebound on machine tool production.

More concretely, it could be argued that the decision to look only at machine tools makes it impossible to consider such variables as the rate of introduction of new machinery, or capital expenditure generally, since there is no way of allocating such expenditure, or such new machines, between different sectors of the firm. On a wider scale, it could be argued that a sector of a firm like Greenwood and Batley, in which machine tool production is only one of a number of activities, cannot be compared with a firm making only machine tools, so that the experience of machine tool production by Greenwood and Batley may not reflect the experience of the industry as a whole. Greenwood and Batley could, for instance, set losses on their machine tools off against profits on their cartridges and horseshoes, and thus survive a period of losses which would have bankrupted a firm making only machine tools.

137

These objections are all, in theory, extremely persuasive. A number of justifications can, however, be adduced for the procedure which has been adopted. Firstly, the firm of Greenwood and Batley organised its production so that one sector was kept separate from other sectors. The works were physically divided into 'shops' which concentrated on different products. When bonus schemes were introduced, they were based on the performance of the individual departments, of which the machine tool department was one, and when reports were given to the directors they were given department by department. Thus in practice machine tool production was separated from the other activities of the firm, and there is no sign in the directors' minutes of any policy of regarding the firm as an integrated whole; indeed it can be argued that the policy of separate departments prevented an efficient use of the resources of the firm. Secondly, the objection that it is impossible to allocate capital expenditure to individual departments is valid; however, no information on capital expenditure by the firm is available until 1889, so that this objection has no force against the isolation of machine tool production up to that date. After 1889 the objection has more force, but it is arguable that the advantages to be gained by looking at capital expenditure by the firm as a whole are outweighed by the advantages of the method of isolating machine tools that has been applied. The capital cost element in the cost of each item was estimated by the firm, so that in the analysis of individual costs capital expenditure can be accounted for, if rather roughly or as a residual item. As to aggregate capital expenditure, and one of its components, the introduction of new machinery, it is doubtful whether its analysis would make sense, simply because of the lack of homogeneity in the products of the firm. Thus it is impossible to assess the effects of any one piece of capital expenditure without knowing its exact function, and the effect on production that it has, and the compilation of statistics of aggregate expenditure will measure not some change in the productive potential of the firm but rather, if it measures anything, simply the amount of capital which the firm has available for new capital expenditure. In other words, the gain in information caused by the ability, when considering the firm as a whole, to look at capital expenditure as a whole, is more apparent than real; any analysis of its effects has to break down the firm into units, which is exactly what the procedure being justified does. Thirdly, it has been shown that many firms in the machine tool industry were similar to Greenwood and Batley in that machine tool production was only one of their interests. Further, the fact that such firms co-existed with specialised machine tool firms in the market must show that the cost structures faced by both types were similar and that at least in terms of production costs and ability to penetrate the market they can be compared. Finally, and most generally, the lack of homogeneity in the products of Greenwood and Batley make it essential, in any analysis of production, markets, innovation, or productivity, to separate one activity from another, as far as it is possible within the limitations of the data. There is no logic in combining as one unit for analysis the production of horseshoes with the production of milling machines; the problem of quality changes, the assessment of changing output, the cost of inputs, contain enough difficulties when only one sector is considered, without attempting to lump together sectors which have little in common beyond their location under adjacent roofs.

Appendix 5.1   Machine tools made by Greenwood and Batley, 1856–1900

The machine tools are listed by main types, e.g. 'lathe', and then by sub-types, e.g. 'screwcutting lathe'.

1. Lathe

1.	Blanshard copying	15.	Grinding
2.	Polishing or surfacing	16.	Disc and surfacing
3.	Screwcutting	17.	Chuck
4.	Hollow-spindle	18.	Tyre turning and boring
5.	Turret or capstan	19.	Break
6.	Roller	20.	Annular
7.	Fluting	21.	Hollow-spindle and capstan
8.	Surfacing and screw-cutting	22.	Spinning
9.	Double	23.	Bushing
10.	Copying	24.	Wheel
11.	Boring	25.	Cutting off
12.	Gap	26.	Face
13.	Eccentric	27.	Drilling
14.	Brass finishing	28.	Quadruple capstan rest

2. Planing machine

1.	Reversing	7.	Roller pad
2.	'Jim Crow'	8.	Vertical
3.	Circular	9.	Profile
4.	'With two tools'	10.	Stud planing
5.	Two tool boxes, two tools each	11.	Screw planing
6.	Circular planing or ending	12.	Side planing
		13.	Rack planing

3. Drilling machine

1.	Pillar	2.	Radial

3. Multiple
4. Wall
5. Column
6. Horizontal
7. Portable
8. Hollow upright
9. Bench
10. Slot drilling
11. Drilling and boring

12. Horizontal drilling and boring
13. Capstan
14. Mitrailleuse
15. Horizontal rotary
16. Horizontal drilling and milling
17. Rack pillar
18. Mortice
19. Armature

4. Milling machine
1. Clamp
2. Edge
3. Screw
4. Universal
5. Sand miller
6. Copy
7. Common
8. Independent
9. Straight
10. Vertical
11. Pointing
12. Rotary
13. Double
14. Face
15. Point

16. Rotating
17. Profiling
18. Cutter
19. Vertical universal straight
20. Cam
21. Multiple spindle
22. Horizontal
23. Keyway
24. Worm wheel
25. Cross
26. Capstan
27. Mortice
28. Thread
29. Milling and planing

5. Grinding machine
1. Twist drill grinder
2. Surface
3. Internal
4. Cylindrical
5. Sand
6. Cutter
7. Copy
8. Spindle
9. Copy cutter

10. Automatic emery
11. Shell
12. Mill
13. Tool
14. Grinding and lapping
15. Universal
16. Grinding and polishing
17. Vertical

6. Shaping machine
1. Flat and circular
2. Circular
3. Flat
4. Universal
5. Milling

6. Double
7. 'Kinders patent'
8. Straight
9. Incline
10. Bevel wheel

7. Slotting machine
1. Horizontal

2. Fallers

3.	Double upright	5.	Compound
4.	Vertical	6.	B.S. screw

8. Moulding machine
1. Moulding and shaping

9. Press

1.	Hydraulic	3.	Punching
2.	Screw	4.	Pressing machine

10. Screwcutting machine

11. Stamping machine

12. Cam-cutting machine

13. Wheel- and gear-cutting machine

1.	Wheelcutting and dividing	3.	Helical
2.	Bevel	4.	Worm

14. Planing and cutting machine

15. Boring machine

1.	Horizontal	9.	Boring and tapping
2.	Double finishing	10.	Capstan horizontal
3.	Vertical	11.	Mitrailleuse
4.	Multiple	12.	Mitrailleuse capstan
5.	Double	13.	Boring and milling
6.	Boring and ending	14.	Barrel boring
7.	Double horizontal	15.	Horizontal boring and milling
8.	Barrel finish	16.	Hollow spindle

16. Punching and shearing machine

1.	Punching and trimming	4.	Circular shearing
2.	Shearing	5.	Guillotine
3.	Punching	6.	Rivet shearing

17. Component parts
Ordered for other machine

18. Tapping machine

1.	Horizontal	2.	Vertical

19. Screwing machine

1.	Capstan	3.	Screwing and lapping
2.	Bolt and nut	4.	Screwing and turning

20. Horizontal boring, cutting and milling machine

141

21. Slitting machine
  1. Screw

22. Groove-making machine

23. Turning machine
  1. Trunnion

24. Dividing machine

25. Screw-making machine
  1. Capstan
  2. Rotary
  3. No. 1
  4. No. 2
  5. No. 3

26. Sawing machine

27. Rifling machine
  1. Capstan rest
  2. Martini—Henry

29. Nut and bolt making machine

31. Threading machine

32. Profiling machine
  1. Horizontal

33. Cutter-sharpening machine
  1. Milling

34. Chasing machine
  1. Mitrailleuse

35. Bolt-making machine
  1. Nut and bolt
  2. Nut, bolt and rivet
  3. Bolt and rivet
  4. Nut
  5. Rivet

37. Twist-drill cutting machine
  1. Double-headed

39. Universal cutter milling and grinding machine

40. File grinding machine
  1. Flat
  2. Round

41. Chamfering, screwing and shaping machine

42. Gunboring, tracing, rifling and lapping machine

43. Boring, turning and rifling machine

44. Gear-cutting machine
Note: The numbers are those used in the recording and processing of the data. Omitted numbers refer to alterations, second-hand machines and odd attachments.

Appendix 5.2 List of records of Greenwood and Batley

(The records listed below are now in the possession of Leeds Public Library, with the exception of items 17 and 18.)
1. Cost books. c. 100 volumes. 1856–1966.
2. Order-books. 60 volumes. 1856–1920.
3. Carriers' delivery books. c. 30 small books. c. 1880–c. 1920.
4. Photographs indexed by machine type. Book A1 c. 1860–c. 1880; Book B1 c. 1880–c. 1903, c. 1904–c. 1915.
5. Sectional order books. c. 25 volumes. c. 1880–c. 1915.
6. Cost and time ledgers (Tool department). 11 volumes from 1911 onwards.
7. Letter books. 3 volumes from period 1870–1910 (incomplete).
8. Letter book of the North Wortley Conservative Association. 1885–95.
9. Patents. 23 boxes of patent specifications.
10. List of photographs (see 4 above). Indexed by works number. 3 volumes, 1857–1966.
11. Sectional ledgers. c. 50 volumes.
12. Departmental cost accounts. 1 volume, 1910–11.
13. Cash and cheque record. 2 volumes from 1900–3 and 1907–8.
14. Costs of sundries ledgers. 10 volumes from 1910–14.
15. Catalogues:
    a. English circulars, 1–160. No date.
    b. English circulars, 161–327. No date.
    c. English circulars, 328–500. No date.
    d. English circulars, 501–660. Dated c. 1902–5.
    e. Two further volumes of English circulars, from 1930s.
    f. German catalogue, c. 1900–10.
    g. Catalogue of machine tools, c. 1920–30.
    h. Machine tool catalogue. No date.
    i. Illustrated catalogue of milling machines, c. 1906.
    j. French 'catalogue illustré des machines à fraiser', 1903.
    k. Illustrated catalogue of bolt and nut machinery, 1896.
    l. Illustrated catalogue of machine tools, 1906.
    m. Catalogue of textile machinery, c. 1920s.
    n. Catalogue of oil mill machinery, c. 1920s.

    o. English circulars, 661–821, c. 1905–c. 1910.

    p. French catalogue, c. 1920s.

16. Two volumes, described as English circulars, but in fact containing press cuttings, advertisements etc. relating to Greenwood and Batley.

17. Minutes of the Board of Directors, 1889–present day.

18. Balance sheets and profit and loss accounts, 1889–present day (incomplete).

Appendix 5.3   Missing data in the cost and sales ledgers of Greenwood and Batley

The total data set consisted of 4961 orders. Of these 4664 orders were for outside customers or for use by Greenwood and Batley itself. The remaining orders were for stock.

    The following table shows the size of the complete data set, in terms of numbers of orders and of numbers of machines, for each of the major variables used in the analysis. Since these missing items are not exclusive, the exclusion from the data set of all orders for which at least one item of data was missing produced the cleaned data set of 2435 orders which was used in most of the calculations in chapter 6.

	No. of items where information given	
Variable	*Orders*	*Machines*
No. of orders	4664	10062
Delivery date	4475	9915
Price	4240	10000
Date of work-start	3219	7522
Labour cost	3670	8203
Weight	3703	8324
Total cost	4265	9622
Times of labour	3683	8208
Price and cost	3893	9018

6. Greenwood and Batley: markets and prices

Demand Conditions

Greenwood and Batley sold machine tools to 653 customers during the forty-five years between 1856 and 1900. In addition, a number of tools were sold through agents, so that the ultimate destination of the tool is not discoverable. These 653 customers ranged geographically from Leeds to Japan, and industrially from the Chinese Imperial Mint to the Ordnance Store of the Tower of London. Since machine tools are producer's goods, bought to manufacture some other metal product, the total demand for machine tools made by Greenwood and Batley was composed of the various demands from disparate industries; these in their turn were created by the demands for metal goods which these industries were facing. To examine the demand for machine tools from Greenwood and Batley it is necessary, therefore, to examine the conditions in the various major markets in which the machine tools were sold.

The most obvious distinction that can be made between customers of Greenwood and Batley is that between customers in the British Isles and customers overseas. Greenwood and Batley were extremely successful in selling their machine tools in export markets. Their first such sale was in April 1857, when Lancelot Kirkup and Co., of St Petersburg, placed an order for a surfacing and polishing lathe worth £155. Thereafter machine tools were exported by the firm in every year except 1865. Table 6.1 shows the total sales of machine tools to each foreign country over the whole period with which this study is concerned, and table 6.2 shows the sales year by year to the major foreign markets. It is apparent that the demand from abroad for machine tools, both in total and from individual countries, was subject to severe fluctuations, as can be seen in figure 6.1, a histogram showing the yearly value of foreign orders to the firm. Nevertheless, as table 6.3 shows, foreign demand was, throughout the period, an important component of total demand for the firm, and in fact made up about 40% of output over the period. Figure 6.2 shows the year by year percentage distribution between home and foreign orders.

The firm was also successful in selling their machine tools throughout

Great Britain, and there is no sign that they were, at any period, restricted to the area around Leeds. In the distribution of orders between the major industrial regions in this country, shown in table 6.4, London predominated, because of the high volume of orders from the arsenals and arms factories around London, but demand was otherwise spread widely through the country, and reflected the industrial development of the different regions, rather than any peculiarity of the demand for tools made by Greenwood and Batley.

Table 6.1   *Greenwood and Batley: total orders from each foreign country, 1856–1900*

Country of destination	No. of machines sold	Value of machines sold
India	114	£10,027
South Africa	32	5015
Australia	11	1160
Canada	6	565
Hong Kong	7	1153
New Zealand	9	2323
Malta	3	255
United States of America	5	404
Russia	1591	156,508
Japan	101	15,822
France	107	11,275
Germany	41	8200
Italy	285	21,127
Switzerland	77	6754
Austria	650	35,969
Belgium	91	9078
Czechoslovakia	2	108
Spain	94	15,355
Portugal	8	1670
Sweden	17	1882
Turkey	83	10,650
Denmark	14	1009
Norway	16	1175
Brazil	32	4114
Hungary	29	2280
Finland	3	455
China	178	28,865
Argentina	75	3187
Honolulu	1	135
Uruguay	1	35
Morocco	1	90
Egypt	10	1434
Afghanistan	37	5166

Notes:
(a) This table refers only to machines sold for which both price and cost are known.   (b) Current prices.

Table 6.2   *Greenwood and Batley: value of foreign orders of machine tools, 1856–1900, by selected countries and by year*

Year	Russia	Japan	Italy	Austria	Spain	China	All other
1856							
1857	31						1655
1858					110		1417
1859							1389
1860							96
1861					643		945
1862	262		145		40		1059
1863	930						285
1864							2322
1865							
1866				677			1469
1867	228			9864	1280		2292
1868	1,430			7573	410		1910
1869	2,767		1080	1550			5494
1870	205			1757	80		6712
1871	34,232	270	600	890			2730
1872	1,312	1200	115	40			855
1873	2,146			6282			775
1874	2,133		230			2795	2164
1875	1,310		375	1475	1605	781	1749
1876	580						390
1877	2,701						410
1878	805	1235			2365		360
1879	3,385				75		35
1880	36	95					5903
1881				110	580		2488
1882	2,300			245			5136
1883			935				3888
1884	855		345				6553
1885				740		132	457
1886	5,060		70			6943	2189
1887		2228	2704			518	1630
1888		340	12,820				300
1889	405	83	473	4310	6702	7440	5436
1890	1,651			301		4885	1785
1891	33,953						215
1892	8,205	75	754				746
1893	5,127				401	75	1035
1894	5,976	104			560	2305	1372
1895	10,787	132		155	216	205	4230
1896	6,773	8265			288	2786	656
1897	2,799	55	185				2065
1898	14,703	1180	296				3641
1899	3,421	140					3279
1900		420					312

Notes:
(a) Figures are in £, in current prices.   (b) Blank signifies no sale in that year.
(c) Individual countries are those with total sales greater than £15,000, see Table 6.1.

Table 6.3   *Home and foreign orders for machine tools from Greenwood and Batley, 1856–1900*

Year	Home orders £	Export orders £	Total £
1856	3,433		3,433
1857	1,279	1,686	2,965
1858	2,499	1,527	4,026
1859	14,937	1,389	16,326
1860	18,109	96	18,205
1861	12,011	1,588	13,599
1862	2,877	1,506	4,383
1863	30,203	1,215	31,418
1864	1,681	2,322	4,003
1865	625		625
1866	5,841	2,146	7,987
1867	3,054	13,664	16,718
1868	1,046	11,323	12,369
1869	5,839	10,891	16,730
1870	14,817	8,754	23,571
1871	13,178	38,722	51,900
1872	23,931	3,522	27,453
1873	3,377	9,203	12,580
1874	11,079	7,322	18,401
1875	11,851	7,295	19,146
1876	5,948	970	6,918
1877	5,691	3,111	8,802
1878	6,845	4,765	11,610
1879	2,170	3,495	5,665
1880	4,004	6,034	10,038
1881	8,674	3,178	11,852
1882	13,951	7,681	21,632
1883	14,646	4,823	19,469
1884	13,522	7,753	21,275
1885	45,199	1,329	46,528
1886	36,772	14,262	51,034
1887	14,710	7,080	21,790
1888	29,466	13,460	42,926
1889	20,746	24,849	45,595
1890	7,820	8,622	16,442
1891	5,645	34,168	39,813
1892	4,726	9,780	14,506
1893	3,777	6,638	10,415
1894	9,070	10,317	19,387
1895	4,783	15,725	20,508
1896	17,257	18,768	36,025
1897	12,925	5,104	18,029
1898	17,461	19,820	37,281
1899	19,868	6,840	26,708
1900	21,520	732	22,252

Notes:
(a) These figures relate only to orders for which both price and cost are given.
(b) Figures are in current prices.

Figure 6.1. Greenwood and Batley: yearly value of foreign orders

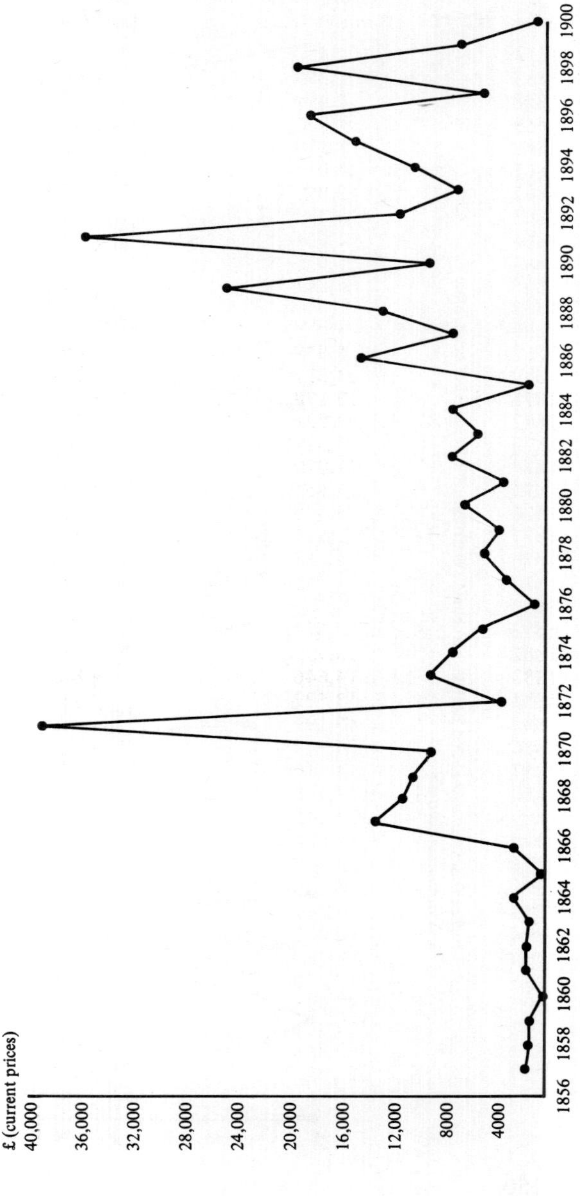

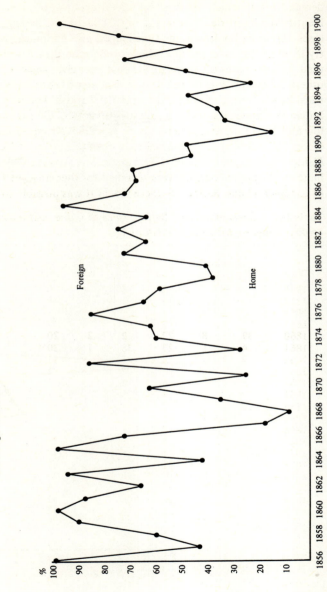

Figure 6.2. Greenwood and Batley: percentage distribution of orders between home and foreign customers

The high level of foreign demand for the machine tools of Greenwood and Batley is of some intrinsic interest; for a closer examination of the demand within which the firm was operating, however, it is necessary to identify the industries to which their 653 customers belonged. In most cases, the order-books and the time ledgers give no indication of the industry in which the machine tool whose production they describe is to be used. In some cases the name of the customer gives some indication, in others the customer is so well known that identification is easy; the Electrical Power Storage Co. Ltd, the Imperial Turkish Armoury, or the Great Indian Peninsular Railway Co., are identifiable by the first method, Waterlow and Sons Ltd, Kynoch and Co. or Friedrich Krupp of Essen by the second. To supplement these methods, the *Directories of Merchants and Manufacturers*, used in chapter 1 above on the structure of the engineering industry during the period, were searched for the names of the customers of Greenwood and Batley. By these means it was possible to identify the

Table 6.4   *Greenwood and Batley: sales to home customers, 1856–1900, broken down by location of customer*

Year	Area								
	1	2	3	4	5	6	7	8	9
1856		1	13	2		20			3
1857	2	11	14	1		6			10
1858	2	2	5			15			3
1859	27	1	12			67			1
1860	39	8	22	2	2	20			2
1861	4	1	23	38	1	30			1
1862	12	1	6	8		11			
1863		70	15	2	1	1	1		1
1864	1	1	40	6		3			1
1865		3	14	3		1			1
1866	3	3	2			23			3
1867		1	5	8		7			
1868			9	1	1	7			
1869	1		8	8	1	15			
1870	2	4	15	18		49			
1871	1	1	18	29		27			1
1872	1	8	23	70	2	20			
1873		5	24	13		3			2
1874	1	3	28	36		32			
1875	5	2	11	13		47			
1876		5	5	7		29			
1877		4	5	18		16			3
1878		1	11	5		27			
1879		2	5			9		1	
1880	7		4	3		13			1
1881	1	14	2	4		23			2

Table 6.4   *Continued*

| Year | \multicolumn{9}{c}{Area} | | | | | | | | |
	1	2	3	4	5	6	7	8	9
1882	9	15	12	6		69			5
1883	15	17	23	3	5	32			4
1884	10	13	12	4		22	1		7
1885	42	3	47	8	1	86			1
1886	23	5	27	6	1	89	1		
1887	14	6	25	6	1	54	2	1	2
1888	8	6	21	17		60			2
1889	4	12	60	9		44	1		
1890	5	3	22	11	1	20			5
1891		5	25	10	2	9	3		1
1892	2	8	14	6		14		1	1
1893	1	2	17	5		17	2		
1894		2	9	5		20	4		2
1895	4	2	12	6	7	11			
1896	10	5	41	25	3	54			1
1897	4	5	19	15	2	21			1
1898	5	3	17	7		14			
1899	10	1	30	7		50	3		
1900	8	3	33	7	3	6	6	6	2

Notes:
    (a) Key to areas: 1. northern England, 2. north-west England, 3. north-east England, 4. Midlands industrial, 5. Midlands agricultural, 6. south-east England, 7. south-west and south England, 8. South Wales, 9. Scotland and Ireland.
    (b) The figures for Leeds, in group 3, includes 'orders' from Greenwood and Batley itself.

majority of the 653 customers, although 112 British and 139 foreign customers could not be positively identified. Fortunately, the more important customers were easier to identify; well over 85% by value of the machine tools sold could be allotted to particular industries. One difficulty was that in some cases machine tools were sold to the multi-product engineering firms described above, such as Whitworth or Armstrong or Krupp, and of course there is no indication of the exact product on which they were to be employed. In these cases, one of three courses could have been adopted. The machine tools could have been allotted to only one of the product or industry groups in which the customer was known to be involved; they could have been allotted to all these groups, either in total or divided up in some arbitrary way; or they could have been relegated to the 'other identified' category. None of these alternatives is entirely satisfactory; the first, and the method of arbitrary division, involves a judgement on the composition of production inside a firm like Whitworth, for which no evidence is available. The method of allocation to all groups produces an element of double counting, and is unsatisfactory particularly if the products of the customer changed markedly over time. The third alternative, relegation to 'other identified', would aggregate the £10,000 worth of machine tools bought by Armstrong, Mitchell in 1885 with the one lathe bought by an amateur turner, F. Boynton, Esq., of Bramley Hill, Croydon, in 1878, thus producing a group of little homogeneity. After experimentation with different methods, it was decided to adopt that of allotting the total volume of sales to a customer like Armstrong or Whitworth to all the industries in which that firm is known to have been involved. The element of double counting is quite large; total sales over the period amounted to £892,318, while the sum of the industry groups listed in table 6.5 is £1,014,305. On the other hand, since the allocation of sales to groups is known, and presented in table 6.5, the effects of this double counting can be discounted in the non-numerical considerations of the experience of the different industries. Since broader categories, which are less likely to be subject to double-counting, are in general used in the numerical investigation of the differences between groups of customers which are described below, and since the element of double counting is important only within a few related groups (such as steam-engine manufacture, hydraulics, pumps and cranes and other home engineering industries) this method seems to have less dangers and to provide more information than the other methods of presentation which were considered.

Table 6.5 shows the result of dividing the sales of machine tools by Greenwood and Batley in terms of the industry of the customer, by the method described, while graphs of sales to some of the major customer groups are shown as figure 3, a–h. The sales shown are in current prices, and it should be remembered that there appears to have been a gradual upward drift of machine tool prices over the period; the sales are, however, not transformed into constant price terms because the evidence is not available which would allow an appropriate deflator to be constructed. Although a general price index is implicitly constructed in the next chapter, problems of quality change, and of mix of machine tools sold to particular customer groups, make suspect the results of applying it to individual groups of customers.

It is clear from these graphs that the pattern of sales over time varied very greatly from one customer group to another, and that analysis of the sales made by Greenwood and Batley needs therefore to be accompanied by description of the demands for the goods made by these customer groups, and their consequent need for machine tools. The best documented demands are those upon the armaments industries, which consumed the majority of Greenwood and Batley's tools, and their experience will therefore be considered at some length. It is unfortunately impossible, in the absence of histories of the other major customer industries, to describe the demands which they exercised on Greenwood and Batley with the same precision.

Table 6.5   *Greenwood and Batley: distribution of customers and sales by industrial group of customer, 1856–1900*

Industry	No. of customers in group	Total sales to group £	No. of years in which sales made	Year First	Last
1. British government	23	169,814	41	1856	1900
2. Colonial governments	13	60,701	40	1859	1899
3. Foreign governments	42	223,514	39	1859	1899
4. Armaments: home	43	166,539	42	1856	1900
5. Armaments: foreign & colonial	19	35,485	23	1867	1900
6. Machine tools: home	33	21,239	34	1857	1900
7. Hand tools: home	30	14,320	30	1860	1900
8. General engineering: home	38	39,929	35	1857	1900
9. Textile machinery: home	29	10,192	28	1856	1899
10. Electrical machinery: home	23	11,204	16	1859*	1897
11. Sewing machines: home	11	3,229	16	1867	1897
12. Agricultural machinery: home	35	3,688	20	1860	1900
13. Cycles: home	20	4,455	6	1890	1897
14. Steam engines: home	48	49,685	41	1857	1900
15. Railways: home	13	15,953	26	1858	1900
16. Railways: foreign & colonial	19	10,958	18	1859	1899
17. Iron and steel trades: home	15	15,952	16	1857	1900
18. Shipbuilding: home	6	1,293	6	1859	1899
19. Hydraulics, pumps & cranes: home	24	51,193	38	1857	1900
20. Printing and paper: home	8	620	7	1857	1897
21. Locks: home	2	484	5	1858	1873
22. Miscellaneous identified	25	3,489	15	1878	1900
23. Unidentified: home	112	31,951	42	1856	1900
24. Unidentified: foreign	139	78,478	41	1857	1899

Notes:

Prices are current prices.

   * This unlikely figure is the result of difficulties in defining exactly the product group to which a particular firm belonged. The next sale to an electrical equipment manufacturer was in 1872, and the major sales to this group occurred after 1880.

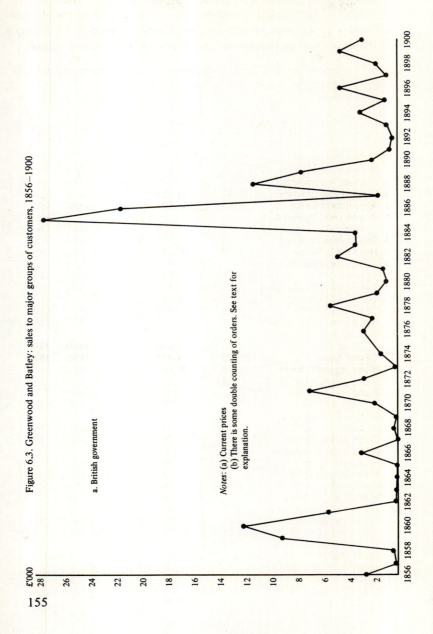

Figure 6.3. Greenwood and Batley: sales to major groups of customers, 1856—1900

a. British government

Notes: (a) Current prices
(b) There is some double counting of orders. See text for explanation.

155

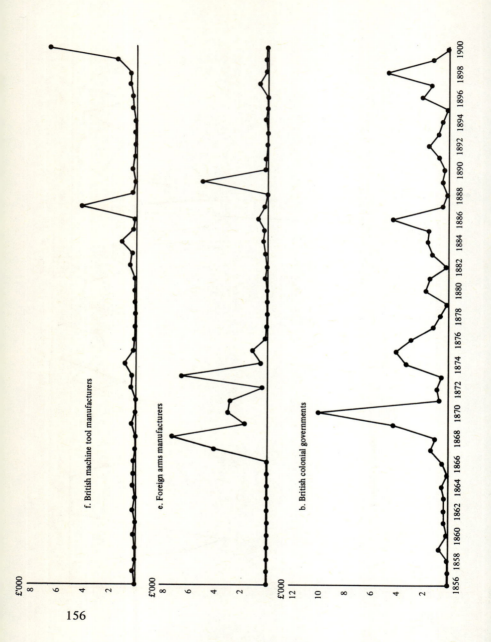

f. British machine tool manufacturers

e. Foreign arms manufacturers

b. British colonial governments

156

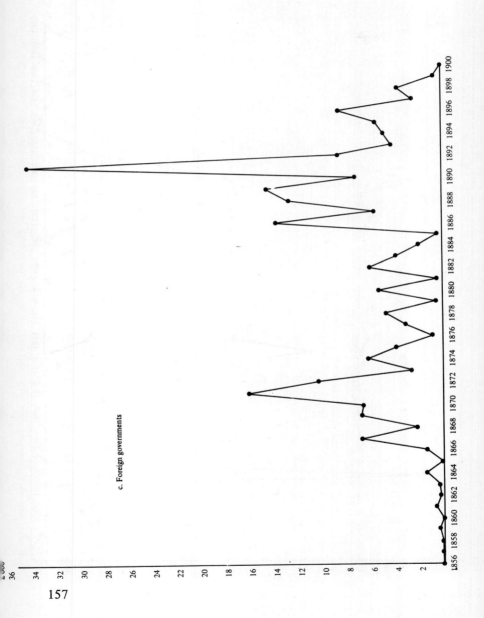

Greenwood and Batley: markets and prices

c. Foreign governments

157

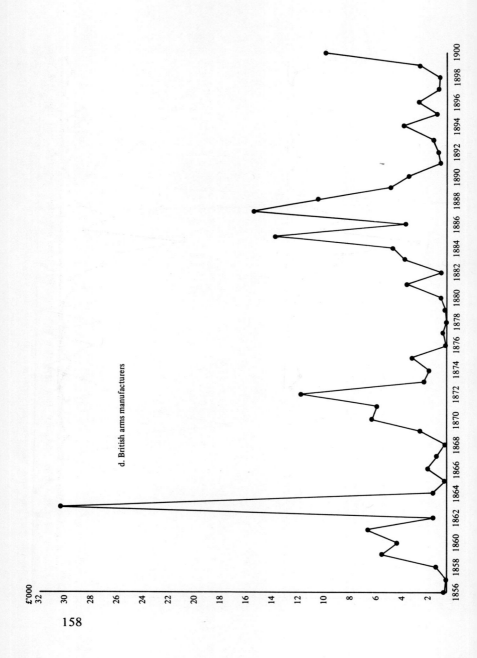

d. British arms manufacturers

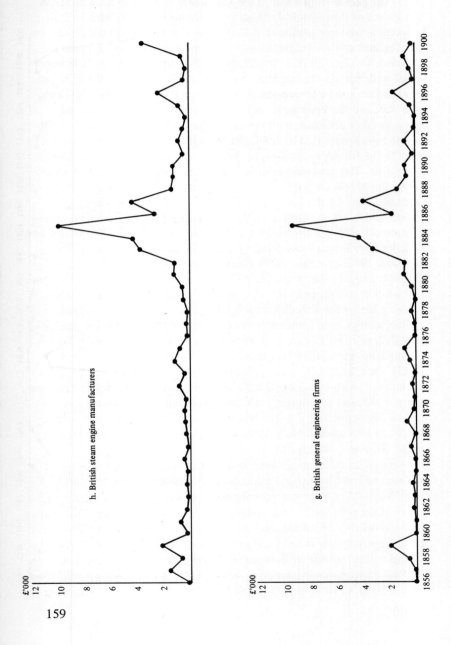

h. British steam engine manufacturers

g. British general engineering firms

Professor Howard has described the development of arms manufacture during the period from 1850 to the first world war as a process in which 'the spread of technological change . . . compelled governments to contemplate a total re-equipment of their armies on an average once every two decades, and confronted navies with still vaster problems of expense' (Howard, 1962, p. 205). In the Crimea, British and French soldiers were armed with muzzle-loading Minie or Enfield rifles, although the Prussian army had adopted a breech-loading 'needle-gun' in 1841. The American Civil War, and the Prussian successes in European wars, spurred experiments in other countries with breech-loading rifles, and the British army adopted the Snider rifle in 1864, the French the Chassepot rifle in 1866. In 1871 the British again changed their equipment, adopting the Martini— Henry rifle. The next change, to repeating, magazine-feeding rifles, came during the 1880s, with rifles of this type being adopted in 1884 by the Germans, 1885 by the French, 1886 by the Austrians, and 1888 by the British (Liddell Hart, 1960, pp. 304—5). Similar transformations occurred in ammunition, with the introduction of metal cartridges in the 1870s, and with the inventions of smokeless powder and the small-calibre bullet (Howard, 1962, pp. 206—7). The introduction of the machine-gun, although dogged by mishandling and technical difficulties, brought another new weapon to European armies from 1867, when the 'mitrailleuse' gun was adopted by the French (Liddell Hart, 1960, pp. 306—7). In land artillery similar developments took place, beginning with the conversion of smooth-bore to rifled guns in the Crimea, and the introduction of breech-loading guns, recoil absorbing gun carriages and new explosives for shells later in the century (Howard, 1962, p. 207). In naval armament progress was equally swift, both in offensive weapons, beginning with the Armstrong gun of 1855, and in defence, with the introduction of armour-plating (Lewis, 1960, pp. 284—5). The Whitehead torpedo, manufactured in Britain by Greenwood and Batley, 'added another element to the naval battle' (Howard, 1962, p. 231).

These technical developments in the art of war were accompanied by, and were to some extent the result of, an expansion during this period of the military strength of the great powers, a corresponding expansion of the power of the military leaders, and a growth in expenditure on armaments. The introduction of conscription by all the major powers except Britain led to large increases in the number of men who could be mobilised, and a corresponding increase in the number of weapons needed to arm them. 'In 1874 Germany had a regular army 420,000 strong and a war establishment of 1,300,000; in 1897 the regular army had increased only by a third, to

545,000, but the war establishment, at 3,400,000 had nearly trebled'. The French war establishment at the latter date was 3,500,000, the Austrian 2,600,000 and the Russian 4,000,000 (Howard, 1962, p. 217). Between 1874 and 1896 total defence expenditure by the major European powers is said to have increased by slightly over 50% (Howard, 1962, p. 240), and it must be remembered that similar increases in expenditure were being undertaken all over the world, in British India, China, Japan, the United States and Latin America. Furthermore, the needs of the armies for transport stimulated expenditure on railway construction, particularly in Russia and Germany.

It is clear that manufacturers of armaments, and of machines to make armaments, were in a fortunate position during this period, as the successes of Krupp, Whitworth and Armstrong, among many others, demonstrate. A rapid rate of obsolescence, combined with an expansion in demand, and an absence of governmental restriction on arms sales, produced what must have seemed at times to be a limitless field for expansion.

This expansion in demand was supplied through a revolution in the methods of manufacture of armaments, the replacement of a traditional craft industry by a factory industry using the most advanced techniques of machining, metallurgy and industrial chemicals.

In the light of this market situation, it seems surprising that the machine tool sales of Greenwood and Batley, which were catering for the international manufacturers of arms, both private and governmental, should exhibit such fluctuations as those shown in figure 6.3, a—e. A complete explanation of such fluctuations would require an examination of the armament policies of the major European and Eastern countries, material on which does not appear to be readily available. In the case of British manufacturers, both government and private, it is possible to discover the course of demand, and the reasons for the fluctuations in demand which can be observed in figures 6.3, a and 6.3, d. The British experience will therefore be examined at some length, and related to the demand facing Greenwood and Batley. Although the precise timing of foreign demand for new armaments and new machinery for making them was different from the British, as shown above, there is no reason to think that the problems of catering for the demand varied very greatly from country to country, and in default of more detailed evidence the British experience must stand as an example.

Machinery for the manufacture and assembly of interchangeable parts for small arms was adopted in Britain during the 1850s. The impetus for this development is normally said to have been the report on the use of interchangeable manufacture in the United States published in 1854 by Whitworth and Wallis as a result of their visit to the New York Exhibition of 1852. This was followed by the visit of John Anderson, later superintendent of the Royal Small Arms Factory at Enfield, to the United States, and the decision by the government to accept his recommendations for the purchase of machine tools from the United States. The buildings to house this machinery at Enfield were begun in 1855, and by 1857 the factory was making arms at the rate of 1000 a week (Mordecai, 1861, p. 106). The majority of the equipment was purchased from the United States, or from Belgium, although a Leeds tradition stated that: 'Owing to the enterprise of Mr. Greenwood, the interchangeable system of manufacture, an American device, was adopted in England' (Sellers, 1912, pp. 400f.). It is possible that Greenwood did design machines for the Woolwich arsenal while working for Sir Peter Fairbairn, but he cannot be credited with such a transformation in manufacturing practice as this statement suggests.

The introduction of the machinery at Enfield, on a larger scale than had at first been contemplated, owing to the needs of the Crimean War, forced the traditional craft gunmakers of Birmingham and the Black Country to consider revising their manufacturing methods. The Birmingham Small Arms Trade, an association of sixteen leading Birmingham gun-makers, had been formed in 1853, partly to protect the traditional trade from the effects of government competition, but in 1860 very little of the gun-making process in Birmingham was carried out by machinery (Allen, 1966, pp. 107–8). The American Civil War, however, during which 'the gun trade . . . was subject to an enormous increase' (Allen, 1966, p. 176), stimulated a switch to more modern methods, and the members of the Birmingham Small Arms Trade:

> organised a company in 1861 to erect a factory at Small Heath, and to equip it with machinery capable of producing interchangeable arms comparable to those manufactured at Enfield. 'Stocking' machinery was purchased from Massachusetts and rifling and boring machinery from Leeds, and thus the famous Birmingham Small Arms Company Limited was set upon its long career. (Allen, 1966, p. 188)

With the setting up of this factory, both the public and the private sectors of the small-arms trade had largely turned to machine-made arms, although the large and prosperous sporting gun section of the Birmingham industry continued to make guns by traditional methods.

The implications of these changes for Greenwood and Batley, as manufacturers of machine tools used in these new factories, can be seen in figure 6.3, a showing the purchases by the government arms factories, and figure 6.3, d showing purchases by private gun-makers. Although much less is known about the manufacture of heavier guns, and the gun carriages needed for them, than about the manufacture of small arms, the heavy orders from Woolwich, from the Royal Carriage Factory, the Rifled Ordnance Department and the Royal Laboratory in 1859 and 1860 show that the introduction of new machine tools to these branches of arms manufacture was being expanded. In the private sector, the expansion of demand for machine tools during the American Civil War is clear in figure 6.3, d. In 1861 the newly established Birmingham Small Arms Company ordered 100 machine tools worth £6101 from Greenwood and Batley, following this in 1862 with orders for five more machines worth £450. The major purchaser in this period was however Fraser Trenholm and Co. of Liverpool, and it seems likely that the 348 machine tools worth £30,319, which they bought in 1863, were in fact shipped to the United States, since Fraser Trenholm were not prominent as manufacturers of small arms. The other major purchases in this period were from makers of larger guns, the Elswick Ordnance Company and Thomas Firth and Sons of Sheffield, the former being involved in the 'Battle of the Guns' between Whitworth and Armstrong at this period.

The ending of the American Civil War produced depression in the private sector of the armaments industry, and through it in sales of machine tools, although the traditional trade, still largely unmechanised, benefited from the Prussian-Danish War of 1865–6 and the Austro-Prussian War of 1868 (Allen, 1966, p. 186). Although B.S.A. were occupied between 1866 and 1868 in the conversion of 100,000 muzzle-loading Enfield rifles to breech-loaders, using the Snider action, they do not seem to have bought new machinery for this purpose, and the government factories were presumably also well-equipped. Purchases of machine tools are thus low in this period. Some recovery in the trade came with the Franco-Prussian War of 1870–1, and Greenwood and Batley received further large orders in this period from B.S.A., and from the two other factory small-arms manufacturers, the London Small Arms Company and Westley Richards Limited, and the latter's successor, the National Arms and Ammunition Company. After the war 'For some years . . . the two Birmingham firms were busy supplying British and foreign governments with the new types of breech-loader . . . ' (the small-bore rifle), and the large orders placed by the National Arms and Ammunition Company for machine tools in 1872 show the effect of this demand in an expansion of capacity in the private industry. However, as Allen states:

. . . after 1876 the cloud descended . . . The leading Continental powers

163

had by that time equipped factories of their own for meeting their needs, and Enfield proved capable of satisfying the peacetime demands of the British services. Consequently, the orders received by the trade were insufficient to occupy more than a small part of their plant.

The National Arms and Ammunition Co. was wound up in 1882, after an attempt by the three leading small-arms companies to share orders had been frustrated by the War Office, and B.S.A. was forced into an early unsuccessful attempt to make bicycles (Allen, 1966, pp. 218–29). Sales of Greenwood and Batley's machine tools show a consequent low level of demand during this period.

The private small-arms and ordnance industries, and the Enfield and other government factories, were rescued from stagnation during the next decade, from about 1884 onwards, by the coincidence of the two types of stimulus to demand for arms, a war scare and the decision by the War Office to change the pattern of arms. As Allen puts it, during 1884.

> Prospects began to improve owing to the proposed adoption by the War Office of the magazine rifle; and then, in 1885, both the Enfield and the private factories were roused to a sudden activity by the danger of a rupture between Russia and England. (Allen, 1966, p. 219)

The results of this burst of activity can be clearly seen in the sales of machine tools by Greenwood and Batley. Purchases by all the government manufacturing establishments pushed orders from this sector to £27,995 in 1885, and £21,852 in the following year, by far the highest levels reached during the whole period from 1856 to 1900. Similarly in the private sector, orders particularly from the heavy ordnance- and shell-makers, Armstrong Mitchell, John Brown, and the Nordenfeldt Gun and Ammunition Co. among others, allowed sales to this sector to rise above £10,000 in 1885, 1887 and 1888.

As in the late 1870s, the expansion of capacity in both the public and the private sectors produced a falling-off in demand for new machine tools in the 1890s, although the private sector of the arms business was kept busy by the adoption of the Lee-Metford magazine rifle by the War Office in 1890 (Allen, 1966, p. 266). Greenwood and Batley continued to receive orders from armaments makers in this country during the decade, although their financial difficulties, during this period, and their difficulties with government purchasers, show that demand was not very buoyant, at least until the outbreak of the Boer War, at the end of the period for which detailed records of the operations of the firm can be used.

It is clear that sales of machine tools by Greenwood and Batley were closely related to the vicissitudes of demand in the armaments industry, although the firm was to some extent shielded from the shifts in demand which so badly affected the private arms firms in the 1876 to 1884 period by their ability to sell to the ordnance as well as small-arms sectors. Greenwood and Batley were, however, as the graphs show, able to maintain a substantial sale of machine tools to public and private arms buyers in the intervals between the abnormal peaks and troughs of demand which have so far been described. That they could do so was due to the constant innovation by the firm of new methods of manufacture, which enabled them to persuade the arms manufacturers to buy their tools, since the old tools were rendered obsolescent, together with the replacement expenditure as machines deteriorated in use.

The process of innovation in the small-arms field is extremely difficult to delineate in detail, largely because, even with the reasonably detailed descriptions of the machines given in the Greenwood and Batley order-books, such descriptions tend to be concerned with the job that the machine tool will do, rather than with the way in which it will do it. Thus a barrel-turning machine sold in 1860 was a different machine from a barrel-turning machine sold in 1880, but the name has not changed; it may be described as a 'No. 2' machine or as being of 'improved pattern', but this does not give enough information to enable any definite conclusions on the pace of technical change to be drawn. However, there is one case in which evidence exists on a technical change in this field which was large enough to render the previous machinery entirely obsolete, and it can be presumed that similar innovations were made in other fields. In evidence to the Morley Committee of 1887 (the Select Committee on the Organisation and Administration of the Manufacturing Departments of the Army), two witnesses spoke of the introduction of new barrel-boring machinery into the Enfield Small Arms Factory. Colonel Henry T. Arbuthnot described in some detail the process by which new machinery was bought for the Factory:

> If I hear of any new machinery which would be of assistance in my particular work I generally go and look at it myself, if it is running any-where else and I try and find out what their experience has been, and I send the foreman of my tool room sometimes to look at the machine and to give me his technical opinion upon it, and if I think it is desirable to try it at Enfield I ask for authority to purchase one perhaps first, and if it answers then I go in for it more largely. That is very much the case with regard to the barrel-boring machines; that was an invention of a member of the firm of Greenwood and Batley; he first applied it in a factory which he fitted up for the Government of Italy at Terni. I saw it

and thought the machine worked all right and it appeared to me to be very good, but the result that he told me they got in Italy appeared to me to be so extraordinarily favourable that I could hardly believe it, but I obtained authority to purchase one machine to try, and I found that he did not over-state the case one bit. I thought perhaps that one machine would not be a fair test, so I got half-a-dozen more, and they all worked just as satisfactorily as the first did, and now the whole of my boring of barrels is done by these machines. I save about ⅓ or ¼ per barrel and one man now does the same work as half-a-dozen did before. (P.P., 1887, Q.7403)

Mr McGee, manager of the Enfield factory, amplified to the committee the evidence of his superintendent. His evidence illustrates not only the high gains of this innovation, but also the difficulty of attributing credit for it to any one person or company.

Q.7754. We have been told that your cost has been reduced, has that come about through your ordering iron nearer the size, or has it partly come about on wages or on improved machinery? — On improved machinery principally.

Q.7755. Who is responsible for designing that improved machinery? — I have had a great deal to do with it. A little while ago we paid 2s. each for drilling gun barrels. We have now introduced a new machine made by Greenwood and Batley which has reduced the cost of that operation to 3d.

Q.7756. By whom was that designed? — In the first place it was a Belgium notion, but it was perfected by Greenwood and Batley and ourselves.

Q.7757. I suppose the principal reason for that machine being a success is that you can work with water at from 60 to 70 lbs. pressure to pump the water to clear the swarf? — That has a great deal to do with it.

Q.7758. Was it the Belgium idea that you should use water for that pressure? — I think it was Greenwood and Batley's notion.

Q.7759. But was it the Belgium idea that you should work from both ends? — Yes. (P.P., 1887)

It is thus clear that Greenwood and Batley were able to sell at least some machinery to the arms manufacturers as the result of technical advance rendering the existing machinery obsolete; the Morley Committee was later told of the necessity of selling the old barrel-boring machinery, probably for scrap. Changes of pattern would also, with the specialised machinery used for small-arms manufacture, make it necessary for new machinery to be bought. Replacement expenditure, the purchase of machinery simply because the old had worn out, is difficult to identify from the Greenwood and Batley records, although in a number of cases orders made reference to previous orders, asking for a machine of the same pattern. Both these types of expenditure, that caused by technical advance, and that for replacements, helped Greenwood and Batley to weather the falls in demand caused by peace or the satisfaction of the army or navy with its existing weapons.

In the case of the machine tools sold to the armaments manufacturers in this country, it is therefore possible to identify quite accurately the exact cause of expansion or decline in demand for arms, and its indirect effect on Greenwood and Batley.

The causes operating to produce orders for machine tools from foreign governments, shown in figure 6.3, c, and from foreign private arms manufacturers, shown in figure 6.3, e, are presumably much the same in origin as those motivating the British arms manufacturers, although the timing differs. The first major peak in sales, in 1867 to 1872 in the case of the governments, and 1867 to 1871 in the case of the private manufacturers, is clearly related to the Austro-Prussian and Franco-Prussian wars of this period, but in the absence of any detailed studies of rearmament during this period in countries other than Britain, explanation of the second major peak, between 1889 and 1891, is more difficult. The major peak in 1891, when machine tools worth £34,896 were sold to foreign governments, is largely the result of sales to the Russian government, but it is not clear why these purchases were made. The construction of the Trans-Siberian railway began in that year, but the majority of the tools sold to Russia were light tools, principally milling machines, together with a number of rifling machines, so it is likely that a small-arms factory was being equipped.

In the remainder of the industrial groups into which Greenwood and Batley's customers can be divided, identification of the exact causes of changes in demand is a haphazard process. Demand for machine tools is essentially a derived demand, and identification of its causes thus depends on identification of demand changes for all the industries to which machine tools are sold. In general, the sales by Greenwood and Batley seem to follow the familiar chronology of the period of the great depression (particularly if the double counting caused by the inclusion of Armstrong, Mitchell in the General engineering and Hydraulics, pumps and cranes groups is discounted, thus removing the boom in these groups in the 1880s). Identifi-

167

cation in the way that is possible in the sales to the armaments industry seems impossible to achieve, if only because Greenwood and Batley are in no sense monopoly suppliers to the other industrial groups, as they became in certain fields of armaments machinery. Thus, in the general engineering groups, a fall or rise in demand for Greenwood and Batley's machine tools may be the result of changes in demand in the industry, or of the attractiveness of a particular tool made by the firm, or of some influence undiscernible at this distance.

In this section the industrial and geographical distribution of the customers for the machine tools made by Greenwood and Batley has been investigated. It has been shown that sales to this country were largely determined by government rearmament policies, and it has been inferred that similar causes determined the pattern of orders from foreign manufacturers of armaments. Non-arms sales are less easy to ascribe to particular changes in demand conditions in the customer industries, in the absence of detailed information on these demand changes, and because of the more competitive nature of the market for machine tools in those fields.

Market differentiation

In the previous section the existence of a number of distinct markets for the machine tools of Greenwood and Batley has been asserted. Identification of these markets has however been solely in terms of the geographical location or industrial involvement of the customers of the firm. In this section, the order and cost data provided by the records of Greenwood and Batley will be examined in order to see whether the market structure which has been described has any other than nominal significance. In other words, did the different markets in which machine tools were sold affect either the profit levels that could be achieved, or the methods needed to penetrate them, or the behaviour of a firm such as Greenwood and Batley which was faced with satisfying the needs of so heterogeneous a selection of customer firms?

A convenient measure of the degree of competition in different markets for machine tools, and the success of Greenwood and Batley in selling to these markets, is the level of profits which could be attained, and maintained over time, in each market. A significantly higher level of profit in one market over some period of time would suggest that Greenwood and Batley was either in a monopoly or oligopoly position in that market, or that it was more efficient in producing for that market than for others. The first topic to be investigated is therefore the profit levels gained by the firm.

Taking first the geographical division of sales, profit levels were in general higher for sales to some foreign countries than for sales to home customers.

Table 6.6, shows the average profit levels realised, over the whole period from 1856 to 1900, on sales to Great Britain and to the major foreign customer countries.

Table 6.6   *Greenwood and Batley: profit levels on sales to foreign customers, 1856–1900*

Country	Average profits as % of sales
Italy	23.0
Japan	18.9
China	17.5
France	13.4
Austria	12.7
Russia	10.8
Germany	6.5
India	−2.6
Belgium	−5.8
Great Britain	5.7

Note: The average profits for Russia and Belgium are reduced by one large loss in each case. Excluding these losses the figures would be 15.1% and 6.3% respectively.

Z-tests for difference of means reveal that, at the 5% level, there are significant differences between the profit levels given in table 6.6 for Britain and those for several foreign countries, while the difference between some foreign countries are not significant. Thus the differences between Britain and France and Britain and Russia are significant, those between Japan and France and France and Russia are not.

Further evidence bearing on the difference in profit levels on sales to home and foreign customers is provided by a comparison of the profit levels on sales to each of the industrial groupings of customers. The relevant comparisons are in government purchases, private arms companies' purchases, railway companies' purchases, and in the unidentified groups, since in all these cases a distinction has been made between home and overseas sales. The average profits as a percentage of total value of sales were 8.31% for home government sales, 5.72% for colonial government sales, and 15.04% for foreign government sales. Within industrial groups the same distinction applied; average profits for sales to home private arms manufacturers were 11.73%, for comparable foreign sales 16.67%. For railway companies the figures are, home −13.99% (i.e. losses overall), foreign 18.93%, and for the unidentified groups profits on home sales averaged 0.23%, and on foreign sales 12.75%.

There are a number of possible explanations for this divergence in profit levels, and they will be considered in turn. Firstly, it is possible that the 'profit' on foreign orders includes within it some element of transport cost. However, it appears from the order-books that in normal circumstances prices were quoted free on board at British ports (or free on rail at Leeds for home orders). Only exceptionally were prices quoted c.i.f., one example being an order for machine tools for a Russian customer where alternative prices were given according to the possibility of rail or sea transport. Normally, therefore, the price quoted would include only a small element of transport cost, and it seems reasonable to reject the first hypothesis that the observed differences in home and foreign profit levels were caused by this factor. A second justification for rejecting this hypothesis is that there is no significant difference in profit levels between sales to nearby and to distant foreign countries; the difference in profit levels between France and Japan, or France and Russia shown in table 6.6 is non-significant. Had transport costs been included in price, it would have been likely that a differential would be observable between close and distant countries; its absence is at least negative confirmation of the rejection of this first hypothesis.

A second hypothesis to explain the difference between profit levels on home and foreign sales would be that the firm used a different pricing policy, perhaps deliberately securing a higher mark-up on foreign sales to compensate it for the volatility of the foreign market referred to above, or alternatively reducing the quality of goods ordered by foreign customers so as to obtain a higher profit margin. An explanation in these terms would require that, for a given machine, the profit level obtained on a home sale would be smaller than that obtained on a foreign sale. It is thus possible to test, for each sub-type of machine, to see whether there is a significant difference in the profit level as a percentage of the value of the machine sold, between home and foreign sales. One difficulty in such a test is the heterogeneity of the machines even within the sub-types by which they are described, a factor that produced very large variances for the calculated mean profits. However, working with these variances and applying again a z-test for difference of means, no machine sub-type shows a significant difference at the 5% level between profit levels on home and foreign sales. Had this second hypothesis been true, that home and foreign sales would show different profit levels for comparable machines, then at least some significant differences should have been found, even with the large variances which have been mentioned. It seems reasonable, therefore, to reject the hypothesis that the firm had some policy which resulted in foreign customers being charged more for their machine tools than were home customers.

The third hypothesis which would explain the observed difference in profit levels between home and foreign sales is that the mix of machines ordered by foreign customers was different from that ordered by home customers, and that sales to foreign customers were composed of machines on which a higher profit level was obtained. In other words, the hypothesis is that the difference was not so much a result of the location of the customer but of the machines which he was buying. In order to test this hypothesis it is necessary to examine firstly the mix of machine tools ordered by home and foreign customers, and secondly the profit levels obtained on different types of machine tools sold.

Table 6.7 sets out the numbers of machine tools sold to home and foreign customers, broken down by the types of machines that were bought. It refers to all machines for which more than ten home and ten foreign orders were received during the whole period from 1856 to 1900, that is the major types of machine tools sold by Greenwood and Batley.

A chi-square test on the data present in table 6.7 permits the rejection,

Table 6.7   *Greenwood and Batley: numbers of machine tools sold to home and foreign customers, broken down by type of machine tool, 1856–1900*

| Machine type | Number sold to: | | Total |
	Home customers	Foreign customers	
1. Lathe	1757	837	2594
2. Planing machine	145	48	193
3. Drilling machine	823	293	1116
4. Milling machine	2255	1644	3899
5. Grinding machine	98	41	139
6. Shaping machine	156	180	336
7. Slotting machine	124	114	238
9. Press	51	15	66
13. Wheel- and gear-cutting machine	83	29	112
15. Boring machine	329	268	597
16. Punching and shearing machine	62	53	115
17. Component parts orders	335	422	757
21. Slitting machine	123	155	278
25. Screw-making machine	366	106	472
27. Rifling machine	132	165	297
33. Cutter-sharpening machine	125	16	141
35. Bolt-making machine	90	34	124
Totals	7054	4420	11,474

at the 5% level, of the null hypothesis that the two groups, machine tools sold to home and to foreign customers, are similar in mix. ($X^2 = 491.99$ with 16 degrees of freedom.) Less rigorously, it is clear that certain types of machines were sold in much greater frequency to foreign customers than the proportions sold in total would suggest. Thus in total, taking the groups of machines given in table 6.7, of the 11,474 machine tools included 61.5% were sold to home customers, 38.5% to foreign customers. Table 6.8 shows the data for table 6.7 converted into percentage form, with the machine tools ranked according to the proportion sold to home customers.

It is thus apparent that there were significant differences in the mix of machine tools sold by Greenwood and Batley to home and to foreign customers. It is possible, therefore, that this difference may explain the observed difference in profit levels obtained from these two groups of customers.

To confirm this, it would be necessary to demonstrate that foreign buyers were buying tools on which higher profit margins were charged. A test of this would be to examine whether, for type of machines, profit level is correlated with a tendency for a machine to be sold abroad. To test this the machines listed in table 6.8 were ranked according to the proportion sold to home customers, that is in the order in which they are given in that table. They were further ranked according to profit level, that is the type with the highest average profit, in fact bolt-making machines, with an average profit of 29%, was ranked highest. The hypothesis would suggest that a correlation analysis between these two sets of ranks should produce a correlation coefficient which would be positive and significantly large. In fact computation of the Spearman rank correlation coefficient gives a value of -0.35; this is non-significant and has a sign opposite to that predicted. It would thus seem that no credence can be attached to the hypothesis that foreign sales were of machines which had higher profit levels than had machines sold to home buyers.

The difficulty remains of explaining why this observed difference in profit levels occurred, if all the hypotheses so far advanced must be rejected. It is conceivable that the explanation lies in a mixture of the second and third hypotheses (with conceivably a slight influence from the first). In other words, the joint effect of the sale to foreign markets of a selection of machines slightly different from those sold to home buyers, combined with a slight tendency to charge higher profit margins on foreign than on home sales, combined perhaps with an element of transport charges in foreign prices, may provide together an explanation of the dif-

Table 6.8   *Conversion of table 6.7 into percentage form (summing across columns)*

Machine type	% sold to home customers	% sold to foreign customers
33. Cutter-sharpening machine	89	11
25. Screw-making machine	78	22
9. Press	77	23
2. Planing machine	75	25
13. Wheel- and gear-cutting machine	74	26
3. Drilling machine	74	26
35. Bolt-making machine	73	27
5. Grinding machine	71	29
1. Lathe	68	32
4. Milling machine	58	42
15. Boring machine	55	45
16. Punching and shearing machine	54	46
7. Slotting machine	52	48
6. Shaping machine	46	54
17. Component parts	44	56
21. Slitting machines	44	56
27. Rifling machine	44	56

Note: The line drawn between lathe and milling machine figures indicates the average proportions found in the totals, that is 61.5 : 38.5.

ference in profit levels, although individually none of these tendencies can provide such an explanation. It is further possible that the testing of these hypotheses on the broad groupings of machines listed in tables 6.7 and 6.8 has, because of the lack of homogeneity within the types, obscured the explanation.

One can combine the hypotheses by examining the profit levels obtained on home and foreign orders for sub-types of machines, within those groups which were sold predominantly to home or predominantly to foreign buyers. Specifically, all sub-types of machines of which more than fifty were sold were selected, a total of thirty-four sub-types (three sub-types, which sold more than fifty in total, but less than ten to one of the categories of home and foreign buyers, were excluded). The machines within these groups were then classified according to whether they were sold to home or to foreign customers, and average profit levels were calculated for each type. These profit levels were then summed over each of the four divisions, home sales in predominantly home sold sub-types, foreign sales in predominantly foreign-sold sub types, home sales in predominantly foreign sold sub-types, and foreign sales in predominantly home sold sub-types. Averages were then calculated for each of these four divisions. If both these hypotheses were interacting, one would expect that the highest profit levels would be found in the foreign sales in the predominantly foreign sold group, and the lowest profit levels in the home sales in the predominantly home sold division, with the other two divisions in between, their order depending on the relative importance of the explanation in terms of mix and the explanation in terms of different pricing policies.

The results of this analysis were:

Group
Predominantly home sold
(22 sub-types):   Sold to home buyers   9%
                                          Sold to foreign buyers 13%

Predominantly foreign
sold (12 sub-types):   Sold to home buyers   10%
                                          Sold to foreign buyers 16%

These figures confirm the suggestion that the explanation for the higher profit levels lies in a mixture of the different types of machines ordered by foreign buyers, and a tendency for orders to foreign buyers to be higher priced regardless of machine type. The difference between the extreme figures, 9% and 16% is statistically significant at the 5% level for a one tail test ($z = 1.88$), which is used since the direction of the difference is predicted. It would also appear, although the differences are not significant, that the influence of different pricing for foreign orders is slightly higher than the influence of the different mix of orders, since the two central figures, 13% and 10%, are in the order shown.

It is thus apparent that Greenwood and Batley sold their machine tools in two markets which were distinguished not only by their geographical location, but also by the level of profits which the firm could attain. It is however, conceivable that the true distinction between the markets in which Greenwood and Batley was involved is not in terms of location of the customers, but is the result of differences in profit levels to be obtained in sales to different industries. It is conceivable, for instance, that if higher profit margins were obtainable on sales to customers involved in the manufacture of armaments, then the importance of such sales, particularly to foreign buyers, could produce the effect which has hitherto been ascribed to the influence of differences between home and export markets. Calculation of the average amount of profit as a percentage of total sales to each industrial grouping of the customers of the firm gives some support to such an explanation. Table 6.9 sets out the results of such a calculation. Calculation of the average profits on the five 'armaments' groups shows that these profits, at 11.5%, are considerably higher than the average profits for the remainder of the industrial groups, which in fact show an average loss of 1.5%. (Average profit on the eleven groups where overall profits were made is 7.3%.) Average profits on sales to the home arms groups were 9.5%, and on the remaining home groups 3.7%. There would therefore seem to be some justification in arguing that Greenwood and Batley were successful in obtaining higher profit levels on foreign sales, and also on sales to producers of armaments, although it is impossible to estimate the relative contribution of these two factors to the differential profit levels which have been observed.

It now remains to explain why profit levels should have differed in the ways which have been considered, and how this pattern of involvement in

Table 6.9   *Greenwood and Batley: profits as a percentage of total sales, broken down by industrial group of customers, 1856–1900*

Industrial group	Profits as % of sales	No. of orders
1. British government	7.05	634
2. Colonial governments	5.72	269
3. Foreign governments	16.03	743
4. Armaments: home	11.82	669
5. Armaments: foreign and colonial	16.67	115
6. Machine tools: home	9.94	91
7. Hand tools: home	−7.58	81
8. General engineering: home	4.71	171
9. Textile machinery: home	−1.67	80
10. Electrical machinery: home	−13.59	81
11. Sewing machines: home	5.04	46
12. Agricultural machinery: home	2.57	31
13. Cycles: home	−6.97	48
14. Steam engines: home	3.20	225
15. Railways: home	−11.05	84
16. Railways: foreign and colonial	18.93	43
17. Iron and steel products: home	8.13	30
18. Shipbuilding: home	−14.38	8
19. Hydraulics, pumps & cranes: home	9.32	201
20. Printing and paper machinery: home	−35.97	9
21. Locks: home	−19.42	7
22. Miscellaneous identified	4.33	41
23. Unidentified: home	1.17	244
24. Unidentified: foreign and colonial	13.17	390

Notes:
(a)   This table is based on all orders for which both price and cost are given.
(b) $N = 4170$.

what can be considered as two different markets for machine tools affected the profitability and the operations of Greenwood and Batley.

The explanation of how Greenwood and Batley were able to obtain higher profits on sales to some customers than to others is likely to lie in differences in the competitive position in different markets. There is a paucity of evidence on the degree of competition in the markets for machine tools, but it would seem likely that the export trades, particularly to countries without their own developed engineering industries, would be less competitive than the market within Great Britain, in which a large number of engineering firms were competing. Within Great Britain, also, there is considerable evidence, some of which was considered in the chapter on the structure of the industry, that machine tool firms, although willing to make almost any tool required, preferred to specialise in tools for a particular trade, and to build up connections with that trade in an effort to ensure a regular flow of orders. Thus the market for, for instance, machine tools for the manufacture of printing machinery might be less competitive than the market for, for instance, machine tools for engine building, simply because, as the market for tools for printing machinery was smaller, not all manufacturers would build up the connections with the printing trade which would enable them to design suitable tools or modifications of tools for this particular purpose. It is likely that this would apply with particular force to the sale of machine tools for arms partly because of the relatively restricted number of customers for such machinery, and partly because of the specialised nature of many of the tools, whether because of their complexity, as with some mass production machinery, or their size, as with large gun-boring lathes, which only a small number of firms could undertake to make.

In the case of Greenwood and Batley, these theoretical considerations which suggest that the market for arms machinery was not perfectly competitive are borne out by direct evidence on the relationship between the firm and the British government. The government, in its desire to build up a stable relationship with a small number of firms, was acting in much the same way as that described by Mr Trebilcock in his study on the supply of cordite (Trebilcock, 1966). In the Report and Minutes of Evidence of the 1887 Committee on the Organisation and Administration of the Manufacturing Departments of the Army, it was stated that tenders for the supply of engineers machine tools for the army were normally requested from twenty-seven firms, and for special machine tools eleven firms were approached. Colonel Barlow, the superintendent of the Royal Laboratory at Woolwich, which supplied ammunition for the army and navy, described to the committee the system that was adopted:

Q.2723. You were saying that the Manager and Assistant Manager designed all your machinery; after having designed it, what course do you take in obtaining new machinery? — One of two courses is taken, sometimes we make the machinery in a great measure in the department or else modify the old plant, which not infrequently happens; otherwise it is put out to contract through the Director of Contracts.

Q.2724. Do you ask two or three different firms to contract for it? — As a rule we endeavour to put as many names in as we can. I would like to mention that there is one maker to whom we generally give the plant for small arms cartridge manufacture, namely, Greenwood and Batley, because they first made this plant, which is rather a specialty of theirs; but as a rule we endeavour to put a large number of names on our contract paper.

Q.2725. May I ask why you went to Greenwood and Batley? — You are going back too long before my time, but I think I may say that they are a firm who are very well known in the trade as manufacturers of that class of plant.

Q.2726. Do I understand you to say that you went to them because they had made for you in previous years? — We went to them partly on that account, but you must remember that I put other names on the paper even in that case; I think, as a matter of fact, you will find that Greenwood and Batley have got our orders for the small arms machinery. In our last contract we put in other names; the thing was gone into with the Director of Contracts, and, on the whole, we thought it was best to go to them.

Q.2727. When you put other names forward and allow them to tender, do you take the lowest tender? — Not invariably; other circumstances may come in and the lowest tender may occasionally be cut out by time; but, as a general rule, unless we can show cause against we take the lowest. (P.P., 1887)

It is clear that in this, and presumably in other fields of government purchases, a free market in the supply of machine tools did not exist, the opportunity to tender for government contracts being restricted. Of course, the restriction of the market in this way does not necessarily imply that the prices charged will be inflated; the object, after all, of competitive tendering is to obtain for the purchaser the lowest possible price. There is however evidence that the restriction of the opportunity of tendering to a

177

small number of machine tool firms, all of them known to each other, allowed these firms, by collusion, to share the market and to fix prices to suit themselves. Evidence on market sharing and price fixing agreements is normally elusive, since the participants in such arrangements naturally preferred them to remain secret, but in this particular case of machine tool supply to arms manufacturers some evidence has survived, in the form of a private out-letter book belonging to the firm of James Archdale and Co. of Birmingham. In view of the exceptional evidence contained in this correspondence on market sharing and price fixing arrangements, it will be quoted at length. It should be remembered that the letters are those sent by Archdale's; the replies have not been preserved.

October 7th. 1889 To Messrs. Wm. Muir and Co.[1]
Dear Sir, We have enquiries from Enfield for the following – Will you please say per return what enquiries you have so that we may arrange matters. Yours truly.
1 Vertical Drilling Machine E30[2]
2 Capstan Machines
2 10″ lathes E43
5 . . . [illegible] drilling machines E28
10 Cross milling machines E11
5 Cross milling machines E12
11 Back-gearèd cross millers E13
1 Screw capstan lathe E18
2 Trimming presses E42
4 Cross millers E14
2 Capstan lathes E44
2 Drilling machines E24
10 Edge milling machines E15
1 Shaping machine 12″ E23
1 6″ shaper E19
2 Shaping machines E22

Oct. 7th 1889 To Arthur Greenwood Esq.[3]
Dear Sir, We have enquiries from Enfield for the following and will you please say per return what enquiries you have, so that we may arrange matters. Yours truly. [There follows the list of machine tools as in the previous letter.]

October 12th 1889 To Arthur Greenwood Esq.
Dear Sir, Thanks for your wire. We have wired 'our Manchester friend',

and he agrees to be at your office on Wednesday afternoon at 3 o'clock. Our Mr. Archdale will also attend at same date and time. Yours truly.

Oct. 14th 1889 To Messrs. Wm. Muir and Co.
Dear Sirs. We thank you for yours of the 12th inst. We wrote to you on Saturday appointing the meeting in Leeds for 3 p.m. on Wednesday at Mr. Arthur Greenwood's office. We note that you are quoting £14.10.0d. for the 12 drills to Smallheath.[4] We are quoting £15 each delivery 3 months. We wired you this afternoon to kindly send us tonight certain the prices you are quoting Smallheath for the special lathes and drills they require. We are holding over our quotation until we know this. Yours etc.

Oct. 15th, 1889 To Messrs. Wm. Muir and Co.
Dear Sirs, Thanks for yours of 14th inst. We have quoted prices etc. as below.

4	6″ backgeared screwcutting lathes	£60 each	4 weeks time
4	6″ plain lathes for cylindrical part of bolt	£45 each	14 weeks time
3	6″ plain lathes for inside of bolt handle	£45 each	14 weeks time
5	6″ copy turning lathes	£55 each	14 weeks time
2	8″ spherical rest lathes, for rough finish turning knob	£45 each	14 weeks time
2	6″ compound slide rest lathes for rough finish turning shank	£38 each	14 weeks time
12	Quick speed drills	£15 each	12 weeks time
3	Horizontal drilling machines	£40 each	14 weeks time
1	Horizontal drilling machine	£40 each	14 weeks time

We confirm our wire of this morning: 'Mr. Archdale will meet Mr. Muir at 2 o'clock tomorrow afternoon Queen's Hotel Leeds'. They can then proceed to Mr. A. Greenwood's office, the meeting being fixed for 3 o'clock. Yours etc.

Oct. 21 1889 To Arthur Greenwood Esq.
Dear Sir, We quoted B.S.A. Co. Smallheath on 14th inst. for machines as follows:– [There follows list as in previous letter, identical except for two small changes in times of delivery.]

Nov. 7th 1889 To Alfred Muir Esq.
Dear Sir. We thank you very much for yours of 6th. Up to the present we have no orders from Enfield. When we hear anything we will at once let you know. Yours etc.

Nov. 12th 1889 To Arthur Greenwood Esq.

Dear Sir, The only orders at present received from Enfield by us are:

2 10″ lathes at £146 each

1 6″ shaper at £42

2 Automatic Bolt-shaping machines at £50 each

1 12″ shaper at £70

What have you received. Yours respectfully etc.

Nov. 12th 1889 To Alfred Greenwood Esq.

Dear Sir, We thank you for yours of 13th inst. Of course we are sorry we have not got a better share of Enfield work but at the same time we are glad to think the prices have been kept up. We received intimation this morning that our tender was declined. If you will kindly favour us with a specification of lathes required we shall have pleasure in quoting or at any rate consider whether we can put in for them or not. — Per same post we send you our catalogue. Yours etc.

Nov. 16th 1889 To Arthur Greenwood Esq.

Dear Sir, Many thanks for your specification returned herewith. As at present situated, we could not quote for the tools required. We thought perhaps you were requiring a largish quantity of 6″ or 8″ lathes and then we could have given you a quotation. You will also do better by buying the stocks and dies direct from the maker (we do not make them). Yours respectfully.

Nov. 16th, 1889 To Arthur Greenwood Esq.

Dear Sir Yours of 14th. re K. and Co. Ltd.[5] The matter we fear will prove rather difficult to adjust to our mutual satisfaction. We don't like the plan of accepting commissions — if you get the order we do not wish any commission. We merely wanted to know if you were tendering and our object was to try and see if we could not keep up the prices. We have already tendered for cutting and cupping and drawing machines for the case and bullet envelopes for .303 cartridges. We now see the difficulty of the position — as your machines probably are not similar to ours of course the prices cannot be similar. Of course we cannot ask you to shew your hand as we should not like to do so ourselves. We fear in this case each must stand on his own merits but if you can throw any light on the matter we shall be pleased to hear from you. You can rely on us acting square. Yours etc.

Nov. 20th, 1889 To Alfred Muir Esq.

Dear Sir, We thank you for yours of 19th. The Gas Block [? partly legible] machine shall be put in hand. Sorry to hear you have been laid up. We have heard from Leeds and of course are vexed we have fared so badly but at same time are glad to have been to some extent the means of keeping up the prices. Yours etc.

May 16th 1890 To Mr. Wurtzburg[6]
Dear Sir, We have an enquiry from Sparkbrook[7] for 20 cross millers, heavy pattern . . . [illegible]. Muir is going to quote £62. We thought of quoting abt £60. As yourselves and Muir got the bulk of the last Enfield enquiry. We think we ought to have this and will you kindly say what enquiries you have got and what you have to propose in this matter? We have also an enquiry for a few other tools as herewith . . . [illegible, possibly 'estimated'], but as Muir has not received and the machines are specified to be of our make we concluded that ourselves only have received it.
1 machine . . . [illegible] shaping.
2 . . . [illegible] copy millers.
3 4 spindle drills
3 2 spindle drills
3 1 spindle drills
6 edge milling machines . . . [illegible]
6 edge milling machines small
3 slot drills
As the tenders have to be posted on the 21st inst. there is no time to lose and hoping to hear from you per return. Yours etc.

May 20th 1890 To J. H. Wurtzburg Esq.
Dear Sir, We thank you for yours of 19th inst. We rather demur however to your claim to the 20 cross millers. You and Muir had the bulk of the last order to our almost . . . [illegible] exclusion. We think therefore you ought to give us a little advantage in this case. The enquiry for 20 millers is worth more than our other enquiry as there are 20 of a kind. However, we will quote £60 . . . [illegible] as you . . . [illegible] abide by the result. We understand Mr. Muir will quote £62. Yours.

May 20th. To Alfred Muir Esq.
Dear Sirs, Mr. Wurtzburg is going to quote £60 for the cross millers and we are going to quote the same. We understand you will quote £62. Yours etc.

June 4th 1890 To J. H. Wurtzburg Esq.
Dear Sir, We beg to advise you that we have received the Sparkbrook

181

order for 20 cross millers at £60 ea. In addition to the special machines that we specified to be of our make and of which we advised you. Yours etc.

June 17th, 1890 To J. H. Wurtzburg

Machines for B.S.A. factory Sparkbrook	Price each	Time of delay
1 Machine radial drilling	135	6 weeks
1 Machine shaping 15″ stroke	170	3 mos.
1 Machine drilling, double geared (heavy)	80	3 mos.
*1 Machine spotting Barrel	140	3 mos.
1 machine special, for drilling cleaning red hole	–	–
3 machines drilling, horizontal double spindle for butts and fore-ends	50	3 mos.
1 machine drilling and tapping butt plate screw holes letting in . . . [illegible] of butt plate	–	–
3 machines milling, Archdales copy	60	3 mos.
*1 Lathe turning barrel finish	100	3 mos.
2 machines clamp milling for end of barrel	–	–
1 machine facing for end of barrel	–	–
7 machines drilling, horizontal, 3 spindles for drilling barrels	–	–
2 lathes for drilling special to centre barrel	–	–
1 set pump and accumulator for screwing barrel plant with fitting complete	–	–

* These prices are same as had by us before for these machines.
Note. tenders to be posted from here on Thursday 20th inst.

June 17th 1890 To Mr. Wurtzburg

Dear Sir, We now enclose prices and time delay we propose putting in. We have ascertained that there are some half dozen firms cutting in for the machine tools and consequently we shall not stand very much chance for them. We find that only *you* and *ourselves* are invited to tender for the remainder. As we shall not stand much if any chance for the ordinary machine tools we think we ought to have the barrel finish turning and the barrel spotting. They are required to be precisely as last made by us but with some alterations and improvements affected by themselves – If you will please let us know what amts. to put down for the other machines we will carry out your wishes. We think however that there had better not be *too great* a difference or it might look suspicious bearing in mind the low prices you have sometimes lately put

in. We hope to hear from you on Wednesday as the matter is urgent.
Yours etc.

The letters which have just been quoted cover a period of just under one year, but it is clear from the tone of the correspondence that the collusion in price fixing and market sharing which they reveal was continuing, and, in the case of these three firms, an efficiently organised practice. It should be emphasised that Archdale's, Muir's and Greenwood and Batley were among the most reputable and most successful makers of machine tools at this period, and judging from their records and advertisements all had a wide sale for their tools both at home and abroad. That the arrangements revealed in the letters were unknown to the government buyers of machinery is confirmed by the evidence of Colonel Barlow, given to the select committee sitting in the same year as these letters were being written. The three firms involved seem to have been satisfied that the arrangement did in fact contribute to 'keeping prices up', and it seems reasonable to conclude that such arrangements are at least partially responsible for the higher profit levels which Greenwood and Batley were, as has been shown, able to obtain on their orders for arms machinery.

It is further likely, although no direct evidence for this exists, that such price fixing arrangements operating in the home market helped to keep up prices in the export field. The prestige attached to supplying the British government must have helped such firms as those named in this correspondence to secure orders from foreign governments (advertisements in trade journals make a special point of mentioning that a firm has supplied the government), and the maintenance of prices on home orders in this way must have allowed the firms to keep up similar or even inflated price levels in export markets.

It should of course be emphasised that such arrangements were probably viable only in the making of machine tools to do a specialised task, as the letter of 17 June 1890 about tools for B.S.A. suggests. However, such orders were obviously of great importance to the firms taking part in the arrangement, and it seems likely that in other specialised fields of machine tool building, similar arrangements, and a similar dependence of machine tool firms on them, may have existed. For Greenwood and Batley, much of whose profits came from sales of machine tools to arms-makers, the arrangements revealed in this correspondence must have been extremely important in maintaining profit levels, especially since the profit margins revealed in their records for other machine tools were so slender.

7. Greenwood and Batley: production

This chapter is concerned with the production by Greenwood and Batley of the machine tools whose sale has been described and analysed in the preceding pages. The production process in an industrial firm can be analysed in numerous ways, through study of the training and management of the labour force, the methods of management of the factory, the rate of building or other capital investment, or through other components of industrial behaviour. The records of Greenwood and Batley do not provide sufficient information to analyse these components separately. One measure, however, which serves to summarise the effects of all these other components, is that of changes in productivity, since the whole productive process, technical advance, and entrepreneurial behaviour contribute together to changes in the productivity of the factors of production.

The measurement of productivity is not only a useful method of summarising the behaviour of an individual firm, but it is also crucial to an understanding of the economic history of an industry, or of a country as a whole. Before presenting the results of an analysis of productivity change in the operations of Greenwood and Batley, it is therefore important to examine the possibility of generalising from the experience of this one firm to the experience of the engineering industry as a whole. If such generalisations can be based on the records of Greenwood and Batley, then it may be possible for these records to contribute towards the solution of the controversial topic of the course of the British industrial economy in the second half of the nineteenth century.

It is difficult to define a 'typical' firm, or to establish whether a firm is 'representative' of the industry of which it forms a part. Luckily, for most purposes it is not necessary to establish whether the firm which is to be studied is 'typical' or 'representative' in all respects; normally it is only necessary to know whether it is so in respect of the particular characteristics or facets of the industry which are to be explored. Thus if the subject of enquiry is the trend of wages in the engineering industry, and it is known that all engineering firms paid the same wages, then the experience of one firm would be a complete guide to the experience of the industry as a whole in this particular respect. That firm may be fifty times larger than any other firm, and totally atypical in all kinds of other ways, but in this particular case of wages it would be typical, and, for a study of wages, that is all that matters.

In most cases, however, the subject of enquiry covers characteristics of firms which cannot be expected to be uniform over all firms, such as size, location, products or age. In these cases, there is a spectrum of firms, from smallest to largest, from north to south, and so on. This is true of productivity change and its causes and results. It is likely that there are, in any industry, some firms whose labour productivity, for example, is very much higher than that of other firms; there will, in the common terminology, be a spectrum of firms ranging from 'best-practice' to 'worst-practice' firms, with respect to this particular characteristic, labour productivity. It would of course be possible to enquire where a particular firm falls along the spectrum, but it is normally very difficult to answer such a question in an historical study, because of the scarcity of evidence on all but a few firms. It is thus normally impossible to say with any degree of confidence whether the experience of one firm at one period of time represents the best or the worst practice at that time, or where it falls on the spectrum. Normally, however, the interest lies not so much in the position of one firm, but in the trends observable in the industry as a whole over a period, for instance in the rise in the productivity of labour over the period. In this case, it would not be necessary to know where the particular firm from whom information is taken lies on the best—worst practice spectrum, but merely whether it maintains whatever position it has over the period. If, for example, a firm begins as technically most advanced, but by the end of the period is generally known as backward and conservative, by comparison with other firms, then naturally its experience does not provide a good base for drawing general conclusions about the industry. If, however, the firm is known to stay, throughout the period, at roughly the same point on the spectrum, then it may be possible to extrapolate from its experience to that of the industry as a whole.

It has already been argued, in chapter 5, that the technical standing of Greenwood and Batley in the machine tool industry was such as to place it among the 'best-practice' firms, and that in spite of its financial difficulties it remained advanced in technical terms at least until 1900. The most relevant characteristic for the purposes of this chapter is not however the standing of the products of the firm, but the relative standing of the methods by which the machine tools were produced. As the comments of the American engineer, Porter, on the Whitworth works, demonstrate, it was quite possible for a high reputation among outsiders to coincide with deplorably backward methods of production. There is however no evidence that Greenwood and Batley were, in their production of machine tools, anything other than the 'best-practice' plant which the praise of their products suggests. Descriptions of the works by outsiders were favourable, and it is clear from the order-books of the firm that the most advanced machine tools were regularly applied to production, being transferred to the 'Utensils Account' of the firm, as well as being sold to outside customers. Although the financial structure of the firm and the control of its commercial operations, were heavily criticised after 1890 both by several of the directors and by outside commentators, no criticisms of technical performance were made, and the impression created by these comments is that many of the commercial difficulties were the result of the technical progress and inventiveness of the firm outrunning demand and the ability of the salesmen to sell the machines. It is clear, therefore, that Greenwood and Batley were, throughout the period, among the 'best-practice' firms in the machine tool industry, both in terms of the products which they made and in terms of the methods which they used.

There is no evidence that Greenwood and Batley differed from other leading firms in the industry in its treatment of, or relations with, its labour force. The engineering industry was heavily and successfully unionised, and the rates of wages paid were common to all firms within a district, although there were minor variations between districts. Greenwood and Batley appear from the Minutes of the Board of Directors, to have paid the wages normal in the engineering trades in Leeds, and they were allied with the other employers in the engineering strike or lock-out of 1897. The firm was also typical in adhering to the practice, apparently normal in Leeds, of giving or taking no notice of leaving employment; a man could be employed, be dismissed, or leave of his own accord, at any meal-break, giving a highly flexible, if insecure, labour force (G. & B. Board, dates in 1896/7). The labour force of the firm was certainly large by the standards of most firms in the engineering industry, reflecting the range of products made, but there is no evidence that it was atypical in any other respects (G. & B. Board, 15 March 1892). The family control of the firm, at least until 1888, and the division of responsibility between the partners, which has been described in chapter 5, also seems normal for a business at this time.

In two respects the firm was certainly atypical. It made, firstly, many more types of engineering goods than was normal. In its organisation, however, the production of each type was segregated, so that it does not appear likely that the scale of the firm as a whole altered the conditions under

which a particular product was manufactured; machine tool production
was quite separate from the rest of the firm. The firm was secondly
atypical in the closeness of its relationship with the government arms factories, a closeness which stemmed from the early work of Thomas
Greenwood in designing and producing tools for these factories. As has
been demonstrated, this connection was valuable for the firm in the larger
profits which it made on arms orders, for the British and foreign governments. In this context, however, of change in methods of production, it
seems likely that the connection was valuable in giving Greenwood and
Batley access to new ideas and designs developed by the government
engineers, and it is possible that this gave it an advantage over other firms.
It does not seem likely, however, that such advantage could be very great,
since any new ideas and designs were apparently quickly publicised in the
trade press, and could be taken up at will by other firms.

Greenwood and Batley seem, therefore, to have ranked among the 'best-
practice' machine tool firms as far as technical advance and the quality of
their products are concerned; in other respects, with the possible exception
of their size and the number of products which they made, they do not
seem to have been atypical in comparison with the leading firms in the
industry. They are clearly unlike the smaller and less technically progressive
firms in the industry, who formed the tail behind the 'best-practice' firms.
Nor are they representative of the specialised firms making machine tools
for such customers as the ship-building industry. Nevertheless, it is clear
that Greenwood and Batley were consistently among the leaders of the
industry in their working methods and in the quality of their products; in
these circumstances, it is reasonable to regard the changes in productivity
of the factors of production which are observable in their records as
roughly representative of trends in 'best-practice' machine tool production
at this time. At the least, the Greenwood and Batley data on productivity
change demonstrate what it was possible for one firm to achieve; at the
most, if it can be regarded as representative, it can provide some information on the nature and causes of productivity change in British engineering as a whole.

The accounting methods of the firm and their relevance to the study of production

The sources for the study of the production of machine tools in this chapter are the records of the firm of Greenwood and Batley, and in particular,
their cost- and order-books. As Greenwood and Batley made many products

besides machine tools, it is impossible in this study to use the aggregate financial records of the firm, where these exist, in any systematic manner; such aggregate records can do no more than give an impression of the progress of the company, and they have been used in this way in chapter 5. Specifically, although the aggregate records give information on the additions to the plant and machinery of the firm which were made during the period, it is impossible to attribute the new machinery which was bought or manufactured to one or other of the lines of production of the firm. It is therefore impossible to calculate, or to obtain from the aggregate records, the capital cost of the machinery or buildings used by Greenwood and Batley to construct their machine tools; it is further impossible, since there is no information about the technical performance, age, or type of machines being used, to establish any technical production functions, the technical relationships between the input of raw materials and the output of finished machine tools or their component parts.

Secondly, the accounting methods used by the firm make the information provided by the cost-books of limited value in exactly the same field, the estimation of the capital inputs. The method adopted by Greenwood and Batley in calculating total costs of production on each order was extremely simple. From records of the number of hours worked by each of the five types of labour employed, the direct labour cost of the order was easily calculated. The metal cost of an order was also directly calculated from a list of the metal inputs used. There remained the problem of calculating the overhead costs, office and sales expenses and other miscellaneous costs, and the capital costs of the machinery employed. To cover these costs Greenwood and Batley adopted the simple method of taking the direct labour cost and adding the same sum into the cost calculations, under the name of 'management cost'; in the accounts of the firm, therefore, with very rare and unimportant exceptions, 'management costs' exactly equalled direct labour costs on each order.

Greenwood and Batley were not alone among contemporary engineering firms in using this method. The whole question of the calculation of management costs was carefully considered by the Morley Committee on the Manufacturing Departments of the Army, apparently because of allegations from private manufacturers that the lower costs of manufacturing recorded by the government factories reflected not greater efficiency but rather a different method of calculating overhead costs.

The Morley Committee was told by the accountant and auditor to the government factories that:

I do not know what practice prevails at present in large manufacturing

188

Establishments of private firms, but in forming an estimate of prices I have been told by several that they take the material and the labour and then add 50%.

In the government factories, however, the practice was to charge indirect expenditure as a percentage of the direct labour cost alone:

The total indirect expenditure is levied as a percentage upon the direct labour charged against each order in the cost ledger of each department. The amount of indirect expenditure is constantly varying according to the amount of work which is being turned out. Last year it amounted to about 48% on direct wages. (P.P., 1887, Q.3429)

This charge was however not intended to cover depreciation or capital expenditure on machinery. After hearing other evidence, the committee concluded in its report that 'In private factories it appears that there is no uniformity in the manner of charging machinery' (P.P., 1887, para. 101).

Accounting manuals of the period gave guidance on the accounting practices which should be adopted, while recognising that the advice was not often followed. A work on 'The management of small engineering workshops', for instance, which was published in 1899, stated that the theory of estimating 'costs of establishment' was that:

$$\text{establishment cost} = \text{wages paid on order multiplied by} \frac{\text{total yearly est. cost}}{\text{total yearly wages}}$$

In practice, however, the method adopted was to: 'add a percentage of the estimated wages cost, which percentage is calculated from the experience of previous years, and it is only an estimate for the current year in a very rough sense' (Barker, 1899, p. 187).

Greenwood and Batley were thus not in any way exceptional in their methods of accounting. The firm does not seem to have realised that, as the Morley Committee pointed out,

As this expenditure is distributed among all the articles produced in proportion to the cost of direct labour expended upon them, it follows that articles which are produced chiefly by manual labour and comparatively cheap machines are charged too highly, while, conversely, articles which require for their construction complicated and expensive machinery, directed by few hands, are charged too little. (P.P., 1887, para. 101)

The directors of Greenwood and Batley seem in fact to have discussed the system on only two occasions. In 1891 Mr Wurtzburg, while discussing the valuation of stocks in hand, explained the system used:

In working out actual costs the Managing Directors always added 100%

189

for expenses and charges, on to the actual cost of labour; so that there was ample margin between the 60% charged on stock and the 100% when the orders came to be weighed up; and therefore the stock was taken at a low and safe rate. He further explained the system of taking quarterly balances and of ascertaining the actual rate of Expenses and Wages, the results showing that in busy times the rate of expense went sometimes as low as 73%, whereas in the quarter April to June last it had been 98% and in the quarter July to September 82%. (G. & B. Board, 30 November 1891)

The Board showed no wish at that time to alter the system, but when it was again discussed, in 1913, they were told that an allowance of 100% on direct wages was no longer enough, and that an increase would have to be considered (G. & B. Board, 29 January 1913).

However normal the system was for engineering firms in the late nineteenth century, it has severe disadvantages from the point of view of an historical analysis of the production of engineering goods. As has been mentioned in the last chapter, it is impossible to assess the true profit rate on any individual order, since on the evidence of Mr Wurtzburg's statement the 'management cost' figure would conceal a hidden profit of up to 27% of direct labour costs, depending upon the utilisation of capacity. While this difficulty does not affect significantly the validity of the estimates of relative profit levels on orders to different types of customers, described in the last chapter, it makes it impossible to construct estimates of the capital cost of any order for use in analysis of the productive process. Although it is possible to construct an index of capacity based on the number of hours worked within a month, the use of such an index to deflate the 'management cost' figure to arrive at a better approximation of capital cost is not sensible; such an index of capacity would assume constant labour productivity, which is too restrictive an assumption. Another difficulty with such a procedure is that even the deflated 'management cost' figure is highly correlated with the direct labour cost.

The accounting methods also have a more general defect, in that for a number of orders data are missing from the cost ledgers on one or other aspect of production, perhaps the weight, or the time taken in production of the order. In the whole of the statistical study of productivity movements, therefore, the results are based upon calculations in a set of data from which all orders with missing information have been removed. Approximately 50% of orders had some data missing, the principal reason for such omission being that the order was for stock or for the use of Greenwood and Batley itself; in these cases the delivery date of the machine or its price, respectively, were normally omitted. This procedure is regrettable in that data are being wasted, but the remaining sample size (over 2000 orders for 5551 machine tools) is so large that it is unlikely that any serious distortion has resulted. An alternative procedure, the insertion of values for the missing data based on the values which can be found, is subject to serious objections which have already been discussed.

In spite of these difficulties, it is still possible to use the records of Greenwood and Batley to describe and analyse changes in the production of machine tools in the late nineteenth century. Changes in production methods are, in essence, changes in the relationship between the human and material resources used in production and the output which they combine to produce. More formally, the relationship between resources and output can be written as a function, of the form

$$Y = f(X_1, X_2, X_3, \ldots, X_n)$$

where Y represents the output and the Xs are different resources combined together in production; such a function is therefore described as a production function. More specifically, it is normal in economic analysis to distinguish three main groups of resources, labour, raw materials, and capital, and to write a specific production function of the form

$$Q = f(L, R, K)$$

where Q represents output, L labour, R raw materials, and K capital. Such a production function is still, however, extremely general, in that it states simply that three resources are used in production, without stating in what proportions or by what means they are combined. A further step in the direction of specificity is therefore to write a function which has these properties. That function which is most commonly used is

$$Q = AL^\alpha R^\beta K^\gamma$$

where Q, L, R and K are defined as before. The constant α is the elasticity of response of output to changes in the labour input, in other words, it is the percentage by which output will change if the labour input is increased by 1 per cent, with the inputs of raw materials and capital held constant. The constants β and γ similarly are the output elasticities respectively of raw materials and of capital.

Technical change is, in essence, a change in the relationship between the term on the left hand side of the production equation Q, and the input terms L, R and K on the right hand side of the equation. Remembering that, by definition, the two sides of the equation must be equal, such

191

change can take place in one of two ways: either there can be a change in the relative importance of the input variables, a decline in the value of K balanced by an increase in the value of L, for example, or there can be a change in the value of the last term, A. A is a term which is designed to capture all change in the relationship between outputs and inputs which is not simply the result of the rearrangement of inputs. We are used to the concept of the productivity of labour, output per unit of labour input, which is used often in economic history as a measure of the changing efficiency of the use of labour. A, sometimes known as the index of total factor productivity, is an analogous measure, but one which tries to measure the changing efficiency in the use of all inputs. This can be clearly seen if we re-arrange the equation into the form

$$A = \frac{Q}{L^{\alpha}R^{\beta}K^{\gamma}}$$

where A is clearly seen to measure the relationship between outputs and inputs.

The equation which we have just rearranged, however, has two deficiencies from the point of view of the economic historian. Firstly, in order to use it to measure the change in the efficiency of an industry we need to be able to measure both output and inputs. Measurement is a problem particularly in the case of the input of capital; while we can measure with ease the number of men employed (although their quality may vary) or the number of tons of iron used, the capital employed in manufacturing industry will probably consist of a motley collection of old and new machines, a factory building and perhaps an office block. It is for this reason that it is often necessary to use what is called a dual of the equation we have stated above, in which inputs and outputs are measured not in physical terms (numbers of men, tons of iron etc.), but in terms of their price. It will be clear that it is easier (though often not much easier) to measure capital employed in terms of the cost than in terms of some physical unit.

$$A = \frac{nw^{\alpha}r^{\beta}i^{\gamma}}{P}$$

Secondly, even if we can satisfactorily measure the relationship between inputs and outputs in price terms, we shall have a measure, from the equations we have stated, of the relationship at one point of time, while for most purposes economic historians are interested in the problem of how the relationship changes over time. It can be shown that the last equation can be transformed to a form which helps us with this problem.

$$\overset{*}{A} = \alpha\overset{*}{w} + \beta\overset{*}{r} + \gamma\overset{*}{i} - \overset{*}{P}$$

In words, this tells us that the percentage rate of growth (denoted by an asterisk over the variable) of A, the index of total factor productivity, is equal to the sum of the rates of growth of the inputs (each weighted by its output elasticity) less the rate of growth of the price of output. Thus productivity is defined as increasing whenever input prices grow more rapidly on average than output prices.

This formulation might seem to be a simple and easy means of establishing whether productivity, or the efficiency of the process, has increased. There are, however, some assumptions underlying the use of these equations, which are often left unstated but should be fully laid out. Firstly, the production function which we have used, and the successive equations which have been derived from it, embody an assumption that the sum of the output elasticities is unity. This is equivalent to assuming that the productive process which the function is describing exhibits constant returns to scale; that is, a doubling of the inputs will produce merely a doubling, not more or less, of the output. In other words, there are no economies of large (or small) scale production. This may be a realistic assumption with many industrial processes, at least over certain ranges of scale, but we need to be certain that it is reasonable before using this method. Secondly, use of the equations which make use of prices implies that we believe that these prices are being set in conditions of perfect competition; clearly, if the producer concerned were a monopolist, he could vary his output prices so as to make nonsense of the assumption that efficiency was measured by the relationship of those artificially set output prices with input prices. Imperfections in labour or capital markets could have the same nullifying effect. In addition, it is normal to measure the output elasticities by calculating the shares of total receipts which are paid to labour, raw materials and capital; this identity, which is extremely useful, holds strictly only when the factor markets are in equilibrium under conditions of perfect competition.

In spite of these assumptions, which are very restrictive, analysis making use of the Cobb–Douglas production function can be very valuable at least as an indication of trends in productivity, and numerous studies have, for that reason, made use of the methods which have been outlined. It does not seem that we would be doing too much violence to these assumptions by using this method to analyse the operations of Greenwood and Batley.

193

As has already been shown, it is reasonable to believe that machine tool production did not show significant economies of scale, and it is also reasonable to assume that Greenwood and Batley was operating in competitive labour and product markets. Although some exceptions to this assumption have clearly been demonstrated in the last chapter, they relate to a comparatively small part of Greenwood and Batley's production, most of which was sold in more competitive markets and which made up, at least in 1907, a small fraction of total sales of British machine tools. Similarly, Greenwood and Batley, although a large employer, were only one among many engineering employers in Leeds and the West Riding, and certainly had no monopsonistic power over supplies of raw material or of capital.

Even if the assumptions of total factor productivity analysis can be satisfied, there still remains the problem of the choice of measures of output and inputs. This choice is, in a sense, complicated by the sheer abundance of the production records of Greenwood and Batley, which offer an unusual choice of both input and output measures. The main requirement of such measures is that they should be, so far as possible, homogeneous both within a given time period and over a different time period. The importance of this requirement is best illustrated by considering the choice of output measures. If we were to measure Greenwood and Batley's output of machine tools by, for example, the average price of machine tools produced, we would be lumping together many different machine tools, of different names, shapes, and sizes; without further enquiry, we would not know whether a rise in the average price of machine tools, from one year to the next, was the result of a change in this mix of products – the production of more expensive and less cheap machines, for example – or of an overall change in the price of all products, such as might originate in a decline in efficiency of production, or, alternatively, in a rise in the quality of the products. The problem is equally acute over long time periods, when the quality of products may change, although their name and many physical characteristics remain the same, and it is particularly acute in an industry such as machine tools, where there are frequent product changes and where few machine tools are made in large numbers. In the case of labour and raw materials, similar problems of aggregation and homogeneity arise, since there are clearly different skills of labour to be employed, and different grades of metal to be used.

In the light of these problems, the most appropriate measure of output which can be derived from the Greenwood and Batley records appears to be that of price per hundredweight of net weight produced. Intuitively, the

194

production of a complicated piece of capital equipment such as a machine tool involves more work, both in design and in manufacture, the larger the piece of equipment which is to be produced. A heavy machine tool is made heavier not simply by hanging chunks of unworked metal on to a light machine tool, but by the use of larger components which require more working. For much the same reason, the amount of work involved in the production of a machine of given weight will not greatly vary, whether the machine is an engine lathe or a planing machine; there will of course be some variation, but weight will be a powerful influence on the amount of effort which will need to be expended. That weight was an important determinant of the amount of work needed to produce a machine tool, and hence of its price, as can be seen by calculating the correlation between weight and price, within years (see table 7.1). The high correlation is a justification for using net weight as an aggregative method, both for individual years and for comparison between years, since changes in net weight produced for a given amount of effort (or inputs) will be an appropriate measure of the productive efficiency of the firm.

Table 7.1   *Greenwood and Batley: correlation coefficients between weight and price of machine tools, selected years*

Year	Correlation coefficient (R)
1858	+0.79
1868	+0.96
1873	+0.95
1888	+0.98
1894	+0.96

Note: These correlations are computed between the weight and price of machine tools in the years given, excluding orders for which any data was missing.

The choice of input measures is less troublesome. It is possible to measure the labour input by the cost of labour per hour worked. Since, however, workmen of different degrees of skill were employed, it is desirable, and possible, to take account of this heterogeneity by weighting the hours worked by each category of labour to produce a composite measure taking account of these skill differences; the appropriate weights are, clearly, the relative wage-rates of the different categories, and these can be used to produce a composite measure of weighted hours, from which an input measure of labour cost per weighted hour can easily be calculated. It would be desirable to do the same for metal inputs, but it was decided at an early stage of data collection that individual metal inputs and their prices would not be recorded; the only measure of metal cost which is, therefore, directly available from the Greenwood and Batley data set is total metal cost per hundredweight of machinery produced. This is, however, not really a relevant measure of input metal costs, since clearly the amount of metal used to produce a given weight of machinery is partly a function of the efficiency of the machining and design process; any changes in productivity in the operations of the firm will therefore be partly reflected in changes in metal cost per unit of output. Since we require a measure of input cost unaffected by productivity changes, metal cost per unit is inappropriate. Since no other measure of metal input costs is directly available from the Greenwood and Batley data set, it is necessary to use an index of raw material costs, in this case an index of iron and steel prices compiled by C. H. Feinstein as a by-product of his work on the British national income. Although Greenwood and Batley made use of other metals, the great bulk of metals used were iron and steel castings, so that it is unlikely that the omission of other metals from the index produces any serious distortion. Lastly, it is necessary to choose a measure of the cost of capital inputs; the cost of capital is a function of the initial money cost of the capital employed, of the rate of depreciation of the capital goods, and of the interest rate. In this particular case, where the input measure which is required is that of the rate of change of capital cost, it is reasonable to argue that the rate is equivalent to the rate of change of the rate of interest. This is because we have no information on the rate of change of depreciation, and can perhaps assume it to have been zero, while if we assume the rate of change of money prices of capital goods to have been zero, we are allowing any changes in price as a result of productivity changes, in this particular industry where capital goods input are the same as the output, to be reflected in output rather than input changes. On this basis, we can make use simply of the rate of change of interest rates as a proxy for capital costs, and use the rate on consols as a proxy for the unknown interest rate applicable to the operations of Greenwood and Batley.

Table 7.2 shows the results of the resulting calculation of total factor productivity. The factor shares are the mean shares of the three factors in the six years 1857–62, at the beginning of the operations of the firm; the resulting figures are very close to the mean shares over the whole period to 1900.

The implication of table 7.1 is that Greenwood and Batley achieved, over a substantial period of time, a considerable increase in the overall efficiency of their production. In reality, the increase may have been slightly higher than 0.9% p.a., since the true fall in materials prices facing Greenwood and Batley's machine tool production may have been less than

Table 7.2   *Total factor productivity in the operations of Greenwood and Batley*

1. *Trends in input variables*	
Labour cost per weighted hour	+1.1% p.a.
Iron and steel prices	−1.5% p.a.
Interest rate	−0.7% p.a.
2. *Weights*	
Labour	37%
Materials	18%
Capital	45%
3. *Trend in output variable*	
Price per cwt of output	−1.1% p.a.
4. *Total factor productivity*	+0.9% p.a.

the −1.5% p.a. shown by the Feinstein index, which relates to semi-manufactured products rather than to the complicated castings used in engineering manufacture. The fall in metal cost per hundredweight of finished machinery produced by Greenwood and Batley was −0.6% p.a., and it seems likely that the true trend relevant to Greenwood and Batley would be between that figure and −1.5%, tending to increase the growth of total factor productivity. It is also relevant that Greenwood and Batley's labour costs rose (at +1.1% p.a.) substantially faster than the overall Spicer index of engineering wages which shows a rise of only 0.5% p.a. over this period, suggesting that Greenwood and Batley were employing a different mix of labour from that normal in the industry as a whole; this would be an expected feature of a highly skilled occupation such as machine tool making, and since skilled labour would also be employed in the production of the castings, may also explain why Greenwood and Batley's metal prices fell by less than the national average. Taking all these factors into account, it seems reasonable to take the overall rise in total factor productivity at approximately 1% per annum.

Some caution is, however, necessary in interpreting these results. Firstly, as has often been pointed out, the measure of total factor productivity is a residual measure; that is, it attempts to measure the difference between rates of growth of inputs and output. Since this is so, it incorporates not only what may be called 'true' changes in the relationship between inputs and output, that is changes in productivity, but also any errors of measurement, or any mistaken assumptions involved in using this crude method of measuring productivity. Secondly, the conclusions which we can draw from the results depend to a great extent on how the increase in total factor productivity was achieved, and how its benefits were passed on to those who used the machine tools of Greenwood and Batley. This is important, and complicated, in the case of the machine tool industry, because that industry is both part of the engineering industry and the supplier of its machinery; an explanation of productivity change in the machine tool industry thus relates directly to similar change in the whole engineering sector. Lastly, the fact that it is so unusual to be able to measure total factor productivity in the operations of a single firm, since few sets of business records as detailed as those of Greenwood and Batley survive, means that the results cannot be compared with those for other firms, in engineering or other industries.

Unfortunately, the explanation of the changes in total factor productivity in the operations of Greenwood and Batley is much more difficult than is its description. Most studies of the causes of productivity change have attempted to decompose that change into such factors as improvements in the quality of labour, increases in the skill of labour, increases in capital per worker, 'embodied' improvements in technology through the introduction of new and improved machinery, and so on. Such explanation is greatly facilitated when either some one identifiable change takes place in the production process, such as, for example, the substitution of a new power source or a new machine, or when, as in the Horndal–Lowell cases, the physical equipment does not change in any way and productivity changes can then be attributed directly to 'learning-by-doing' (David, 1975, pp. 174–95).

By contrast, productivity changes in Greenwood and Batley's production of machine tools seem to have been steady and more generalised, difficult to attribute to any single cause or to partition among several causes. Although it is impossible to identify the introduction of new capital equipment into the production of machine tools, the evidence of the sales records is that the firm constantly made machine tools for its own use, in some branch of its factory. It is thus a reasonable inference that it equipped its machine tool shops with new equipment as it seemed necessary to do so, rather than engaging at any one time in a major re-equipment. Further support for this inference of gradual change can come from table 7.3, which shows the relative use of different types of workers in machine tool production. If there had been any spectacular changes in the firm's production methods, such as the introduction of automatic or semi-automatic machine tools, it would be natural to expect that this would have been reflected in this table; the desire to economise on skilled labour was, in fact, the reason normally given by contemporaries for the use of such new machine tools, and it was for this reason that the 1897 engineering strike was called by the

Amalgamated Society of Engineers. In fact, as table 7.3 shows, there was very little change in the relative use of different types of labour.

A second possibility is that the changes were the result of the achievement by the firm of economies of scale or specialisation. There is some danger of confusion in using this explanation, since it will be recalled that our evidence for an improvement in total factor productivity stems from an analysis which assumes that there were constant returns to scale. Nevertheless, it is useful to examine again the possibility that there were returns to scale, in case they can be shown to have been important for Greenwood and Batley, as distinct from being important for the industry as a whole. Unfortunately, the nature of the evidence is such that no conclusive judgement can be given. If production measured by hundredweights produced per man-hour is regressed upon numbers of hundredweights produced, an $R^2 = 0.5500$ (or 0.5524 if the weighted hours measure is used) is obtained. This is some slight confirmation of the existence of economies of scale. Since, however, the method used in the compilation of the data set used in this chapter involved the exclusion of all cases for which any information was missing, this measure is probably a lower bound since many of the orders excluded would have contributed to whatever economies of scale were achieved. It is also possible to reason that such economies could have been achieved in two ways, firstly by the manufacture of some machine tools, in particular straight milling machines, edge milling machines, cutter grinding machines and rifling machines, in large numbers, which must have led to economies in design costs and through the familiarity of the labour force with the production processes, and secondly by the manufacture of sectional parts in large numbers, to be supplied later to the fitters working on particular orders. This process was not, however, taken very far by Greenwood and Batley before 1900, and it seems unlikely that it was more than a minor cause of improvements in productivity. A further reason, however, for attributing some at least of the increase in productivity to economies of scale is that such an explanation would be consistent with the tendency of all unit costs to move together over time, and also for the use of different types of labour to remain stable, although this evidence would also be consistent with explanations based on learning-by-doing.

The third possibility is that the increase in total factor productivity stemmed from technical change in the sense of improvements in the design and use of the machine tools which were used by Greenwood and Batley to make machine tools. It has already been suggested, in chapter 2, that there were major technical improvements in machine tool design during the

Table 7.3   *Proportions of total hours worked by each category of labour,
Greenwood and Batley, 1856–1900*

(Totals do not necessarily sum to 100 in each year, because of rounding errors.)

Year	Boys	Planers and borers	Turners and fitters	Boy joiners	Men joiners
1856	20	15	64	0	1
1857	27	20	51	0	2
1858	26	20	53	0	2
1859	20	21	52	1	6
1860	28	20	49	0	2
1861	30	20	45	0	4
1862	31	21	43	0	4
1863	26	20	50	0	4
1864	29	22	45	1	4
1865	31	20	46	1	2
1866	19	16	54	2	9
1867	22	22	53	0	3
1868	23	19	54	1	3
1869	22	16	58	1	3
1870	22	19	54	1	5
1871	22	15	59	1	3
1872	27	11	60	1	2
1873	27	9	62	1	1
1874	25	11	61	1	2
1875	25	10	60	2	4
1876	21	6	58	4	11
1877	29	8	56	2	4
1878	28	20	46	1	4
1879	19	33	44	1	4
1880	10	38	46	1	5
1881	17	34	45	0	3
1882	16	22	54	1	7
1883	24	18	55	0	4
1884	24	17	50	1	8
1885	21	17	52	1	8
1886	26	16	51	1	6
1887	21	19	53	1	6
1888	23	24	50	1	3
1889	24	19	54	0	2
1890	23	15	59	0	2
1891	22	16	58	1	3
1892	29	15	55	0	1
1893	23	14	59	1	3
1894	24	14	57	1	4
1895	19	19	57	1	4
1896	21	12	63	1	4
1897	21	12	63	1	3
1898	24	18	53	1	4
1899	23	18	54	1	3
1900	27	13	56	2	2

nineteenth century which widened the possibilities of machining metal accurately, which greatly increased machining speeds, and which reduced the costs of such machining. It is also clear that Greenwood and Batley were an innovative firm in their output, which is some warrant for believing that they may have been an innovative firm in their use of new ideas in production. In addition, it is clear from studies of machine tool design that the improvements in this period came slowly, in the form of minor improvements to existing plant, rather than in the form of dramatic new developments; this would be consistent, at the least, with the picture of gradual changes in total factor productivity which have been observed.

Lastly, it is possible, and even likely, that the firm benefited from the increasing experience of its labour force through a process of learning-by-doing. As David has shown, when by chance the effects of learning-by-doing can be isolated, they can be shown to be quite significant, and there seems no reason why productivity should not have increased at least in part because the labour force employed by Greenwood and Batley became more experienced and better at its job (David, 1975).

It is thus impossible to reject any of the most obvious explanations for the rise in total factor productivity found in the records of Greenwood and Batley, and impossible also to allot to any of them any definite and quantified role. What can be said is that the rise in productivity appears to have been reflected in a falling price for machine tools supplied by the firm, which must have benefited its customer industries. In addition, to the extent that the measure of output which has been used does not capture improvements in the quality of the tools, the customers were additionally receiving those benefits.

Greenwood and Batley were among the 'best-practice' firms in the machine tool industry during the years to which these calculations of productivity change relate. It is likely therefore that the increases in productivity, both in labour productivity and in total factor productivity, were also achieved by other leading firms in the industry, both those making machine tools and those producing other engineering products, and that similarly the benefits of such increases were passed on to customers both for machine tools and for engineering goods in general. If this is so, then the British machine tool industry must have been making a substantial contribution to increasing productivity in the metal-working and machinery using industries.

The size of this contribution, if it is adequately represented by Greenwood and Batley's achievements, can be compared with productivity changes found in aggregate in the British economy at this period. In terms of labour productivity alone, the measure which has normally been used in discussion of the British economy, the Greenwood and Batley data shows a rise of 2.3% per annum in labour productivity between 1856 and 1900, as compared with the Feinstein index, which shows a growth of 1.2% per annum over that period (Feinstein, 1972, p. T51). In terms of total factor productivity, a growth of 1.0% per annum represents less of a departure from the national average, since estimates of McCloskey and Aldcroft, based on Feinstein's data, show rates of growth which are very similar to that. Whichever measure is chosen, it does not seem that the British machine tool industry was failing, although it would be more instructive to be able to make comparisons with rates of growth of productivity achieved by machine tool industries in other countries.

Conclusion

This book cannot pretend to be a complete history of the machine tool industry in Britain between 1850 and 1914, for too much has been omitted. Either for reasons of space, or because of lack of data, there has been no discussion of the labour force of the industry nor of several of its major foreign competitors, and many important firms and entrepreneurs have been given only passing mention. Instead, three aspects of the industry have been studied in detail: the growth of the machine tool industry and its relationship to the mechanical engineering industries as a whole, the place of the British machine tool industry in international trade, and the production and organisation of one of the most successful of British machine tool firms.

The main conclusion of this study is that, even with a considerable amount of evidence, it is impossible fully to delineate and explain the course of structural and technical change in so complex an industry as that making machine tools. On the other hand, it is clear that any such description and explanation must take great account of the exact nature of an industry's structure and of its relationship with its customers; discussion of technological change in the guise of shifts in the aggregate production function cannot take account of the constant modification of existing machinery and methods which was the characteristic form of change in the machine tool industry. Nor is aggregate analysis helpful in explaining the influence of prior decisions to specialise in particular ways on future decisions to develop new types of machine tools. Innovation by the British machine tool industry was patchy and uneven, and different from that in the United States, not because of entrepreneurial weakness or technical incompetence, but because it was a response to the particular needs, at particular times, of particular customers.

Similarly, this study suggests the need to be careful in undertaking aggregate analysis of Britain's performance in international trade, and to resist the temptation to speak generally of 'lack of British competitiveness' without closely investigating the exact chronology of trade and the market conditions in international commerce. Nor is it obvious, at least on the somewhat slender basis of the Greenwood and Batley evidence, that the British machine tool industry was failing its customers in the late nineteenth century, even if the overall performance of the British economy was disappointing.

These conclusions are of interest mainly to economic historians and to economists interested in explaining the process of technological change. More generally, the discovery and use of so much, admittedly disparate, quantitative material may encourage other historians to use such materials, and the statistical and theoretical methods which necessarily accompany them; quantitative enquiry is not a substitute for the more traditional methods of historical scholarship, but it is an indispensable adjunct to it. At the very least, this study is, I hope, an adequate refutation of the view of J. Richards, who told the readers of the *American Machinist* in 1899 that:

> It is not probable that a history of machine tool making will ever be written or published, at least not in an accurate or impartial way . . . the expense and time required to collect and collate the facts over such a wide field are not warranted.

List of works cited

(A fuller bibliography of works concerned with mechanical engineering and the machine tool industry can be found in Floud (1971).)

Abbreviation: *P.I.M.E.* = *Proceedings of the Institution of Mechanical Engineers.*

Addy, G. 1890. On milling cutters, *P.I.M.E.*, 1890.
Allen, G.C. 1966. *The Industrial Development of Birmingham and the Black Country*, 2nd edition (London).
Ames, E. and Rosenberg, N. 1969. The Enfield Arsenal in theory and practice, *Economic Journal*, xxix.
Anon. 1867. Engineers' tools, *Engineering*, 25 October 1867.
  1876. *Report of the United States Commissioners to the International Exhibition held at Vienna* (Washington, D.C.).
  1887. Memoir of Sir Joseph Whitworth, *P.I.M.E.*, February 1890.
  1889. Memoir of Richard Peacock, *P.I.M.E.*, January 1889.
  1890a. English criticisms on American engineering work, *Engineer*, 12 December 1890.
  1890b. *Official Description of the Paris Exhibition of 1889* (Paris).
  1895. Sales by Charles Churchill and Co., *American Machinist*, 7 February 1895.
  1896. Report of address by Samuel Dixon on machine tools, *Colliery Guardian*, 2 April 1896.
  1897. Article in *American Machinist*, 5 August 1897.
  1898a. English and American machine tools, *Engineer*, 2 December 1898.
  1898b. Memoir of Joseph Whitworth Hulse, *P.I.M.E.*, April 1898.
  1899a. British and American machine tools: their comparative cost, continued *Engineer*, 15 December 1899.
  1899b. Memoir of Thomas Elliott, *P.I.M.E.*, February 1899.
  1899c. Sales of American machine tools to Europe, *American Machinist* (American edition), 13 July 1899.
  1900. English and American methods, *Engineer*, 31 August 1900.
  1902a. Memoir of Alfred Muir, *P.I.M.E.*, May 1902.
  1902b. Memoir of John Shepherd, *P.I.M.E.*, December 1902.
  1902c. Modern machine methods, *P.I.M.E.*, January 1902.
  1903a. Memoir of Henry Bates, *P.I.M.E.*, May 1903.
  1903b. Memoir of Samson Fox, *P.I.M.E.*, December 1903.
  1907. Delays in delivery of American machine tools, *The Times* Engineering Supplement, 16 January 1907.
  1909. Memoir of Charles Scriven, *P.I.M.E.*, February 1909.
  1910a. A description of the Wolseley Company, *P.I.M.E.*, 1910.

205

1910b. Brussels Exhibition of 1910, *The Times* Engineering Supplement, 31 August 1910.

1910c. Olympia Exhibition of 1910, *The Times* Engineering Supplement, 14 September 1910.

1910d. Memoir of Arthur Greenwood, *P.I.M.E.*, January 1910.

1912. Olympia Exhibition of 1912, *The Times* Engineering Supplement, 16 October 1912.

1914. Greenwood and Batley, *Financial Mail*, 4 September 1914.

1917. Obituary of James Ryder Butler, *Halifax Evening Courier*, 20 August 1917.

1920. *Who Was Who, 1897–1915* (London).

1921–2. History of the Ministry of Munitions. Typescript, held in copyright libraries.

1929. *Who Was Who, 1916–1928* (London).

1938. *Peerless Planes and Plows* (Halifax: John Stirk and Sons).

1941. *Who Was Who, 1929–1940* (London).

1965a. Charles Churchill, 1865–1965, *Machine Shop and Engineering Manufacture*, XXVI.

1965b. 100 Years of machine tool building, *Machine Shop and Engineering Manufacture*, XXVI.

Barker, A.H. 1899. *The Management of Small Engineering Workshops* (London and Manchester).

Barr, J.H. 1893. *Report of the U.S. Commissioners to the Paris Exposition of 1889*, Executive Documents, House of Representatives, 1889–90, vol. 40, 1893. Vol. III, 'Machine tools'.

Blake, W.P. (ed.) 1870. *Reports of the United States Commissioners to the Paris Universal Exposition, 1867* (Washington, D.C.).

Board of Trade. 1907. Report from the commercial attaché in Madrid, *Board of Trade Journal*, 28 November 1907.

1910a. Report for 1909 of H.M. consul at Lyons, *Board of Trade Journal*, 26 May 1910.

1910b. Report for 1909 of H.M. consul at Kharkov, *Board of Trade Journal*, 18 August 1910.

1960. *The Machine Tool Industry* (London).

Brown, A.B. (ed.) 1868. *Engineering Facts and Figures for 1868* (London).

Burn, R.S. 1860. *Modern Mechanical Engineering and Machine Making* (London)

Buxbaum, B. 1960. Der amerikanische Werkzeugmaschinen- und Werkzeugbau im 18 und 19 Jahrhunderts. *Beiträge zur geschichte der Technik und Industrie*, X (Berlin).

Byrne, O. 1873. *Spon's Dictionary of Engineering* (London).

Cairncross, A.K. 1953. *Home and Foreign Investment, 1870–1913* (Cambridge).

Carden, G.L. 1909–10. *The Machine-tool Trade in . . . [Various countries]* (Washington, D.C.).

Churchill, C. 1899. Letter about sales of American machine tools to Europe, *American Machinist* (American edition), 30 March 1899.

1902. The American tool business in Great Britain, *American Machinist* (American edition), 6 November 1902.

List of works cited

Clark, D.K. 1864. *The Exhibited Machinery of 1862* (London).

Cox, H. 1903. *British Industries under Free Trade* (London).

Dans, C. 1898. American machine trade in Europe, *American Machinist* (European edition), 13 January 1898.

David, P. 1975. *Technical Choice, Innovation and Economic Growth* (Cambridge).

Feinstein, C.H. 1972. *National Income, Expenditure and Output of the United Kingdom, 1855–1965* (Cambridge).

Floud, R.C. 1971. The Metal Working Machine Tool Industry in England, 1850–1914 Unpublished D.Phil thesis, Oxford University.

1974. The adolescence of American engineering competition, 1860–1900, *Economic History Review*, XXVII.

Fontaine, H. 1874. *Machinery Exhibited at Vienna, 1873* (Paris).

Foster, F. 1906. *Engineering in the United States* (Manchester).

Frevert, H.F. 1906. How machine tools are sold, *Machinery* January 1906.

Garanger, A. 1961. *Petite histoire d'une grande industrie* (Neuilly-sur-Seine).

Glover, F.J. 1956. The growth of transport in Leeds, *Leeds Journal*, 1956.

Green, R.E. 1964. Willson Lathes Ltd, *Machinery*, 3 June 1964.

1965. Craven Brothers (Manchester) Ltd, *Machinery*, 3 February 1965.

Grierson, E. (n.d.) *A Little Farm Well Tilled* (London).

Habakkuk, H.J. 1962. *American and British Technology in the Nineteenth Century* (Cambridge).

Hawke, G. 1975. The United States tariff and industrial protection in the late nineteenth century, *Economic History Review*, XXVIII.

Herbert, Sir A. (n.d.) Machine Chasers. A MS autobiography.

Horner, J. 1897. Some lessons of the Stanley Show, *American Machinist* (American edition), 20 December 1897.

Howard, M.E. 1962. The Armed Forces, ch. VIII of *New Cambridge Modern History*, vol. XI, ed. F.H. Hinsley (Cambridge).

Jefferys, J.B. 1946. *The Story of the Engineers* (London).

Lewis, M. 1960. Armed Forces and the Art of War: Navies, ch. XI of *New Cambridge Modern History*, vol. X, ed. J.P.T. Bury (Cambridge).

Liddell Hart, B.H. 1960. Armed Forces and the Art of War, ch. XII of *New Cambridge Modern History*, vol. X, ed. J.P.T. Bury (Cambridge).

Lipsey, R.E. 1963. *Price and Quantity Trends in the Foreign Trade of the United States* (Princeton).

MacDougall, D. 1966. Machine tool output, 1861–1910, in *Output, Employment and Productivity in the United States after 1800*, National Bureau of Economic Research, Studies in Income and Wealth (New York and London).

Miller, F.J. 1897. American and other machinery abroad, *American Machinist* (American edition), 20 May 1897, 27 May 1897 and 17 June 1897.

Mordecai, A. 1861. *Report of Major Alfred Mordecai of the United States Military Commission to Europe, 1855–6*. House of Representatives executive document, 36th Congress, 2nd session (Washington, D.C.)

Morgan, B.H. 1902. *Report on the Engineering Trades of South Africa* (London).

207

Orcutt, H.F.L. 1899. Machine shop management in Europe and America, *Engineering Magazine*, XVII.

Parliamentary papers (P.P.):

1867–8. Report of the Royal Commission on the Paris Exhibition of 1867. Report on 'Machine Tools' by John Anderson. P.P., 1867–8, XXX, p. 701.

1874a. Report of the British Commissioners to the Vienna Exhibition of 1873, P.P., 1874, LXXIII.

1874b. Technical Reports on the Vienna Exhibition of 1873, by W.H. Maw and J. Dredge. P.P., 1874, LXXIII.

1877. Reports on the Philadelphia International Exhibition of 1876. Report on 'Machines and Tools for Working Wood, Metal and Stone' by John Anderson. P.P., 1877, XXXIV, p. 306.

1880. Report of the British Commissioners of the Paris Universal Exhibition of 1878. P.P., 1880, XXXII.

1882. Report of the Royal Commission for the Melbourne Exhibition of 1880. P.P., 1882, XXVIII.

1887. Minutes of Evidence to the Committee on the Organisation and Administration of the Manufacturing Departments of the Army (The Morley Committee). P.P., 1887, XIV.

1901. Report of the Royal Commission to the Paris Exhibition of 1900. Report on 'Machine Tools' by C.W. Burton. P.P., 1901, XXXI.

1906. Report of the British Commissioners to the Exhibition at St Louis, 1904. P.P., 1906, LIV.

1912–13a. Report of the British Commissioners on the Exhibitions at Brussels, Rome and Turin, 1910 and 1911. P.P., 1912–13, XXII.

1912–13b. Final Report of the Census of Production, 1907. P.P., 1912–13, CIX.

1918. Report of the Committee appointed to consider the position of the Engineering Trades after the War. P.P., 1918. XIII.

Payne, P.L. 1967. The emergence of the large-scale company in Great Britain, 1870–1914, *Economic History Review*, XX.

Porter, C.T. 1908. *Reminiscences of Life as an Engineer* (New York and London).

Porter, W.T. 1880. *Report of the U.S. Commissioners to the Paris Exhibition of 1878*, Executive Documents, House of Representatives, 1880, vol. IV 'Report on Machines, Apparatus and Machine Tools'.

Pratten, C.F. 1971. *Economies of Scale in Manufacturing Industry* (Cambridge).

Richards, J. 1899. Machine tools, *American Machinist* (American edition), 4 May 1899.

Riddell, W.G. 1948. *The Thankless Years* (London and Glasgow).

Rolt, L.T.C. 1965. *Tools for the Job* (London).

Rose, J. 1886–7. *Modern Machine Shop Practice.*

Rosenberg, N. 1963. Technological change in the machine tool industry, 1840–1910, *Journal of Economic History*, XXIII.

Saul, S.B. 1967. The market and the development of the mechanical engineering industries in Britain, 1860–1914 *Economic History Review*, XX.

List of works cited

1968a. The engineering industry, in D.H. Aldcroft (ed.), *British Industry and Foreign Competition, 1870–1914* (London).

1968b. The machine tool industry in Britain to 1914, *Business History*, X.

Sellers, M. 1912. Industries, iron and hardware, in *Victoria County History of Yorkshire*, vol. II (London).

Shadwell, A. 1908. Machine tools *The Times* Engineering Supplement, 19 February 1908 and 4 March 1908.

Shelley, C.P.B. 1885. *Workshop Appliances* (London).

Sidders, P.A. 1961a. Thomas Ryder and Sons Ltd, *Machinery*, 27 December 1961.

1961b. William Asquith Ltd, *Machinery*, 22 November 1961.

1962a. Fredk. Pollard and Co. Ltd, *Machinery*, 11 April 1962.

1962b. H.W. Kearns and Co. Ltd, *Machinery*, 4 July 1912.

1962c. James Archdale and Co. Ltd, *Machinery*, 25 April 1962.

1964. Giddings and Lewis-Fraser Ltd, *Machinery*, 11 November 1964.

1965. J. Parkinson and Son (Shipley) Ltd, *Machinery*, 17 February 1965.

Sigsworth, E. and Blackman, J. 1968. The woollen and worsted industries, in D.H. Aldcroft (ed.), *British Industry and Foreign Competition, 1870–1914* (London).

Smiles, S. 1885. *Autobiography of James Nasmyth* (London).

Spicer, R.S. 1928. *British Engineering Wages* (London).

Spon, –. 1873. *Spon's Dictionary of Engineering* (London).

Steeds, W. 1969. *History of Machine Tools, 1700–1910* (Oxford).

Thurston, R.H. (ed.) 1876. *Report of the United States Commissioners to the International Exhibition held at Vienna, 1873*. Vol. III, 'Engineering' (Washington).

Tinbergen, J. 1951. Business cycles in the United Kingdom, *Verhandelingen der koninklijke Nederlandse Akademie van Wetenschappen*, N.S. LII, 4.

Trebilcock, R.C. 1966. A 'special relationship' – government, rearmament and the cordite firms, *Economic History Review*, XIX.

United States Consular Reports. 1899. Report from U.S. Consul Halstead, Birmingham. U.S. Consular Reports, LIX (Washington, D.C.).

Wagoner, H.D. 1968. *The U.S. Machine Tool Industry from 1900 to 1950* (Cambridge, Mass.).

Walker, S.F. 1907a. Starting an engineering business, I, *The Practical Engineer*, XXXV.

1907b. Starting an engineering business, II, *The Practical Engineer*, XXXV.

Webb, H. 1898. English and American methods in the engineering and iron trades, *Engineer*, 21 January 1898.

Weissenborn, G. 1861. *American Engineering* (New York).

Woodbury, R.S. 1958. *History of the Gear-Cutting Machine* (Cambridge, Mass.).

1959. *History of the Grinding Machine* (Cambridge, Mass.).

1960. *History of the Milling Machine* (Cambridge, Mass.).

1961. *History of the Lathe to 1850* (Cambridge, Mass.).

Notes

1. The engineering industries

1. *History of Ministry of Munitions*, vol. VIII, part III, p. 38. P.L. Payne (1967) attributes specialisation generally in British industry to product differentiation designed to achieve oligopolistic control, and implies that there was a growing number of firms adopting the strategy.
2. The firms included were Archdale, Butler, Asquith, Parkinson, Herbert, Lang, Craven, Ward, Richards and Greenwood and Batley. Details of output for all except the last were kindly provided by Professor Saul, and were obtained by him from the records of the firms. For details of Greenwood and Batley output see chapter 6. The total output of these firms was £858,000 in 1907 (of which Herbert provided £324,000), and the Census of Production showed total output of the industry as £2,936,000 (P.P., 1912–13b, p. 126).
3. This information on the methods used by the compilers of Kelly's Directories was given to me by Mr F. G. Barkway, then Manager of the U.K. Division of *Kelly's Directory of Merchants and Manufacturers*.

3. The machine tool industry: structure and explanation

1. Papers of Sir Alfred Herbert. 'Machine Chasers' – a typescript autobiography. Section headed 'Alfred Herbert Ltd.', pp. 4–5. After describing his acquisition of the steel tube agency, Sir Alfred concludes 'It was our good fortune to make a sufficient profit from the tube business to set us on our feet, and we used it to extend and equip our growing machine tool industry.
2. Fontaine, 1874, p. 127, gave as the reason for Whitworth's failure to exhibit machine tools at Vienna that the firm was making only arms machinery, but at least two other writers describe Whitworth tools later in the century, in terms which suggest they were of recent manufacture. Rose, 1886–7, vol. I and Shelley, 1885, p. 185.

5. Greenwood and Batley: history, records and methods

1. According to the 'Agreement for the sale of the assets of the Partnership', sixty-seven British and Foreign Patents were held by the partnership dating from 1875 to 1888. Six, referring to armaments machinery, were taken out by Arthur and George Greenwood.
2. Greenwood and Batley Prospectus 1888. The first issue was of £80,000 in debentures, 8000 £10 7% cumulative preference shares and 14,000 £10 ordinary shares, the managing directors taking 'one third of the debentures and of each class of shares in part payment'.
3. The valuation of £265,000 was given in the Prospectus of 1888. Expenditure on alterations was described to the Board on 13 June 1891. On 6

May 1890 the Chairman had reported to the Board that 'the inconvenience caused by the work going on had disorganised the workshops and greatly increased the difficulty of moving work from one shop to another and also the cost of turning it out'.

4. Greenwood and Batley Board Minutes on 28 March, 6 June and 8 December 1898 and 9 June 1899 describe the initial discussions. The de Laval Company was thereafter frequently discussed by the Board, the original proposal being accepted in parts on 6 February, 19 June and 8 December 1903.

5. The application to promote a railway was reported to the Board on 13 May 1898. The subject was discussed on 3 November 1898 and 5 July 1902, when it was reported that 'The Company was engaged in designing a small self-contained Electrical Train' for use on branch lines, and on 19 June 1903, 10 March 1904 and 15 June 1905. On 19 January 1909 the Chairman proposed that the railway, the Colne and Trawden light railway, should be disposed of; on 8 March 1910 it was said that 'it might prove a considerable loss'. The railway was finally sold to Colne Corporation in 1914, the sum paid to Greenwood and Batley being £9,367 12s 11d.

6. Greenwood and Batley: markets and prices

1. A machine tool firm in Manchester. Muir formerly worked for Archdale's, according to Mr Clements, a former employee of James Archdale and Co.
2. These numbers presumably refer to patterns.
3. Chairman and Managing Director of Greenwood and Batley Ltd.
4. The Birmingham Small Arms Co. factory at Smallheath, Birmingham.
5. Presumably Kynoch and Co. Ltd., small-arms ammunition makers.
6. A Managing Director of Greenwood and Batley Ltd.
7. The Royal Small Arms Factory at Sparkbrook, Birmingham.

Index